INFORMATION LAW SERIES – 14

COPYRIGHT AND HUMAN RIGHTS

Freedom of Expression – Intellectual Property – Privacy

edited by Paul L.C. Torremans

*City Solicitors' Educational Trust Professor of Intellectual Property Law,
School of Law, University of Nottingham, United Kingdom, and
Professor of Private International Law,
Faculty of Law, University of Gent, Belgium*

2004

KLUWER LAW INTERNATIONAL

The Hague • London • New York

A C.I.P. Catalogue record for this book is available from the Library of Congress.

ISBN 90-411-2278-8

Published by:
Kluwer Law International
P.O. Box 85889
2508 CN The Hague
The Netherlands
Tel.   +31-70-308-1500
Fax   +31-70-308-1515
E-mail   sales@kluwerlaw.com
http://www.kluwerlaw.com

Sold and distributed in North, Central and South America by:
Aspen Publishers, Inc.
7201 McKinney Circle
Frederick, MD 21704
United States of America
Tel.   +1-877-529-5427 (Customer care)
Fax   +1-301-698-7159
E-mail   customercare@aspenpubl.com
http://www.kluwerlaw.com

Sold and distributed in all other countries by:
Extenza-Turpin Distribution Services
Stratton Business Park
Pegasus Drive
Biggleswade
Bedfordshire SG18 8QB
United Kingdom
Tel.   +44-1767-604958
Fax   +44-1767-601640
E-mail   kluwerlaw@extenza-turpin.com
http://www.extenza-turpin.com

Printed on acid-free paper

Printed and bound in the Netherlands

Table of Contents

Preface

On 6 March 2002 I organised a conference on 'Rights in Information' on behalf of the British Association for Canadian Studies Legal Studies Group. The idea was to bring together the human rights and the intellectual property legal communities and to provide a transatlantic bridge. The conference turned out to be a success and many of the papers contained such interesting leads for further analysis that all involved wanted to take things further. This collection of essays is very much the result of that further work. Ysolde Gendreau, who delivered the key not speech at the conference, as well as Alison Firth, Peter Jaffey, Jonathan Griffiths and Patrick Masiyakurima built upon their original papers and what they gained in the debate and the further analysis that followed in writing their essays for this book. To complement these additional essays were commissioned from Wendy Gordon and Michael Birnhack in order to provide contrasting perspectives. And I tried to provide an introductory, broad but provocative perspective. We all realise that we have by no means exhausted the topic, but we will feel satisfied if it turns out that we have made a contribution to the growing debate on the interaction between the areas of human rights and intellectual property law.

Such a contribution is obviously based on the expertise of the authors, but I would also like to thank them for the exemplary way in which they facilitated my work as editor of the book. None of this would however have been possible without the encouragement and the support that I received from the Canadian High Commission in London through their Academic Relations Officer Michael Hellyer and my colleagues on the Executive Committee of the BACS Legal Studies Group in developing this theme of the interaction between intellectual property and human rights. I am therefore immensely grateful to them and to Bernt Hugenholtz, who helped me greatly in developing the research leading to this volume in his Information Law Series further. Gwen de Vries and her colleagues at Kluwer Law International then provided the much appreciated skills of turning the manuscript into the book you now have in front of you.

In the book a number of themes are developed. We start by looking at the Human Rights credentials of Copyright. Then attention is turned to the interaction between specific aspects of human rights law and copyright. Four papers look at the relationship between copyright and freedom of speech and freedom of expression. Two of them do so primarily from a North American perspective and the two others are firmly rooted in English-European law. We then look specifically at the question whether anyone has the right to speak with another's language in the light of the US Supreme Court's decision in *Eldred* on the issue of the constitutionality of the duration of copyright and that essay is balanced from a European perspective by a close look at the role of the public interest defence in copyright as a tool to protect fundamental rights and freedoms. In a final paper attention is turned to issues surrounding the fundamental rights of privacy when put into practice in an intellectual property environment.

Paul Torremans
Leicester, 8 December 2003.

Chapter 1

Copyright As A Human Right

*Paul L.C. Torremans**

I.   Introduction

When the Canada House conference in which this collection of essays is rooted was set up and subsequently when the topics and the essential components of a book treating the issue of copyright, and other intellectual property rights, and human rights were discussed amongst the series editor, the editor of this collection and the contributors it seemed obvious to think of the issue as one involving copyright and intellectual property rights in general on the one hand and human rights on the other hand. The first impression was inevitably one of two elements being involved and of the task ahead being the study of the interaction between these two elements.

That interaction between copyright and intellectual property rights on the one hand and human rights on the other hand is in truth not a new phenomenon. This essay will demonstrate that the roots of this interaction go back a long time and are of a fundamental nature, but at least in the United Kingdom it gave the impression of being something new. No doubt this was a consequence of the introduction of a formal Bill of Rights in the form of the Human Rights Act 1998, which provided a sharp focus on human rights in the English legal system. It is true though in a broader international context that copyright and intellectual property rights on the one hand and human rights on the other hand for quite a while seemed to develop in virtual isolation.[1] Each discipline seemed to stand on its own and had very little interest in the development of the other, let alone in the development of any interaction. It is in this respect sufficient to have a look at the vast majority of copyright and intellectual property rights standard texts. No reference to human rights is found[2] and similarly most standard texts on human

---

*   City Solicitors' Educational Trust Professor of Intellectual Property Law, School of Law, University of Nottingham (UK) and Professor of Private International Law, Faculty of Law, University of Gent (Belgium).

[1]   L.R. Helfer, 'Human Rights and Intellectual Property: Conflict or Coexistence?', in *Minnesota Intellectual Property Review* 5 (2003) 47-61, available at http://mipr.umn.edu/archive/v5n1/Helfer.pdf; Loyola-LA Public Research Paper No. 2003-27; Princeton Law & Public Affairs Working Paper No. 03-15, p. 3.

[2]   P.B. Hugenholtz, 'Copyright and Freedom of Expression in Europe', in R. Cooper Dreyfuss, D. Leenheer Zimmerman and H. First, *Expanding the Boundaries of Intellectual Property: Innovation Policy for the Knowledge Society*, Oxford University Press (2001), 343-363, at 350.

P.L.C. Torremans (ed.), Copyright and Human Rights, 1–20
© *2004 Kluwer Law International. Printed in the Netherlands.*

rights law do not seem to refer to copyright and intellectual property rights either. In other words, the interaction between the two areas of law may well not be a new phenomenon, but it is one the study of which has only attracted attention in earnest in recent years.[3]

Two approaches to this interaction can be distinguished.[4] The first approach is based on the conflict model and sees copyright and intellectual property rights as in fundamental conflict with human rights. The proponents of this approach argue that strong intellectual property rights are bound to undermine human rights and in particular economic, social and cultural aspects of human rights. This leads to an incompatibility that can only be resolved through the recognition of the primacy of human rights whenever a conflict arises. This solution imposes itself in the view of its proponents because in normative terms human rights are fundamental and of higher importance than intellectual property rights.[5] It is submitted that this approach focuses, maybe unduly so, primarily on the practical effects of certain forms of intellectual property rights in specific situations. In doing so it does not address the broader picture, involving the function and nature of the elements involved in the interaction. The second approach comes to the interaction between intellectual property rights and human rights from this broader perspective. Looking at it from that perspective, both intellectual property rights and human rights deal with the same fundamental equilibrium. On the one hand there is a need to define the scope of the private exclusive right that is given to authors as an incentive to create and as recognition of their creative contribution to society broadly enough to enable it to play its incentive and recognition function in an appropriate and effective way, whilst on the other hand there is the broader interest of society that the public must be able to have adequate access to the fruits of authors' efforts. Both intellectual property law and

---

[3] See e.g. the expansion of the treatment in the second edition of J.A.L. Sterling, *World Copyright Law*, Sweet & Maxwell (2003) in comparison to the first edition of the book (1999). See also G. Schricker (ed.), *Urheberrecht: Kommentar*, Verlag C.H. Beck (2nd ed., 1999), § 97, Nos. 19-25, pp. 1500-1504 to which P.B. Hugenholtz, 'Copyright and Freedom of Expression in Europe', in R. Cooper Dreyfuss, D. Leenheer Zimmerman and H. First, *Expanding the Boundaries of Intellectual Property: Innovation Policy for the Knowledge Society,* Oxford University Press (2001), 343-363, refers as an example at 351; and M. Vivant, 'Le droit d'auteur, un droit de l'homme?', in *RIDA* 174 (*Revue Internationale du Droit d'Auteur*) (1997) 60.

[4] L.R. Helfer, 'Human Rights and Intellectual Property: Conflict or Coexistence?', in *Minnesota Intellectual Property Review* 5 (2003) 47-61, available at http://mipr.umn.edu/archive/v5n1/Helfer.pdf; Loyola-LA Public Research Paper No. 2003-27; Princeton Law & Public Affairs Working Paper No. 03-15, p. 1-2.

[5] See e.g. United Nations, Economic and Social Council, Commission on Human Rights, Sub-Commission on the Promotion and Protection of Human Rights, Resolution 2000/7 on Intellectual Property Rights and Human Rights, E/CN.4/Sub/2/2000/L.20, preamble § 11 and R. Howse and M. Mutua, *Protecting Human Rights in a Global Economy: Challenges for the World Trade Organization,* International Centre for Human Rights and Democratic Development, Policy Paper, (2000), at 6.

human rights law try to get the private-public rights balance right and as such there is no conflict. Both areas of law may however not define that balance in exactly the same way in all cases. There is therefore a compatibility between them, rather than a consensus.[6]

The other essays in this collection will deal in detail with the various aspects of the interaction between intellectual property rights and human rights. In this essay I would like to examine whether or not it might be too restrictive to see intellectual property rights and human rights solely as two sets of distinct rights between which there is an interaction along the lines of any of the two approaches or models set out in the previous paragraph. Maybe we are overlooking the fact that one way or another intellectual property rights and more specifically copyright may be considered as a Human Right. We will therefore have to examine whether or not copyright can indeed be considered as a Human Right, both at international and at national level. Additionally we will need to examine whether any conclusion on this point necessarily applies to the whole of copyright or only to certain aspects of copyright and whether it applies to all aspects in the same way. Whatever the outcome of such an analysis may be and wherever it may lead us, we will inevitably have to come back to the issue of the interaction between copyright and human rights. The question will have to be answered whether our findings can be reconciled with the idea of interaction as defined above. And if the interaction idea involves a balancing of interests we will have to determine where and how balancing is to take place. The question whether the balancing of interests can maybe also take place inside a broadly conceived human rights portfolio will arise unavoidably. But let us now first turn to the question whether there are indications in international legal instruments that allow us to define copyright as a Human Right.

II. The Human Rights Approach to Copyright in International Instruments

Let us for a moment leave behind legal concepts and consider the factual starting point. Broadly speaking we are essentially concerned here with creative works, creations of the mind and elements of cultural heritage which are of particular value to society. Society finds it is therefore in its best interest to offer some form of protection to the creators of these works. Interests in material goods are protected by means of physical possession of the goods, which then gains legal

---

[6] See e.g. United Nations, Economic and Social Council, Commission on Human Rights, Sub-Commission on the Promotion and Protection of Human Rights, 52nd session, Item 4 of the Provisional Agenda, Economic, Social and Cultural Rights – The Impact of the Agreement on Trade-Related Aspects of Intellectual Property Rights on Human Rights, Report of the High Commissioner, E/CN.4/Sub/2/2001/13, at 5.

recognition in the form of a property right. Whoever produces the goods and has them in his or her possession will be given a property rights in the goods. Similarly protection for creative works is offered along the property route. As these works are immaterial in nature[7] the factual element of physical possession is not available here and cannot form the basis of the property right. That (intellectual) property right is therefore created as a legal fiction, but it serves the same purpose. It is important to note though that the way society and the legal system on its behalf deal with creative works is to turn them into property rights. Behind any property stands an owner and it is important to note also at the outset that the legal fiction that is copyright as a property right refers in this respect to the creator or author behind the work in the absence of the concept of a person having the physical goods in his or her possession in relation to immaterial property. This is important to keep in mind in a human rights context. Apart from the obvious references to copyright as such, the debate will also need to deal with the human rights aspects of property rights and personality rights.[8]

The importance of the act of creation and the link with the creator in relation to rights that may flow from it has also been emphasized by René Cassin, one of the architects of the current Human Rights framework. In his view the ability and the desire to develop intellectual and creative activities from which copyright works may result is potentially found in all human beings. As such it deserves therefore respect and protection in the same way as all other basic faculties that are common to all men. This would mean that creators can claim rights by the very fact of their creation. This is a broad statement and it is by no clear that such rights are by definition Human Rights and that they must cover all creations and necessarily take the format of an exclusive right in such creations.[9] Further analysis is therefore warranted.

II.1. The Universal Declaration of Human Rights

The first key provision in an international instrument that identifies copyright as a Human Right is found in Article 27 of the Universal Declaration of Human Rights.[10] According to Article 27 everyone has first of all 'the right to the protection of the moral and material interests resulting from and scientific, literary or artistic production of which he is the author'. But it is equally important to note

---

[7] They are indeed to be distinguished from their material support of carrier.

[8] See A.R. Chapman, 'Approaching Intellectual Property as a Human Right (obligations related to Article 15(1)(c))', in *Copyright Bulletin* Vol. XXXV, No. 3 (2001), 4-36, at 5.

[9] R. Cassin, 'L'intégration, parmi les droits fondamentaux de l'homme, des droits des créateurs des oeuvres de l'esprit', in *Mélanges Marcel Plaisant: Etudes sur la propriété industrielle, littéraire et artistique*, Sirey (1959), at 229 and M. Vivant, 'Le droit d'auteur, un droit de l'homme?', in *RIDA* 174 (1997) 60, at 87.

[10] See J.A.L. Sterling, *World Copyright Law*, Sweet & Maxwell (2nd ed., 2003), p. 43.

another element of the same article where it is stated in its first paragraph that 'everyone has the right freely to participate in the cultural life of the community, to enjoy the arts and to share in scientific advancement and its benefits'.

This first paragraph of Article 27 clearly has historical roots. The Universal Declaration of Human Rights was drafted less than three years after the end of the Second World War and science and technology as well as copyright based propaganda had been abused for atrocious purposes by those who lost the war. Such an abuse had to be prevented for the future and it was felt that the best way forward was to recognize that everyone had a share in the benefits and that at the same time those who made valuable contributions were entitled to protection. That process was of a human rights nature, as the series of rights and claims made in Article 27 are considered to be universal and vested in each person by virtue of their common humanity. It should in this context also be remembered that the human rights that were articulated in the Universal Declaration of Human Rights are held to exist independently of implementation or even recognition in the customs or legal systems of individual countries. They are after all such important norms that they create prima facie obligations to take measures to protect and uphold these rights. This obligation particularly applies to governments, as they are supposed to act in the common interest of humanity.[11] And '[b]ecause a human right is a universal entitlement, its implementation should be measured particularly by the degree to which it benefits those who hitherto have been the most disadvantaged and vulnerable'.[12] It should not simply serve one group in society that already occupies a privileged position. The benefit that is produced for 'everyone' should also go beyond the ability to draw some benefit from the applications of intellectual property, i.e. the better goods and services that are made available as a result. Enjoyment of the arts and especially participation in the cultural life of society are clearly broader concepts that go further and involve elements of sharing at all levels and stages.

That brings us back to paragraph two of Article 27. This is not inasmuch a tool to implement paragraph one as a complimentary provision that sets up a right to the protection of moral as well as material interests. The protection of moral and material rights of authors and creator is clearly exactly what is covered by the area of law know as copyright and this second paragraph of Article 27 of the Universal Declaration of Human Rights must therefore be seen as elevating copyright to the status of a Human Right, or maybe it is more appropriate to say that the article recognizes the Human Rights status of copyright. The roots of this second paragraph of Article 27 go back to two influential elements. In the first place there

---

[11] See J.W. Nickel, *Making Sense of Human Rights: Philosophical Reflections on the Universal Declaration of Human Rights*, University of California Press (1987), p. 3.

[12] A.R. Chapman, 'A Human Rights Perspective on Intellectual Property, Scientific Progress, and Access to the Benefits of Science', WIPO Panel Discussion on Intellectual Property and Human Rights (8 November 1998), at 2, available at www.wipo.org.

was the original suggestion made by the French delegation which had a double focus. On the one hand the emphasis was placed on the moral rights of the author, which centred around his or her ability to control alterations made to the work and to be able to stop misuses of the work or creation. On the other hand there was the recognition of the right of the author or creator to receive a form of remuneration for his or her creative activity and contribution.[13] Secondly, the Mexican and Cuban members of the drafting committee argued that it made sense to establish a parallelism between the provisions of the Universal Declaration of Human Rights and the American Declaration on the Rights and Duties of Man that had at that stage been adopted very recently.[14] Article 13 of the latter dealt with intellectual property rights by stating that:

> '[E]very person has the right to take part in the cultural life of the community, to enjoy the arts, and to participate in the benefits that result from intellectual progress, especially scientific discoveries. He likewise has the right to the protection of his moral and material interests as regards his inventions or any literary, scientific or artistic works of which he is the author'.[15]

Despite these rather clear and explicit roots, it is not necessarily clear what motivated those who voted in favour of the adoption of the second paragraph of Article 27 of the Universal Declaration of Human Rights. What we know is that the initial strong criticism that intellectual property was not properly speaking a Human Right or that it already attracted sufficient protection under the regime of protection afforded to property rights in general was eventually defeated by a coalition of those who primarily voted in favour because they felt that the moral rights deserved and needed protection and met the Human Rights standard and those who felt the ongoing internationalization of copyright needed a boost and that this could be a tool in this respect.[16]

This is of course not the strongest basis for a strong argument that copyright is beyond doubt a Human Right and in theory things are not helped a great deal either by the fact that as a United Nations General Assembly action the Universal Declaration of Human Rights is merely aspirational or advisory in nature. But where initially Member States were not obliged to implement it on this basis, it has now gradually acquired the status of customary international law and of the single

---

[13] See J. Morsink, *The Universal Declaration of Human Rights: Origins, Drafting and Intent*, University of Pennsylvania Press (1999), at 220.

[14] A.R. Chapman, 'Approaching Intellectual Property as a Human Right (obligations related to Article 15(1)(c))', in *Copyright Bulletin* Vol. XXXV, No. 3 (2001) 4-36, at 11.

[15] American Declaration of the Rights and Duties of Man, Approved by the Ninth International Conference of American States, Bogota, Colombia, 30 March to 2 May 1948, Final Act of the Ninth Conference, pp. 38-45.

[16] J. Morsink, *The Universal Declaration of Human Rights: Origins, Drafting and Intent*, University of Pennsylvania Press (1999), at 221.

most authoritative source of human rights norms. That has in turn greatly enhanced the standing of copyright as a Human Right, even if the economic, social and cultural rights, of which copyright is one, are still seen as weaker provisions than those dealing with basic civil and political rights.[17] The exact ramifications of Article 27 of the Universal Declaration of Human Rights are also no always clear[18], but what is clear that copyright as a Human Right requires there to be a balance between the concepts expressed in Article 27(1) and those expressed in Article 27(2) as they are linked in the drafting of the provision. Nevertheless, national courts have used it to protect the interests of authors on a couple of occasions.[19] For example, in a judgment dated 29 April 1959 the Court of Appeal in Paris granted Charlie Chaplin, a British national, the rights of a Frenchman in France in relation to his moral rights on the basis of an assimilation based on Article 27(2) of the Universal Declaration when he wished to object to the unauthorized addition of a sound track to one of his movies.[20] Similarly Article 27(2) played a prominent role in the granting of the status of author and with it moral rights in the first judgment in the John Huston – Asphalt Jungle saga where colour rather than sound was added to the movie.[21] Whilst both cases deal primarily with moral rights, the concept of authorship also has economic rights aspects and it is clear that Article 27 covers both economic and moral rights and therefore the whole of copyright.

II.2. THE INTERNATIONAL COVENANT ON ECONOMIC, SOCIAL AND CULTURAL RIGHTS

This Covenant is to be seen as a follow up action on the Universal Declaration of Human Rights. Important though is the fact that this follow up action took the form of a Treaty and that as such it can impose legally binding obligations to implement its provisions on States that became contracting parties to it. Article 15

---

[17] A.R. Chapman, 'A Human Rights Perspective on Intellectual Property, Scientific Progress, and Access to the Benefits of Science', WIPO Panel Discussion on Intellectual Property and Human Rights (8 November 1998), at 7, available at www.wipo.org.

[18] R. Cassin, 'L'intégration, parmi les droits fondamentaux de l'homme, des droits des créateurs des oeuvres de l'esprit', in *Mélanges Marcel Plaisant: Etudes sur la propriété industrielle, littéraire et artistique*, Sirey (1959), at 225.

[19] See F. Dessemontet, 'Copyright and Human Rights', in J. Kabel and G. Mom, *Intellectual Property and Information Law: Essays in Honour of Herman Cohen Jehoram*, Kluwer Law International (1998), Volume 6, Information Law Series, 113-120.

[20] *Société Roy Export Company Establishment et Charlie Chaplin c/. Société Les Films Roger Richebé*, in *RIDA* 28 (1960) 133 and *Journal du Droit International* (1960) 128, annotated by Goldman.

[21] Tribunal de Grande Instance de Paris, judgment dated 23 November 1988, in *RIDA* 139 (1989) 205, annotated by Sirinelli, and *Journal du Droit International* (1989) 1005, annotated by Edelman.

of the Covenant is very clear in this respect and imposes a number of responsibilities and steps to be taken on Contracting States in the following way:

'[...]
(2) The steps to be taken by the States Parties to the present Covenant to achieve the full realization of this right shall include those necessary for the conservation, development and the diffusion of science and culture.
(3) The States Parties to the present Covenant undertake to respect the freedom indispensable for scientific research and creative activity.
(4) The States Parties to the Present Covenant recognize the benefits to be derived from the encouragement and development of international contacts and cooperation in the scientific and cultural fields'.

These obligations apply to the substantive rights granted in paragraph one of Article 15 of the Covenant and which are very much based on Article 27 of the Universal Declaration of Human Rights. As such they comprise the rights of everyone (a) to take part in cultural life, (b) to enjoy the benefits of scientific progress and its applications and, most importantly for our current purposes, (c) to benefit from the protection of the moral and the material interests resulting from any scientific, literary or artistic production of which he is the author. However, this provision no doubt gains in importance in the light of the absence in the Covenant of a provision dealing with property, which at the time of the Universal Declaration was still seen as clearly the stronger and more obvious Human Right which could also cover most of the intellectual property issues.

If we look in a bit more detail at the substantive provision contained in Article 15.1(c) of the Covenant the clear starting point is that an obligation is imposed upon the Contracting Parties to protect the moral and material interests of authors and creators.[22] In essence there is therefore an obligation to implement copyright as a Human Right and to put in place an appropriate regime of protection for the interests of authors and creators.[23] But a lot of freedom is left to Contracting States in relation to the exact legal format of that protection. The Human Rights framework in which copyright is placed does however put in place a number of imperative guidelines:

– Copyright must be consistent with the understanding of human dignity in the various human rights instruments and the norms defined therein.
– Copyrights related to science must promote scientific progress and access to its benefits.

---

[22] A.R. Chapman, 'A Human Rights Perspective on Intellectual Property, Scientific Progress, and Access to the Benefits of Science', WIPO Panel Discussion on Intellectual Property and Human Rights (8 November 1998), at 15, available at www.wipo.org.
[23] See also A. Bertrand, *Le droit d'auteur et les droits voisins*, Dalloz (2nd ed., 1999), at 81.

- Copyright regimes must respect the freedom indispensable for scientific research and creative activity.
- Copyright regimes must encourage the development of international contacts and cooperation in the scientific and cultural fields.[24]

In looking at this framework it should not be forgotten that its genesis was troubled and cumbersome. Various proposals were made to include intellectual property rights in the Covenant, all of them attracted severe criticism and some were rejected. However, whenever a draft Covenant without an intellectual property rights clause in it was submitted for further discussion a new proposal to include intellectual property rights was tabled and in the end the incorporation into the International Covenant on Economic, Social and Cultural Rights of an intellectual property clause was approved by a vote of 39 to 9, with 24 Member States abstaining.[25] The Covenant then came into force several years later on 3 January 1976.[26]

It is of course interesting to look back at these instruments that enshrine copyright as a Human Right and the way in which they came into being, especially as the copyright community all too often simply ignores this aspect of copyright. However, one should not look at this simply as a historical accident. One should also try to identify its implications for copyright and the conclusions that should be drawn from it. The first thing to note is that copyright has a relatively weak claim to Human Rights status, as its inclusion in the international Human Rights instruments proved to be highly controversial. And in the end the copyright and intellectual property components of the various articles were only included because they were seen as tools to give effect to and to protect other stronger Human Rights. The second conclusion flows from this first one. The various elements in the Articles dealing with copyright and intellectual property are interrelated, which means for example that the rights of authors and creators must be understood as essential preconditions for cultural freedom and for the participation and access to the benefits of scientific progress. The fact that the rights of authors and creators can also stand in their own right is instead an ancillary point. The third point takes this interaction one step further. Copyright and intellectual property rights are not simply preconditions. Not only do they need to exist to facilitate cultural participation and access to the benefits of scientific progress, they should also make sure that the other components of the

---

[24] A.R. Chapman, 'A Human Rights Perspective on Intellectual Property, Scientific Progress, and Access to the Benefits of Science', WIPO Panel Discussion on Intellectual Property and Human Rights (8 November 1998), at 13, available at www.wipo.org.

[25] M. Green, 'Background Paper on the Drafting History of Article 15(1)(c) of the International Covenant on Economic, Social and Cultural Rights', submitted for the Day of General Discussion on Article 15(1) of the Covenant, 9 October 2000, E/C.12/2000/15, at 8-12.

[26] The International Covenant on Economic, Social and Cultural Rights, 993 UNTS 3, GA Res. 2200(XXI), 21 UN GAOR Supp. (No. 16), p. 49, UN Doc. A/6316 (1966), was adopted on 16 December 1966.

relevant articles in the international Human Rights instruments are respected and promoted. In this sense the rights of authors and creators should not only enable, but also facilitate rather than constrain cultural participation and access to scientific progress. A fourth implication of all this is that the international Human Rights instruments deal with copyright and intellectual property rights as such.[27] They do no delineate the scope and the limits of copyright. The determination of the substance of copyright is an issue that is left to the legislature.[28]

Maybe it is worth adding at this stage that one can only talk in terms of a Human Right when the pre-normative state of a claim has been turned into a normative state that is recognized by the social group concerned. Additionally the norm must fit the existing normative order in a coherent way, it must be considered to represent a basic freedom, i.e. an essential social condition for the better development of the individual, and finally it must be perceived as being of universal reach.[29] Broadly speaking copyright seems to meet these requirements and its inclusion in the international Human Rights Instruments seems justifiable on that basis, but it remains to be seen how all these elements really fit together in practice in relation to copyright.

The common theme that seems to emerge and an understanding of which seems to be essential to understand how copyright operates as a Human Right is that of the balancing of rights and interests. Two kinds of balancing act appear to be necessary. The first one relates to the balance that is inherent to copyright itself and that involves both the private interests of authors and creators and the wider public interests of society as a whole.[30] We will now turn our attention to this particular balancing act. But on top of that one has to acknowledge that copyright as a Human Right is just one element in the international Human Rights instruments. Surely copyright as a Human Right will also have to be seen in relation with other Human Rights. Here again a balancing of rights, albeit be it of a different nature will be unavoidable and we will deal with this at a later stage.

III. Balancing Private and Public Interests

III.1. THE NEED FOR A BALANCING ACT

As Audrey Chapman put it:

'To be consistent with the full provisions of Article 15 [of the International Covenant on Economic, Social and Cultural Rights], the type and level of

---

[27] A.R. Chapman, 'Approaching Intellectual Property as a Human Right (obligations related to Article 15(1)(c))', in *Copyright Bulletin* Vol. XXXV, No. 3 (2001) 4-36, at 13.
[28] See H. Schack, *Urheber- und Urhebervertragsrecht*, Mohr Siebeck (1997), at 40.
[29] M. Vivant, 'Le droit d'auteur, un droit de l'homme?', in *RIDA* 174 (1997) 60, at 73.
[30] See J.A.L. Sterling, *World Copyright Law*, Sweet & Maxwell (1998), p. 40.

protection afforded under any intellectual property regime must facilitate and promote cultural participation and scientific progress and do so in a manner that will broadly benefit members of society both on an individual and collective level'.[31]

The emphasis here is on the broad public interest of society, but any level of intellectual property protection will also give rights to the individual rightholder. The private interest of the author, creator and eventually of the copyrightholder is an inevitable component of the equation. Somehow a balance will need to be struck between these interests, as stronger individual rights inevitably impinge on the interests of society as a whole and vice versa.[32] This balance between public and private interests is not an external element for copyright or indeed any other intellectual property right. On the contrary it has been internalized by copyright and it is part of its fundamental nature.[33] Copyright is therefore familiar with this balance of interests.[34] On the one hand there is the need to protect the individual interest of the author in order to encourage further creation that results in the author being given a certain amount of exclusivity in relation to the exploitation and use of his or her work and on the other hand there is the public interest of society as a whole to have access to culture and to copyright works as a tool for progress and improvement.

The need for a balance that takes us away from granting a kind of unrestricted monopoly property right is also inherent in the wording of Article 15 of the International Covenant on Economic, Social and Cultural Rights where it requires States to make sure that everyone will be able 'to benefit from the protection of the moral and material interests resulting from any scientific, literary or artistic production of which he is the author'. Enjoying a benefit from such protection is clearly not the same as enjoying an unrestricted monopoly property right. In practice copyright insures the balance in many ways, for example by means of limitations and exceptions to copyright infringement rules. This is an example of an attempt to strike the balance by drafting the rule in such a way that its effect in all practical cases is to achieve a proper balance between the various interests. On top of that there are also external correction mechanisms that interfere whenever the

---

[31] A.R. Chapman, 'Approaching Intellectual Property as a Human Right (obligations related to Article 15(1)(c))', in *Copyright Bulletin* Vol. XXXV, No. 3 (2001) 4-36, at 14.

[32] See H. Schack, *Urheber- und Urhebervertragsrecht*, Mohr Siebeck (1997), at 41.

[33] Compare in this respect the wording of Article 1, Paragraph 8, Section 8 of the Constitution of the United States of America in which Congress is vested with the power 'To promote the Progress of Science and useful Arts, by securing for limited Times to Authors and Inventors the exclusive Right to their respective Writings and Discoveries'.

[34] United Nations, Economic and Social Council, Commission on Human Rights, Sub-Commission on the Promotion and Protection of Human Rights, 52nd session, Item 4 of the Provisional Agenda, Economic, Social and Cultural Rights – The Impact of the Agreement on Trade-Related Aspects of Intellectual Property Rights on Human Rights, Report of the High Commissioner, E/CN.4/Sub/2001/13, at 5.

rule would not achieve the balance in a particular, i.e. peculiar, set of circumstances. What we are dealing with them bears close resemblance to the abuse of rights scenario. The use of competition principles in relation to copyright can serve as a good example to clarify the concept of balancing interests in copyright.

III.2. COMPETITION PRINCIPLES AS AN EXAMPLE

III.2.1. PRINCIPLES AND JUSTIFICATION

It would indeed be a serious error to see copyright (and other intellectual property rights), as essentially a private monopoly right, and competition law, as defender of the public interest against inappropriate behaviour, as irreconcilable opponents that fight for supremacy. Instead one should start by looking at the way in which intellectual property rights and in particular copyright fit into our modern society and how their existence can be justified.[35] Why are these intangible property rights such as copyright created? Economists argue that if everyone would be allowed to use the results of innovative and creative activity freely, the problem of the 'free riders'[36] would arise.[37] No one would invest in creation or innovation, except in a couple of cases where no other solution would be available,[38] as it would give them a competitive disadvantage.[39] All competitors would just wait until someone else made the investment, as they would be able to use the results as well without investing money in creation and innovation and without taking the risks that the investment would not result in the creative or innovative breakthrough it aimed at.[40] The cost of the distribution of the knowledge is, on top of that,

---

[35] See in general P.L.C. Torremans, *Holyoak and Torremans Intellectual Property Law*, Butterworths (3rd ed., 2001), pp. 12-25.

[36] See R. Benko, *Protecting Intellectual Property Rights: Issues and Controversies*, American Enterprise Institute for Public Policy Research (AEI Studies 453) (1987), at 17.

[37] Inappropriability, the lack of the opportunity to become the proprietor of the results of innovative and creative activity, causes an under-allocation of resources to research activity, innovation and creation: see K. Arrow, 'Economic Welfare and the Allocation of Resources for Invention' in National Bureau for Economic Research, *The Rate and Direction of Inventive Activity: Economic and Social Factors*, Princeton University Press (1962), at 609–625.

[38] E.g. a case where the existing technology is completely incapable of providing any form of solution to a new technical problem that has arisen.

[39] See H. Ullrich, 'The Importance of Industrial Property Law and Other Legal Measures in the Promotion of Technological Innovation', in *Industrial Property* (1989) 102, at 103.

[40] One could advance the counter-argument that inventions and creations will give the innovator an amount of lead time and that the fact that it will take imitators some time to catch up would allow the innovator to recuperate his investment during the interim period. In many cases this amount of lead time will, however, only be a short period, too short to recuperate the investment and make a profit. See also E. Mansfield, M. Schwartz and S. Wagner, 'Imitation Costs and Patents: An Empirical Study', in *The Economic Journal* Vol. 91, Issue 364 (1981) 907, at 915 *et seq.*

insignificant.[41] As a result the economy would not function adequately because we see creation and innovation as an essential element in a competitive free market economy. In this line of argument creation and innovation are required for economic growth and prosperity.[42] In this starting point one recognizes very clearly elements of public interest, i.e. as the needs of society. Property rights should be created if goods and services are to be produced and used as efficiently as possible in such an economy. The perspective that they will be able to have a property right in the results of their investment will stimulate individuals and enterprises to invest in further cultural and artistic creation as well as in research and development.[43] These property rights should be granted to someone who will economically maximize profits.[44] It is assumed that the creator or inventor will have been motivated by the desire to maximize profits, either by exploiting the creation or invention himself or by having it exploited by a third party, so the rights are granted to them.[45]

But how does such a legally created monopolistic exclusive property right fit in with the free market ideal of perfect competition? At first sight every form of a monopoly might seem incompatible with free competition, but we have already demonstrated that some form of property right is required to enhance economic development as competition can only play its role as market regulator if the products of human labour are protected by property rights.[46] In this respect the exclusive monopolistic character of the property rights is coupled with the fact that these rights are transferable. These rights are marketable; they can, for example, be sold as an individual item. It is also necessary to distinguish between various levels of economic activity as far as economic development and competition are concerned. The market mechanism is more sophisticated than the competition/monopoly dichotomy. Competitive restrictions at one level may be necessary to promote competition at another level. Three levels can be distinguished: production, consumption and innovation. Property rights in goods enhance

---

41 See R. Benko, *Protecting Intellectual Property Rights: Issues and Controversies*, American Enterprise Institute for Public Policy Research (AEI Studies 453) (1987), at 17.

42 See R. Benko, *Protecting Intellectual Property Rights: Issues and Controversies*, American Enterprise Institute for Public Policy Research (AEI Studies 453) (1987), chapter 4 at 15, and US Council for International Business, *A New MTN: Priorities for Intellectual Property*, (1985), at 3.

43 J. Lunn, 'The Roles of Property Rights and Market Power in Appropriating Innovative Output', in *Journal of Legal Studies* (1985) 423, at 425.

44 M. Lehmann, 'Property and Intellectual Property – Property Rights as Restrictions on Competition in Furtherance of Competition', in *IIC* (*International Review of Industrial Property and Copyright Law*) (1989), 1, at 11.

45 For an economic-philosophical approach see also E. Mackaay, 'Economic and Philosophical Aspects of Intellectual Property Rights', in M. Van Hoecke (ed.), *The Socio-Economic Role of Intellectual Property Rights*, Story-Scientia (1991), pp. 1-30.

46 M. Lehmann, 'Property and Intellectual Property – Property Rights as Restrictions on Competition in Furtherance of Competition', in *IIC* 1 (1989), at 12.

competition on the production level, but this form of ownership restricts competition on the consumption level. One has to acquire the ownership of the goods before one is allowed to consume them and goods owned by other economic players are not directly available for one's consumption. In turn, intellectual property imposes competitive restrictions at the production level. Only the owner of the copyright in a literary work may for example produce additional copies of that work and exploit it in any other way. These restrictions benefit competition on the creation level. The availability of property rights on each level guarantees the development of competition on the next level. Property rights are a prerequisite for the normal functioning of the market mechanism.[47] Copyright and the restrictions on copying and communication to the public which it imposes are needed to enhance further creation of copyright work, which is clearly what is required and desirable from a public interest point of view. This is the only way in which copyright can in the words of the American Constitution play its public interest role 'to promote science and the useful arts'.[48]

Not only does this go a long way in demonstrating that the copyright system right from its inception is influenced heavily by public interest imperatives and that the balance which it tries to achieve between the interest of the rightholders and of the users-public is based on public interest considerations. Competition law is also used as a tool to regulate the use that is made of copyright in a later stage. Excesses that can not be reconciled with the justification for the existence of copyright, i.e. that do not serve to achieve the public interest aims of copyright, will come to be seen as breaches of competition law. Yet again the public interest is involved, this time in regulating the use of the exclusivity granted by copyright.[49] The *Magill*[50] and *IMS*[51] cases are good examples in this area.

III.2.2. MAGILL AND IMS HEALTH

Magill was concerned with the copyright in TV listings. The broadcasters that owned the copyright refused to grant a licence to Magill, which needed it to be able to produce a comprehensive weekly TV listings magazine for the Irish market.

---

[47] M. Lehmann, 'The Theory of Property Rights and the Protection of Intellectual and Industrial Property', in *IIC* (1985) 525, at 539.

[48] US Constitution , Article 1, section 8, clause 8.

[49] See P.L.C. Torremans, *Holyoak and Torremans Intellectual Property Law*, Butterworths (3rd ed., 2001), pp. 302-309.

[50] Joined cases C-241/91 P and C-242/91 P *Radio Telefis Eireann and Independent Television Publications Ltd* v. *EC Commission* [1995] ECR I-743, [1995] All ER (EC) 4161.

[51] Case C-481/01 *IMS Health* v. *NDC Health*, pending, the Advocate General delivered his opinion on 2 October 2003, available at http://curia.eu.int/; Order of the President of the Court of Justice of 11 April 2002 in case C-481/01 P(R); Order of the President of the Court of First Instance of 10 August 2001 in case T-184/01 R and Order of the President of the Court of First Instance of 26 October 2001 in case T-184/01 R both available at http://curia.eu.int/.

The case shows clearly that there is nothing wrong with the copyright as such. The problem is clearly situated at the level of the use that is made of the copyright. Here again the starting point is that it is up to the rightholder to decide which use to make of the right and that as such a refusal to licence does not amount to a breach of competition law. But the Court of Justice argued that a refusal might in exceptional circumstances constitute an abuse.[52] These exceptional circumstances involved the following in this case. The broadcasters' main activity is broadcasting; the TV guides market is only a secondary market for them. By refusing to provide the basic programme listing information, of which they were the only source, the broadcasters prevented the appearance of new products which they did not offer and for which there was a consumer demand. The refusal could not be justified by virtue of their normal activities. And, by denying access to the basic information which was required to make the new product, the broadcasters were effectively reserving the secondary market for weekly TV guides to themselves.

In essence, the use of copyright to block the appearance of a new product for which the copyright information is essential and to reserve a secondary market to oneself is an abuse and cannot be said to be necessary to fulfil the essential function (reward and encouragement of the author) of copyright. Here again one clearly sees the public interest input. Competition law is used to make sure that copyright is used according to its proper intention, i.e. in the public interest. Any abuse of the right against the public interest, even if it would further enhance the exclusive monopoly style property right of the copyrightowner by giving it full and unfettered control over the work and its use, will constitute a breach of competition law.[53]

IMS Health[54] is the current complex follow up case. IMS Health had developed a brick structure to facilitate the collection of marketing data on the German pharmaceutical market. It owned the copyright in that brick structure and refused to grant a licence to its potential competitors. In comparison with *Magill* a number of complicating factors arise. First of all it is not entirely clear whether there is a secondary market involved at all, as IMS Health and its competitors both whished to operate on the primary market for the collection of pharmaceutical data in Germany and secondly it is also not clear whether in the circumstances the emergence of a new product would be blocked, as the competitors were only

---

[52] Joined cases C-241/91 P and C-242/91 P *Radio Telefis Eireann and Independent Television Publications Ltd* v. *EC Commission* [1995] ECR I-743, [1995] All ER (EC) 4161, at paragraphs 54 and 57.

[53] P.L.C. Torremans, *Holyoak and Torremans Intellectual Property Law*, Butterworths (3rd ed., 2001), pp. 302-309.

[54] Case C-481/01 *IMS Health* v. *NDC Health*, pending, the Advocate General delivered his opinion on 2 October 2003, available at http://curia.eu.int/; Order of the President of the Court of Justice of 11 April 2002 in case C-481/01 P(R); Order of the President of the Court of First Instance of 10 August 2001 in case T-184/01 R and Order of the President of the Court of First Instance of 26 October 2001 in case T-184/01 R both available at http://curia.eu.int/.

interested in copying IMS's block structure without necessarily providing the user with a different product as a result of such use. The main point in *IMS Health* is however not as much the question whether the requirements of reserving a secondary market to oneself and of blocking the emergence of a new product can be defined in a more flexible way, but rather the question whether these two requirements need to be met cumulatively or whether meeting one of them is sufficient to trigger the operation of competition law. The definitional problems really come down to defining the boundaries of the public interest on this point and the question whether the requirements apply in a cumulative manner defines when the threshold for an intervention by competition law in defence of public interest concerns is met. This latter case shows clearly that striking the balance is not a straightforward or easy task and that the facts of any new situation may require further fine-tuning of the balance.

As *Magill* and *IMS Health* show clearly, society has a strong interest to have access to information and this interest can be impeded by the private interest of the rightholder to enhance its exclusive monopoly style property right by giving it full and unfettered control over the work and its use. But it is not just passive access for society as a whole that is required. Each individual member of society also must have a right of access and a right to borrow (ideas and some expression) in order to exercise its fundamental freedom to create in order in turn to be able to exercise his or her Human Right to benefit from copyright in his or her creative effort. Copyright therefore simply cannot prohibit any and all borrowings.[55] This is another element that is to be taken into account in the fine-tuning of the balance.

III.2.3. NOT ONLY ECONOMIC CONSIDERATIONS COUNT

Be that as it may, what is clear is that copyright has a number of built in mechanisms to balance the private and public interests.[56] Further complications arise though as up to now we have almost exclusively looked at economic interests at either side. This is however not the only interest involved.[57] From a Human Rights perspective the author or creator assumes also a lot of importance. This

---

[55] F. Dessemontet, 'Copyright and Human Rights', in J. Kabel and G. Mom, *Intellectual Property and Information Law: Essays in Honour of Herman Cohen Jehoram*, Kluwer Law International (1998), Information Law Series Volume 6, 113-120.

[56] United Nations, Economic and Social Council, Commission on Human Rights, Sub-Commission on the Promotion and Protection of Human Rights, 52nd session, Item 4 of the Provisional Agenda, Economic, Social and Cultural Rights – The Impact of the Agreement on Trade-Related Aspects of Intellectual Property Rights on Human Rights, Report of the High Commissioner, E/CN.4/Sub/2/2001/13, at 5.

[57] See A.R. Chapman, 'A Human Rights Perspective on Intellectual Property, Scientific Progress, and Access to the Benefits of Science', WIPO Panel Discussion on Intellectual Property and Human Rights (8 November 1998), at 2, available at www.wipo.org.

manifests itself in the work produced by these authors or creators being acknowledged as having an intrinsic value as an expression of human dignity and creativity.[58] In terms of copyright law this is reflected by the balance between economic and moral rights, with the latter being a recognition of the fundamental link between the work and the author or creator. Moral rights survive as rights of the author or creator even when the latter transfers the economic rights in the work, thereby preserving the fundamental link.[59] The moral rights of paternity, i.e. the right to be identified as author of the work, and integrity, i.e. the right to object to the distortion or mutilation of the work that could affect the author's reputation,[60] operate as fundamental minimal rights that do not normally stand in the way of the normal exploitation of the work and the economic rights in it, but that allow the author to object to clearly abusive use of the work that would deny or distort his or her contribution as an expression of his or her human dignity and creativity.[61] This way a fair balance with the economic rights is provided, but this is also clearly another important aspect of the overall balancing act that is required if copyright is to operate properly as a Human Right. '[T]he question essentially is [and remains] where to strike the right balance'.[62]

IV. Copyright's Relationship with Other Human Rights

We already suggested above that a second part of the balancing act relates to the relationship between copyright and other Human Rights. Already intuitively one assumes that Human Rights must have equal value when compared to one another and that one cannot simply overrule the other. This must add yet another factor to consider when one works out the balance between public and private interests. The way we have looked at that balance up to now reflects very much the content of Article 27 of the Universal Declaration of Human Rights and Article 15 of the International Covenant on Economic, Social and Cultural Rights in both of which elements referring to the public as well as the private interest are brought together.

---

[58]   A.R. Chapman, 'Approaching Intellectual Property as a Human Right (obligations related to Article 15(1)(c))', in *Copyright Bulletin* Vol. XXXV, No. 3 (2001) 4-36, at 14.

[59]   See P.L.C. Torremans, *Holyoak and Torremans Intellectual Property Law*, Butterworths (3rd ed., 2001), chapter 13, pp. 220-228.

[60]   As enshrined in Article 6*bis* of the Berne Convention.

[61]   See P.L.C. Torremans, *Holyoak and Torremans Intellectual Property Law*, Butterworths (3rd ed., 2001), chapter 13, pp. 220-228 and P.L.C. Torremans, 'Moral Rights in the Digital Age', in I.A. Stamatoudi and P.L.C. Torremans (eds.), *Copyright in the New Digital Environment*, Sweet & Maxwell (2000), Perspectives on Intellectual Property Series, pp. 97-114.

[62]   United Nations, Economic and Social Council, Commission on Human Rights, Sub-Commission on the Promotion and Protection of Human Rights, 52nd session, Item 4 of the Provisional Agenda, Economic, Social and Cultural Rights – The Impact of the Agreement on Trade-Related Aspects of Intellectual Property Rights on Human Rights, Report of the High Commissioner, E/CN.4/Sub/2/2001/13, at 5.

But one needs to add to that that the balance between these interests must be struck with the primary objective of promoting and protecting Human Rights. That must be the overall aim of the international Human Rights instruments of which the clause considering copyright as a Human Rights forms part.[63]

Article 5(1) of the International Covenant on Economic, Social and Cultural Rights backs this up from a legal point of view by stating that

'[n]othing in the present Covenant may be interpreted as implying for any State, group or person any right to engage in any activity or to perform any act aimed at the destruction of any of the rights or freedoms recognized herein, or at their limitation to a greater extent than is provided for in the present Covenant'.

Copyright and its balance between public and private interests must therefore put in place a regime that is consistent with the realization of all other Human Rights.[64] The right of freedom of information and of access to information[65] provides a good example of another fundamental Human Right that needs to be respected, but the implementation of which alongside the implementation of copyright as an exclusive right in some of that information might create problems in a number of circumstances and will therefore call for a careful balancing of all the rights and interest.[66] The aim must be to respect both rights to the optimal or maximum extent possible. Maybe the suggestion of the German Constitutional Court that the freedom of access to information can still be guaranteed in those cases where whoever seeks access does not get that access for free but against the payment of a fee in respect of the copyright in the information can serve as an example here. Access is guaranteed, but it is not entirely free access and on the other hand copyright is respected by means of the remuneration whilst giving up the right to refuse to grant a licence as a part of the exclusive right in the work.[67]

The same kind of balance between various Human Rights is also found in a slightly different context when attention is turned to National Constitutions and the way in which they protect Copyright as a Human Right. Some of them such as the Swedish[68] and the Portuguese[69] Constitutions have a direct copyright clause, but most of them protect copyright as a Human Right by bringing aspects of it under other constitutional provisions covering other fundamental rights. The German Constitution is an example in point. The German Constitutional Court

---

[63] *Ibidem.*

[64] A.R. Chapman, 'Approaching Intellectual Property as a Human Right (obligations related to Article 15(1)(c))', in *Copyright Bulletin* Vol. XXXV, No. 3 (2001) 4-36, at 14.

[65] As found for example in Article 19 of the Universal Declaration of Human Rights.

[66] A. Bertrand, *Le droit d'auteur et les droits voisins*, Dalloz (2nd ed., 1999), at 81.

[67] H. Schack, *Urheber- und Urhebervertragsrecht*, Mohr Siebeck (1997), at 42.

[68] Chapter 2, § 19 of the Swedish Constitution of 1 January 1975.

[69] Article 42 of the Portuguese Constitution of 2 April 1976.

has intervened in copyright cases on many occasions despite the fact that the German Constitution does not have a copyright clause. Instead, there is a consensus in Germany that parts of copyright are covered by the property clause in the Constitution. Especially the economic rights part of copyright can be considered as immaterial property and is hence entitled to protection under the right of fundamental respect for property.[70] Moral rights on the other hand refer to the author and show a strong overlap with personality rights.[71] The latter are also specifically protected by the German Constitution.[72] These separate aspects of fundamental rights protection then have to be put together to come to an overall protection for copyright as a fundamental Human Right. This clearly does not simply amount to an adding up exercise.[73] The individual components may overlap and they protect different interest which may enter into conflict with one another when pushed to extreme heights of protection. Here too a balancing of these different fundamental rights will be required.

Exactly how this balancing works out and exactly where the balance lies depends also from case to case. The higher the level of creativity and the more important the input of the creator is, the stronger the Human Rights claim of copyright will be. Not all works and not all situations will give copyright the same strength in its claim to Human Rights status and in its balancing exercise with other Human Rights.[74]

V. Conclusion

This essay set out to demonstrate that copyright really has a claim to Human Rights status. We have shown that there clearly is a basis for such a claim in the international Human Rights instruments, but it has also become clear that the provisions in these instruments that could be said to be the copyright clauses do not define the substance of copyright in any detail. Instead one is left with a series of conclusions and implications for copyright and its substance as a result of its Human Rights status. The most important points are the balance that needs to be

---

[70] H. Schack, *Urheber- und Urhebervertragsrecht*, Mohr Siebeck (1997), at 40-43.

[71] See G. Schricker (ed.), *Urheberrecht: Kommentar,* Verlag C.H. Beck (2nd ed., 1999), Vor §§ 12 ff., Nos. 1-13, pp. 243-247; A. Lucas and H.-J. Lucas, *Traité de la propriété littéraire et artistique*, Litec (2nd ed., 2001), at 303, § 367; Poullaud-Dulian, 'Droit moral et droits de la personnalité', in *JCP éd. G* (*Jurisclasseur périodique, édition générale*) (1994) I, p. 3780 and *Anne Bragance c/. Michel de Grèce*, Court of Appeal Paris, judgment dated 1 February 1989, in *RIDA* Issue 4 (1989) p. 301, annotated by Sirinelli.

[72] H. Schack, *Urheber- und Urhebervertragsrecht*, Mohr Siebeck (1997), at 39-40.

[73] See G. Schricker (ed.), *Urheberrecht: Kommentar,* Verlag C.H. Beck (2nd ed., 1999), Vor §§ 12 ff., Nos. 14-17, pp. 247-249.

[74] See M. Vivant, 'Le droit d'auteur, un droit de l'homme?', in *RIDA* 174 (1997) 60, at 103 and 105.

achieved between private and public interests and the equilibrium that needs to be achieved with other Human Rights.

This balancing of rights can be seen as inherently internal to copyright as a Human Right. The analogy – example of the operation of competition principles in relation to copyright that was set out above demonstrates this clearly. Instead it can also be seen in most instances as the impact of other Human Rights on copyright. It is with that impact or interaction in each specific case that the other contributions in this collection will deal in considerable detail.

Chapter 2

Copyright and Freedom of Expression in Canada

Ysolde Gendreau*

I. Introduction

The year 2002 marked an important date in the history of Canadian constitutional law: the 20th anniversary of the Canadian Charter of Human Rights and Freedoms. Adopted at the same time as the Canadian constitution was 'repatriated' from the UK parliament, the Charter includes section 2 (b) that guarantees freedom of expression: 'Everyone has the following fundamental freedoms: ... (b) Freedom of thought, belief, opinion and expression, including freedom of the press and other media of communication'. The relationship between copyright law and freedom of expression is an obvious one and it increasingly attracts much scholarly attention. This has indeed been the case in the neighbouring country, the United States, but not in Canada. Yet, one could have expected that the richness of the discussions in that country would have been quickly borrowed in Canada in order to have a headstart on the analysis when the Charter became a reality. That it did not happen is perhaps another manifestation of the traditional reluctance on the part of some Canadian copyright jurists to a *rapprochement* with US law.[1]

Independently of a concern over the importation of foreign understandings, one may wonder why there has been no real homegrown analysis of the impact of the Charter on copyright law in Canada. Perhaps one reason could be that the Charter is very much a public law instrument. The Charter has beyond doubt impacted much on several public law areas, such as constitutional law, criminal law, procedure or administrative law, and perhaps less so on private law matters,

---

* Professor, Faculty of Law, Université de Montréal. This text has also been the basis of two talks given in July 2002 under the auspices of the Intellectual Property Research Institute of Australia in Melbourne and Sydney. The author wishes to thank Ms Caroline Ouellet (LL.M., U.Montreal) for her help in the research that this text required.
1 A recent example of this attitude can be found in the Federal Count of Appeal decision in *CCH Canadian Ltd* v. *Law Society of Upper Canada*, 2002 18 C.P.R. (4th) 161, where the Court was obviously suspicious of the analysis of the originality concept by the US Supreme Court decision in *Feist Publications, Inc.* v. *Rural Telephone Service Company, Inc.*, 498 U.S.808 1991.

P.L.C. Torremans (ed.), Copyright and Human Rights, 21–36
© *2004 Kluwer Law International. Printed in the Netherlands.*

matters that include copyright law. Such a lesser impact on copyright could further be explained by the hypothesis that copyright law already incorporates freedom of expression values through its own mechanisms. There would then be less need for an open confrontation between the two sets of rules. The first part of this paper will thus examine the situation from the perspective of these private law mechanisms, i.e. seek to understand how the Copyright Act internalises freedom of expression. In the second half, one will attempt to appreciate how the Charter, a public law instrument, has been affecting the relationship between copyright and freedom of expression.

II. Freedom of Expression Within the Copyright Act

Today, copyright law and freedom of expression are generally perceived as conflicting sets of values. Yet, one should not forget that the first modern copyright statutes could be perceived as elements of a certain triumph of the authors' freedom of expression over the control exerted by the stationers, in England, or through the privilege holders, in pre-Revolution France. The idea that copyright protection can act as a vehicle for freedom of expression took on an importance of its own and can be said to have reached its high point with Article 27(2) of the Universal Declaration on Human Rights:

> 'Everyone has the right to protection of the moral and material interests resulting from any scientific, literary or artistic production of which he is the author'.

This statement is echoed in Article 15(1)(c) of the United Nations Covenant on Economic, Social and Cultural Rights:

> 'The States Parties to the present Covenant recognize the right of everyone: [...] (c) To benefit from the protection of the moral and material interests resulting from any scientific, literary or artistic production of which he is the author'.

In this light, copyright has become a human right equal to freedom of expression.

However, if copyright can be regarded as a human right, a more contemporary understanding of that particular human right can lead one to see it as a human right for the 'happy few', i.e. for a small group within society, authors who are thus protected, that is pitted against the rest of society at large, those to whom their works are destined. It is because of this antagonism that the copyright system can be so often challenged by free speech partisans. Yet if authors are indeed protected, one can readily observe that their protection is already in itself limited by rules whose existence owes much to concerns about the freedom of expression of third parties. It is thus possible to read the Copyright Act with 'freedom of expression glasses' with particular attention to the rules governing (a) the identity of the protected work; (b) ownership; (c) term; and (d) all the prerogatives comprised within copyright.

II.1. Identity of the Protected Work

Several rules operate together so as to ensure that some works – or products of intellectual activity – do not come within the scope of copyright protection. When this happens, the works or products belong to the public domain and anyone may use them free of copyright considerations.

The first of such rules, of course, is the distinction that is made between ideas and facts, on the one hand, and works or expression, on the other hand. It is a fundamental precept of copyright that has precisely evolved in order to foster the possibility for all to voice their opinions on a shared commons of ideas and facts. Closely related to that premise is the requirement of originality: not only must the work be a 'work' as opposed to an idea or a fact, it must also be endowed with the quality of originality. However originality is defined in a country,[2] it should not be forgotten that the very existence of a criterion that is meant to determine if a work is protected or not entails that some works will not meet the requirement and thus will not be protected. Part of the concern over the sui generis right for databases, as devised in the European directive on these productions,[3] stems from the fact that it is precisely aimed at the creation of a scheme of protection for objects that would escape copyright protection.

In copyright countries, two other factors circumscribe the protection of works. The first one is the requirement of fixation: a work must be fixed in a tangible medium in order to be protected.[4] Again, depending on how stringently one defines this notion, a greater or lesser number of works will pass the test. The current interpretation of fixation, however, makes for a very broad criterion that encompasses virtually anything that is found on some medium,[5] though it still has

---

[2]   It is expected that the forthcoming decision of the Supreme Court of Canada in *CCH Canadian Ltd* v. *Law Society of Upper Canada* (see *ibid* for the appeal decision) will settle the matter in Canadian law.

[3]   Directive 96/9/EC of the European Parliament and of the Council on the legal protection of databases, 11 March 1996, *O.J.* No L 77/20, 27 March 1996.

[4]   On this issue in general, see Y. Gendreau, 'Le critère de fixation en droit d'auteur', in *RIDA* 159 (*Revue Internationale du Droit d'Auteur*) (1994) 111.

[5]   This situation results from the definition of fixation in the US *Copyright Act*: 'A work is fixed in a tangible medium of expression when its embodiment in a copy or phonorecord ... is *sufficiently permanent or stable to permit it to be perceived, reproduced, or otherwise communicated for a period of more than transitory duration*', 17 U.S.C.§ 101 (emphasis added). See *MAI Systems Corporation* v. *Peak Computers Inc.*, 991 F.2d 511 [1993]. The current concern over 'temporary or permanent' reproductions, as well as 'transient or incidental' ones, as found in the 2001 European directive on the information society can be traced back to this interpretation.

not come to terms with problem areas such as oral works.[6] Copyright countries whose legislations are directly inspired by UK statutes, i.e. essentially Commonwealth countries, face another hurdle: the strict division of works according to specific categories. Should it not belong to any of the defined literary, dramatic, musical, or artistic groups, a 'work' cannot be considered protected by copyright.[7] When a work can fit in a category, the identification of that category may have an impact on the exercise of copyright in that work.[8]

All in all, it is important to remember that not all products of creativity in the literary and artistic domain obtain protection under the Copyright Act. While the preoccupation with categories in Commonwealth countries can hardly be said to stem directly from a need to ensure that some works are not protected, the other conditions can be perceived as reflections of such a policy.

II.2. OWNERSHIP

It is perhaps less conventional to think of copyright ownership rules as concepts that incorporate freedom of expression values. Yet, this is particularly true in countries that distinguish ownership from authorship and wherever a legal definition of authorship is provided that differs from the traditional understanding of the author as the human creator of a work. The reason why such a link exists is that the award of ownership to someone other than the natural author determines who decides how the work is to be used. An author who is deprived of copyright ownership is being silenced in favour of someone whose judgement as to the exploitation of the work is favoured.

Canadian copyright law is rich in examples. In addition to a standard provision that grants copyright ownership in an employee's work to the employer,[9] there is an exception to that rule in favour of employed journalists who may want to exploit their works in a context other than a newspaper, magazine, or other periodical.[10] The Canadian statute, unlike the British Copyright Designs and Patents Act 1988, still retains the rule that awards copyright ownership to the person who commissions engravings, photographs, and portraits.[11] An examination of the

---

[6] See D.J. Brennan & A.F. Christie, 'Spoken Words and Copyright Subsistence in Anglo-American Law', in *IPQ* 4 (*Intellectual Property Quarterly*) (2000) 309.

[7] See *Creation Records Ltd.* v. *News Group Newspapers Ltd.*, in *EMLR* (*Entertainment and Media Law Reports*) (1997) 444, where the set-up for a photograph for an album jacket could not be classified under any heading.

[8] For instance, the general classification of cinematographic works as 'films' in the United Kingdom, as opposed to 'dramatic works', leads to different rules with respect to ownership, term, rights, and exceptions.

[9] *Copyright Act,* section 13(3).

[10] *Ibid.*

[11] *Copyright Act,* section 13(2).

case law that has spawned from this rule reveals how important are the privacy concerns of the commissioning parties in those instances.[12]

The most obvious situation is perhaps that of Crown copyright. Like the United Kingdom, Canada has a provision that grants to the Crown the copyright in material that is either prepared for it or published under its authority.[13] Section 12 of the Act thus allows for a continuing interrogation on the status of court judgements and statutory materials, for instance: to what extent can the State intervene to allow or, more importantly, prevent the dissemination of these texts? A prime example of the control over expression that copyright ownership rule can play can be found in a relatively recent attempt to expand the scope of Crown copyright. In 1997, a bill entitled An Act to amend the Criminal Code and the Copyright Act (profit from authorship respecting a crime) was introduced in Parliament.[14] Its purpose was to deprive convicted criminals, who had prepared or collaborated in the creation of a work 'substantially based on the indictable offence or the circumstances of its commission', of the copyright in that work. The copyright would vest in the Crown for the entire duration that would exist for that person's work. The aim was thus to prevent the convicted person from telling his story again and, at the same time, from profiteering from crime. One can well imagine that ownership of the copyright by the Crown would mean that the work would not be published.

This latter example offers a clear case of state censorship where one person's freedom of expression is thwarted by 'nobler' ideals. Yet, the other cases of employees' works and commissioned works can also be regarded as instances of 'private' censorship that exist for business or privacy reasons.

II.3. TERM OF PROTECTION

In contrast to ownership rules, term of protection is one of the classic examples of the trade-off between copyright protection and freedom of expression. At the end of a set period of time, works are no longer protected and anyone may use them as the basis of their own expression. People get used to the expectation that the works will become free of all copyright control at the end of a well-known length of time. The familiarization is shared by all and any change to the accepted rule can ignite emotionally charged debates, particularly when the term of protection is increased. Maybe because of the very real need for harmonization of term of protection, the change from 'life plus 50' to 'life plus 70' in 1993 in the European Union did not provoke the same furor as in 1998 in the United States. The European countries

---

[12] See, in general, Y. Gendreau, 'Copyright Ownership of Photographs in Anglo-American Law', in *EIPR* 15 (*European Intellectual Property Review*) (1993) 207.

[13] *Copyright Act,* section 12.

[14] Bill C-220, 36th Parl., 1st Session, 46 Eliz. II, 1997 (passed by the House of Commons: 1 October 1997).

were used to the 'life plus 50' rule for quite some time: it had been introduced in the Berlin 1908 revision of the Berne Convention and become compulsory with the 1948 revision in Brussels. In contrast, US law provided for a set term of 28 years upon publication renewable for another similar period until the coming into force of the Copyright Act 1976. It was only at that time that the 'life plus 50' rule was introduced. Less than twenty-five years later, that term was extended, partly in reaction to the European move, to 'life plus 70'.In a much shorter period of time, then, than in countries that have belonged to the Berne Union for a long time, the US term of protection changed from '28 + 28' to 'life plus 70'.It is hardly surprising, in such circumstances, that the debate on the relationship between copyright and freedom of expression, as expressed through the issue of the term of protection, took on such intensity.[15]

Special terms of protection for particular instances reflect similar policy considerations on a smaller scale. The Phase II amendments to the Canadian Copyright Act in 1997 changed the term for posthumous publications. Whereas it used to provide for a protection of fifty years from publication, the Act now has a series of rules that should gradually bring those cases in line with general rule on the term of protection.[16] At the other end of the spectrum is the issue of Crown copyright, which has a term of fifty years from publication.[17] One of the consequences of this rule is that a Crown copyright work that is never published, never has the opportunity to fall in the public domain. When one considers the potential scope for the application of this provision, it becomes clear that Crown copyright can be exercised to silence some authors whose opinions would be judged undesirable by public authorities.

II.4. COPYRIGHT PREROGATIVES

Just as not all creations are protected by copyright for eternity, not all acts that are done in relation to a work come within the scope of the copyright prerogatives. Of course, limitations on the exercise of copyright prerogatives are usually conceived in light of economic rights; but, especially in copyright countries, limitations also exist with respect to moral rights with the avowed aim to give greater freedom to third parties.

---

[15] The *Eldred* case has marked the judicial highpoint of this debate: *Eldred* v. *Ashcroft,* 123 S.Ct. 769 [2003].

[16] *Copyright Act,* section 7. In light of the looming end of a first transitional period, pressure has been brought on the government to postpone the expiration of the protection period. It has led to the introduction of a bill to that effect which breeds similar reactions, but on a much smaller scale of course, as the 'life plus 70' debate in the United States. See *An act to establish the Library and Archives of Canada, to amend the Copyright Act and to amend certain Acts in consequence,* Bill C-36, 37th Parl., 2nd Session, 51-52 Eliz. II, 2002-2003 (1st reading: 8 May 2003).

[17] *Copyright Act,* Section 12.

Exceptions to economic rights are not the only method through which the freedom of expression of others can be seen to thwart the copyright owner's rights. The very definition of the rights themselves can provide inherent containment. For instance, the performing right is always a shortened form of the 'right of public performance'. A recent Canadian example of definitional harness came with the Supreme Court decision in *Théberge* v. *Galérie d'art du Petit Champlain* where the right of reproduction was at stake.[18] The issue was the lamination onto blank canvases of posters and greeting cards based on the plaintiff's paintings. The majority of the Court found that no reproduction took place in the process because the colors were transferred from one medium to the other and the 'originals' were left blank: no multiplication of copies took places. Since no reproduction occurred, the copyright owner could not rely on the corresponding right to seek redress for what he perceived had been an encroachment of his rights. For the dissenting judges, however, the defendant's activities did constitute reproductions because, over time, new manifestations of the work were made. The definition of the right can thus determine in a very concrete manner the extent to which third parties may include a work in their own expression.

The most direct reflection of freedom of expression concerns in the field of copyright rights is to be found, of course, in the exceptions to these rights. In a Commonwealth country like Canada, the prime example will be the fair dealing exception with its specified purposes of 'research or private study', 'criticism or review', and 'newsreporting'.[19] There are also two specific exceptions that can be said to bear directly on the furtherance of free speech: one is to allow the report of a public lecture for the purposes of news reporting or news summary and the other is to allow the report of an address of a political nature given at a public meeting for similar purposes.[20] Both can be regarded, like many of the other exceptions, as specific applications of a general fair dealing principle just like, for instance, the exceptions concerning the public performance of music by religious, educational, fraternal, or charitable organizations in furtherance of their religious, educational or charitable objects.[21]

Compulsory licenses constitute another form of limitation on a copyright owner's rights. Indeed, their use can come in handy when it is judged impractical to request individual consent for the use of a work; but this latter form of approach is already a rationale for collective management without the element of coercion. When one goes beyond the efficiency considerations to set up a system of compulsory license, it is because the legislator wants to deny the copyright owner the possibility to refuse his consent to the use of the work. Those who want to use

---

[18] *Théberge* v. *Galerie d'art du Petit Champlain*, [2002] 17 C.P.R. (4th) 161 (S.C.C.).
[19] *Copyright Act*, Sections 29-29.2.
[20] *Copyright Act*, Sections 32.2(1)(c) and (e).
[21] *Copyright Act*, Section 32.2(3).

the work may not do so for free, but at least they need not worry about the copyright owner's whims.

The author's whims were very much at the forefront of the preoccupations of the Canadian legislator when moral rights, initially introduced in 1931, were revamped in the Phase I amendments of 1987. As in all copyright countries, the moral rights that are recognized are subject to important qualifications: the right to paternity can only be asserted 'when reasonable in the circumstances';[22] likewise, the right of integrity is only infringed when the use of the work prejudices 'the honor or reputation of the author'.[23] These limits, which are actually part of the definition of these rights, are designed to prevent authors from exercising their rights to the fullest because 'unhindered' moral rights are perceived as instruments that can impede the free flow of works. The right of integrity, in particular, can act as a real break on the re-utilization of a protected work by third parties.

Freedom of expression concerns are perhaps most openly articulated through the exceptions to copyright. Yet one can see that they inherently shape many of the copyright rules to some extent. Nowadays, this kind of barnessing from within is perceived as insufficient, probably because it is not upfront enough. In this kind of context, a text like the Charter of Human Rights and Freedoms has the potential to be an instrument that makes freedom of expression interests more obvious in the interpretation of the Copyright Act.

III. The Canadian *Charter* and the Copyright Act

The question to be put is the following: to what extent does the Charter change the balance that is already struck by the Copyright Act? The short answer is: not much. Copyright legislation has been around for nearly three centuries; the Charter is a much more recent phenomenon and has not yet really managed to make its mark on copyright law.

One should not forget that it is not the first time that a public law rule is likely to come in conflict with copyright law. There is a fairly long history of run-ins with the regulation of obscene works.[24] The first Canadian Copyright Act after Confederation in 1867 excluded from protection any 'immoral, licentious, irreligious, treasonable or seditious book or any other . . .work'.[25] This prohibition lasted till the coming into force, in 1924, of the Copyright Act that forms the basis of today's legislation. Nevertheless, the obscenity of some works has been questioned in some post-1924 court decisions. In *Pasickniack* v. *Dojacek*, the trial

---

[22] *Copyright Act*, Section 14.1(1).

[23] *Copyright Act*, Section 28.2(1).

[24] On this topic in general, see R.G. Howell, 'Copyright and Obscenity: Should Copyright Regulate Content?', in *IPJ* 8 (*Intellectual Property Journal*) (1994) 139.

[25] *The Copyright Act, 1868*, S.C. 1868, chapter 54, Section 3.

judge found a book on the interpretation of dreams obscene and thus denied it protection; on appeal, the court reversed the decision on its facts and thus accepted that the work was protected since it was not obscene.[26] Nearly sixty years later and five years after the adoption of the Charter, another defendant raised the obscene nature of videotapes he had copied without authorization to deny accusations of infringement. The court recognized that the prohibition on the protection of obscene works had disappeared from the Act; yet it found that the plaintiff could only be entitled to an injunction and to damages or other monetary compensation because the sale of the tapes was an illegal activity.[27] A similar defence was raised in criminal proceedings the following year to deflect the accusations, but to no avail in those circumstances.[28] The court did refer to the Charter in that case: the 'supremacy of God', to which it alludes in its opening provision, cannot be thwarted by a freedom of expression that manifests itself through grossly immoral pornographic material that is contrary to the standards of tolerant Canadians.

While they confirm that public law rules may interfere with the application of the Copyright Act, these examples do not really lead to a fundamental challenge of the underpinnings of the statute. With the Charter provision on freedom of expression, however, a potential conflict has indeed emerged over time. Two particular problem areas have become apparent in judicial proceedings: (a) Crown copyright material; and (b) fair dealing.

III.1. CROWN COPYRIGHT MATERIAL

The advent of the Charter has not led to a questioning of the existence of Crown copyright per se. In particular, one could have expected or even welcomed a debate on the relevance of Crown copyright over statutory and judicial materials where the notion of freedom of expression could shed new light on state control over these texts that are so essential to the working of a democratic justice system.[29] The discussion that has come the closest to this issue is one that pertains to the access to court judgments. Otherwise, one must mention a fundamental, and rather early, case on a government publication.

In *Wilson & Lafleur Ltée* v. *SOQUIJ*,[30] a private publisher of law reports was at odds with a government agency, SOQUIJ, that both collects and publishes court judgments. As far as the collecting of judgments is concerned, SOQUIJ operates in a state monopoly environment for it is the only entity which is entrusted by law to

---

[26] *Pasickniack* v. *Dojacek*, [1928] 2 D.L.R. 545.
[27] *Aldrich* v. *One Stop Video Ltd.*, [1987] 17 C.P.R. (3rd) 27.
[28] *R.* v. *Ghnaim*, [1988] 28 C.P.R. (3rd) 463.
[29] On this debate, see J.A.L. Sterling, 'Crown Copyright in the United Kingdom and Other Commonwealth Countries', in *IPJ* 10 (1996) 157; J. Frémont, 'Normative State Information, Democracy and Crown Copyright', in *IPJ* 11 (1996) 19.
[30] [1998] R.J.Q. 2489.

operate an activity that allows it to obtain all judgments rendered by courts in Quebec. With such 'raw materials', SOQUIJ publishes various series of law reports. A person who wishes to obtain the judgments as they were issued by the courts may ask for a copy and pay a charge of CAN $ 2.00 per page. This fee applies to published as well as unpublished judgments. The publishing arm of SOQUIJ, however, gets the judgments at cost. Wilson & Lafleur claimed that the situation was discriminatory and prevented it from doing business on the same grounds as SOQUIJ the publisher. In particular, it claimed that it wanted access at cost to judgments that are being left aside by SOQUIJ and that therefore its products would not be competing with those of SOQUIJ.

The freedom of expression argument was used in the following manner. Wilson & Lafleur considers itself a member of the legal press and includes freedom of the press within freedom of expression. The high costs charged by SOQUIJ prevent it from running its business on an equal footing with what is admittedly the largest legal publisher of the province. Therefore, these costs constitute a hindrance to its freedom of expression. The Superior Court of Quebec did not respond favorably to this line of argument. It found that Wilson & Lafleur's expression was not being restrained, but rather that the publisher merely suffered economic harm. Access to judgments was not being denied since it could obtain them like any other person. SOQUIJ's pricing policy does not restrain the right to information, the freedom to gather judgments, access to courts, the freedom to talk about the functioning of the justice system, and so forth. In short, freedom of expression was being trumped up as an excuse for claims of unfair competition. It is nevertheless worth noting that it was used in a context where the subject matter that was being fought over was Crown copyright material.

More to the point – and actually the earliest case on the conflict between copyright and freedom of expression – is the Federal Court of Appeal decision in *R. v. James Lorimer &Co. Ltd.*[31] The object of contention was a one-volume abridgement of a seven-volume report titled *Canada's Oil Monopoly* that had been prepared by the Director of Investigation and Research under the then Combines Investigation Act (the former Competition Act). According to the Copyright Act, such a text was subject to Crown copyright.[32] The defendant raised three separate defences to the infringement action: fair dealing for the purposes of review; public interest; freedom of expression according to the Charter.

All three defences were rejected. The Court did not find that this was a situation where the defence of fair dealing was applicable because the use of the original work was not minimal.[33] Likewise, the common law defence of public interest

---

[31] [1984] 77 C.P.R. (2nd) 262.
[32] *Copyright Act*, Section 12.
[33] It is often said that it is very difficult to rely on the fair dealing defence successfully. So far, there seems to be only one reported case where the defendant won on the basis of that defence: *Allen v. Toronto Star Newspapers Ltd.*, [1997] 78 C.P.R. (3rd) 115.

could not come into play because enough free copies of the report were available throughout the country; people could thus easily have access to the ideas put forth in the report.[34] The innovative aspect of the decision lies in the recognition that the Charter of Human Rights and Freedoms could form a defence to copyright infringement. Moreover, this seems to be the case independently of the other defences that could be available. Despite this openness towards this new type of argument in copyright litigation, the court nevertheless concludes that the Charter was of no avail to the defendant in that particular instance because the abridgement contained so little of its own thoughts, beliefs, opinions, and expression. The defendant's activity had been more akin to an act of appropriation than to one of self-expression. The freedom of expression that was to be protected by the Charter to the benefit of the defendant had to be *Lorimer*'s expression and the mere abridgement of another's work could not warrant reliance on the Charter.

The *Lorimer* decision has proved to be a lucid forerunner of the later decisions on copyright and freedom of expression according to the Canadian Charter. Without stating so openly, it set the stage for the conflict between contents and form or, to put it in standard copyright parlance, between idea and expression. The Charter is probably more designed to protect contents (idea) rather than form (expression); since copyright does not protect ideas, it is likely that the spheres of protection do not really clash. A second observation is that the Charter argument, though independent, was made together with arguments based on the public interest defence and on the fair dealing exception. Although the public interest argument is much more difficult to put forward in Canada than in the United Kingdom, fair dealing has been the mainstay of the confrontation between copyright law and freedom of expression.

III.2. FAIR DEALING

One should not expect here a plethora of decisions that finely dissect the relationship between copyright and freedom of expression. Of the five cases that refer to it, only one provides substantial reasoning. Moreover, the relatively cursory dismissal of the Charter argument in the *Lorimer* case, an appeal decision, can only have had the effect of curbing what initial enthusiasm there could have been in the early years. Direct references to the Charter have however been made in cases that all arose during labour disputes. They essentially revolved around corporate logos or trademarks that had been 'distorted' by the employees' unions at times of labour unrest. That a Charter argument has been made in that context is maybe a reflection of the greater familiarity of labour law lawyers with this legal

---

[34] Unlike UK copyright law (*Copyright, Designs and Patents Act* 1988, section 171(3)), the public interest defence in Canada has no statutory connection. On this defence in general, see G. Davies, *Copyright and the Public Interest*, London, Sweet & Maxwell (2nd ed., 2002) 63 *et seq.*

instrument. Only one case in this group of five is not labour-related: it dealt with a porn version of the most popular television soap opera in Quebec where the defendant tried unsuccessfully to rely on the exception of fair dealing for the purpose of criticism.[35] In its analysis of the exception, the Quebec Court of Appeal declared that one needed to draw a distinction between humorous imitation for criticism or comment and appropriation for commercial opportunism, having regard to 'copyright protection as well as freedom of expression'. The reference to freedom of expression is here very general and even independent of the Charter itself. Yet, its mere mention may be regarded as a reflection that the inroads into legal reasoning that have been made in the other cases may be starting to produce a more general effect on the analysis of fair dealing beyond the narrower context of labour disputes.[36]

Soon after the *Lorimer* decision came two other attempts to invoke the Charter protection of freedom of expression as defences to alleged infringement by the workers' union through the modification of company logos. In both instances, the argument was cursorily dismissed, though the courts paid lip service to the possibility that it could be relevant. 'While there may be situations where the guarantee of freedom of expression in paragraph 2(b) of the Canadian Charter of Rights and Freedoms may properly limit the protection otherwise given to the owners of copyright, I do not believe this represents such a situation'.[37] Similarly, the Charter was found inapplicable in a case where an injunction was sought to prevent the use of the parodied logo of a roast chicken restaurant chain. The court considered that the grant of the injunction would not prevent the union from informing the public about its position in the labour dispute; thus, the freedom of expression was not violated by the exercise of copyright in the logo.[38]

Together with the *Lorimer* case, these two decisions seemed to indicate a general unwillingness to explore the reasoning required by this line of argument, an argument which forces all parties to rethink the concepts of infringement and the role that defences that are extraneous to the Copyright Act can play. Although unmentioned, one can again perceive the tension between contents and form where copyright protection and the Charter might be operating on two different fields. The decisions make no reference to the fair dealing defence. Yet, they are regularly

---

[35] *Productions Avanti Ciné-Vidéo Inc.* v. *Favreau*, [1999] 1 C.P.R. (4th) 129 (Que. C.A.).

[36] The *Avanti* decision is but two years after the more fundamental *Michelin* case. See, *infra*, the text accompanying note 40.

[37] *Canadian Tire Corporation Ltd.* v. *Retail Clerk Union, Local 518 of United Food & Commercial Workers Union*, [1985] 7 C.P.R. (3rd) 415, at p. 420.

[38] *Rôtisseries St-Hubert Ltée* v. *Le Syndicat des Travailleurs(euses) de la Rôtisserie St-Hubert de Drummondville (C.S.N.)*, [1986] 17 C.P.R. (3rd) 461, at p. 476.

cited when the next case is discussed, most probably because of the similarity in the fact patterns.[39]

The *Michelin*[40] case, about a parody of the Bibendum man, is indeed the most explicit decision on the conflict between copyright protection and freedom of expression as guaranteed by the Charter. Thirteen years after the *Lorimer* decision, it bravely renews with an analysis that combines the freedom of expression defence with a pleading of fair dealing. Once again, the fair dealing exception is set aside: the court refuses to consider that parody can come within the notion of criticism and insists on the technical identification requirements of the statute. The analysis of the Charter argument is handled separately as the Court wonders if the parodies are protected by the Charter provision on freedom of expression. Its answer is both specific to the case and general; and the outcome is, once again, favorable to the copyright owner.

The first step in the reasoning is a property argument. The Court considers that one cannot use another's private property right (copyright protected material) to express one's self. If one does use such property, then he must demonstrate a use that is compatible with the function of that good. That function of copyright calls into question a second consideration, i.e. the general purpose of copyright protection. Framed in a Charter perspective, it leads to an interrogation as to the nature of copyright law along the following lines: is the object or effect of the Copyright Act to restrict freedom of expression? The answer to that question is negative because the rights that are granted by the Act are justified in a free and democratic society (language that directly refers to the first article of the Charter). The objectives sought by a statute like the Copyright Act are important enough to justify the suppression of a fundamental right and the means that are used to implement these objectives are in themselves reasonable and justified.

In comparison with the earlier case law, the *Michelin* decision is more explicit and articulates its reasoning according to a more usual Charter language. It also avoids the contents/form discourse that underlay the conflicts as they were presented. However, the conclusion it draws with respect to the general appreciation of the Copyright Act in light of the Charter seems to put a break on any further analysis of the relationship between the two sets of rights. If copyright law as a whole can withstand the pressure of the freedom of expression value that is enshrined in the Charter, how can a single notion within copyright law itself, however fundamental it is, fare better? One can only expect that

---

[39] See D. Vaver, *Copyright Law*, Toronto, Irwin Law (2000) p. 193, footnote 109; J.S. Mc Keown, *Fox on Canadian Law of Copyright and Industrial Designs*, 3rd ed., Toronto, Carswell (2000), p. 585, footnote 118. One should also appreciate that the fair dealing defence has been almost ignored by litigants until the 1990s.

[40] *Cie Générale des Établissements Michelin – Michelin & Cie* v. *C.A.W. Canada*, [1996] 71 C.P.R. (3rd) 348.

copyright litigants and courts will pay lip service to the Charter, just as happened in the *Avanti* decision two years later.[41]

Indeed, the last case in this Canadian survey is already a reflection that the Charter argument does not lead anywhere in a copyright analysis; it may however become more useful in 'peripheral' reasoning. During interlocutory injunction proceedings over alleged copyright infringement by a union whose web site had similar interface, logos, addresses, etc. as the plaintiff's own, a fair dealing defence was raised and met with the same result as *Michelin*.[42] The Charter right to freedom of expression was also pleaded by the union, but in a different manner than what had been done previously. The union argued that its right to freedom of expression was being limited by its inability to appropriate or get at the plaintiff's intellectual property rights. The argument was rejected in relation to copyright, but accepted with respect to passing off: the common law was not to be interpreted in a way that unreasonably infringes a person's freedom of expression. Consequently, the injunction sought by the plaintiff was not granted because, furthermore, the balance of convenience favored the union.

IV. Conclusion

At the end of this exercise, it feels like being back to square one. Although there have been some attempts to come to grips with a fundamental right like freedom of expression, Canadian copyright law remains unaffected. Is this Canadian experience unique? At this point, it might be worth looking at recent developments in this area in the United Kingdom, a country that shares with Canada both constitutional and copyright roots. Moreover, despite some differences, there are interesting similarities in the way copyright law is confronted with freedom of expression in both countries. The European Convention on Human Rights was signed in 1950, but implemented in the United Kingdom only through the Human Rights Act 1998 which came into force in 2000. The Human Rights Act thus incorporates the right to freedom of expression in a statute separate from the Copyright Act and, like its Canadian counterpart, allows for this right to be overridden by other concerns.[43] However, that separate statute does not have in

---

[41] *Production Avanti Ciné-Vidéo Inc.* v. *Favreau, supra,* note 35.

[42] *British Columbia Automobile Association* v. *Office and Professional Employees' International Union, Local 378,* [2001] 10 C.P.R. (4th) 423.

[43] On this issue in UK law in general, see J. Griffiths, 'Copyright Law and Censorship – The Impact of the Human Rights Act 1998' in E.M. Barendt & A. Firth (eds.), *The Yearbook of Copyright and Media Law 1999,* Oxford, Oxford University Press (1999), p. 3; T. Pinto, 'The Influence of the European Convention on Human Rights on Intellectual Property Rights', in *EIPR* (2002) 209; M. D. Birnhack, 'Acknowledging the Conflict between Copyright Law and Freedom of Expression under the Human Rights Act', in *Entertainment Law Review* (2003) 24; C. Ryan, 'Human Rights and Intellectual Property', in *EIPR* (2001) 521; J. Griffiths, 'Copyright in English Literature: Denying the Public Domain', in *EIPR* (2000) 150. From a

UK law the constitutional stature of the Canadian Charter of Human Rights and Freedoms. Another difference in this debate is that the public interest defence in the United Kingdom has some statutory basis in the Copyright, Designs and Patents Act 1988.[44] It is relevant in the present context because many cases that are brought to court and that pit copyright against freedom of expression combine arguments based on both fair dealing and public interest. Lastly, the UK cases often refer to breach of confidence or breach of fiduciary duty, as well as to passing off, something to which the Canadian fact patterns did not lend themselves easily.

Before the coming into force of the Human Rights Act, allusions have been made to the protection of the freedom of expression guaranteed by the European Convention on Human Rights in some major cases of copyright infringement. In both the *Spycatcher*[45] and the *Blake*[46] decisions, defences that were somewhat related to freedom of expression were of no serious avail. The situation changed, however, with the Human Rights Act since that statute had become very clearly part of the law of the land. So far, the high point of judicial analysis on the relationship between the freedom of expression of the Human Rights Act and copyright law has been the appeal decision in the *Ashdown* case.[47] In this case about the publication of the verbatim transcript of private meetings between high profile politicians, both the fair dealing and the public interest defences even rejected. The Court then examined the impact of the Human Rights Act on copyright law. It found that the Copyright Act already restricts rights in a necessary fashion in light of freedom of expression concerns and that conflicts will occur only in rare cases. It seems to tie freedom of expression to the public interest defence, but recognizes that it may stand alone as a factor to consider, especially when an injunction is sought. Similar general observations are made, but with an even less interventionist approach, in a subsequent case where an interim injunction was sought to restrain the publication of some confidential

---

cont.

more general European perspective, see H. Cohen Jehoram, 'Freedom of Expression in Copyright Law', in *EIPR* (1984) 3; C. Caron, 'La Convention européenne des droits de l'homme et la communication des œuvres au public: une menace pour le droit d'auteur?' in *Communication, Commerce Électronique* No. 1 (1999) 9; F. Dessemontet, 'Copyright and Human Rights' in J.J.C. Kabel & G.J.H.M. Mom (eds.), *Intellectual Property and Information Law-Essays in Honour of Herman Cohen Jehoram*, The Hague, Kluwer (1998), p. 113; P.B. Hugenholtz, 'Copyright and Freedom of Expression in Europe' in R.C. Dreyfuss, H. First & D.L. Zimmerman (eds.), *Innovation Policy in an Information Age*, Oxford, Oxford University Press (2000), p. 1.

[44] See, *supra*, note 34.
[45] *Attorney General* v. *Guardian Newspapers Ltd*, [1990] 1 A.C. 109.
[46] *Attorney General* v. *Blake*, [1998] 1 Ch. 439.
[47] *Ashdown* v. *Telegraph Group Ltd.*, [2001] 4 All E.R.618. See L. Joseph, 'Human Rights versus Copyright: the Paddy Ashdown Case', in *Entertainment Law Review* (2002) 72.

documents.[48] There, the fair dealing defence is immediately rejected and the consideration of the public interest defence leads to the conclusion that the end result would favour the plaintiff. The Court is also of the opinion that courts have already been taking into account freedom of expression interests well before the Human Rights Act and that this Act does not change the emphasis that is to be put on that principle in the interpretation of the law.

From the foregoing, one cannot say that, in Canada as well as in the United Kingdom, the official recognition of freedom of expression has revolutionized copyright law. There is no enthusiastic embracing that has led to the revisiting of the statutes. Because of a very weak public interest defence in Canada, recourse to freedom of expression analysis is less extensive in that country than in the United Kingdom. Yet, despite the possibilities to reason in the context of special doctrines within copyright law, the courts in both countries have not hesitated to comment on the overall scheme of the copyright statutes. Given the kind of language that can be found in the latest decisions, one suspects that the high point in this debate has already been reached and that freedom of expression arguments will be relegated to last ditch marginal pleadings.

This attitude is quite different from what continues to happen in the United States where references to free speech arguments continue to be made regularly.[49] How can one explain such a phenomenon? The reason may lie in the history of the relationship between copyright law and freedom of expression. The first US copyright statute dates from 1790 while the First Amendment to the Constitution, which protects free speech, came the following year. Not only have both concepts evolved along each other from their very beginnings, but both share a constitutional legitimacy which has no equivalent in Canadian and, *a fortiori*, in UK copyright law. It should take a very long time before Canadian law evolves to such a point as to close the gap between such differences.

---

[48] *Imutran Ltd.* v. *Uncaged Campaigns Ltd*, [2001] All E.R.(D) 08.

[49] See, for instance, the case about *The Wind Done Gone,* the novel based on Margaret Mitchell's *Gone With the Wind: Suntrust Bank* v. *Houghton Mifflin Co.*, 268 F. 3d 1257 (11th Cir. 2001).

Chapter 3

Copyrighting Speech: A Trans-Atlantic View

*Michael D. Birnhack**

I.   Introduction

In the 'information age', the volume of human knowledge and its dissemination are greater than ever before and this is surely a cause for celebration. At the same time, however, our public sphere continues to shrink. More and more areas are carved out of the public sphere and enclosed behind digital locks, contracts and property rights; more speech is commodified and commercialized, excluding those who cannot afford access. The masters of the enclosed domain might exercise control over cash flow, but they also control others' cultural opportunities to express themselves and participate in the public discourse. If the masters do not like someone's use of their property, they have an arsenal of technological and legal means to prevent that use. One of the main legal tools of enclosure is copyright law. Hence, there is a conflict between copyright and speech.

The digital world is global, and this is old news. However, despite the expansion of global arrangements of copyright law,[1] it still remains a territorial law, and so does free speech jurisprudence: it differs from one place to another. This chapter examines the way in which the conflict between copyright and free speech is addressed in courtrooms on both sides of the Atlantic and suggests an explanation for the different attitudes.

Two intuitions come to mind. Firstly, we know that some European countries protect the moral rights of authors, and at the expense of an over-generalization, we can say that they explain copyright law on a natural rights theory. Secondly, we recall the almost religious way in which the First Amendment is followed in the US Under these intuitions, we would expect that in cases of a free speech/copyright conflict, the copyright owners would prevail in Europe and lose in the US. At

---

*   Lecturer, Faculty of Law, Haifa University, Israel. LL.B., 1996, Tel Aviv University; LL.M., 1998, New York University; J.S.D., 2000, New York University. The author thanks Jonathan Griffiths for helpful comments, and Martijn DeKeizer, Khalid Genayem and Gavan Gravesen for assistance with materials in Dutch and German.
[1]   Especially the World Trade Organisation's Agreement on Trade Related aspects of Intellectual Property Rights (TRIPS) and the WIPO Copyright Treaty (1996) (WCT).

P.L.C. Torremans (ed.), Copyright and Human Rights, 37–62
© *2004 Kluwer Law International. Printed in the Netherlands.*

least, we would assume that the First Amendment would be taken into consideration and would be less surprised if in Europe free expression is not directly considered.[2] However, the current legal status of the conflict discourse is opposite. Free speech is more likely to be considered explicitly by European courts and less likely to be considered in the US. This puzzle motivates this chapter.

Two recent cases illustrate this trans-Atlantic difference: *Eldred* v. *Ashcroft* in the US, in which the Supreme Court found that the Copyright Term Extension Act of 1998 (CTEA), an act which extended the duration of protection from 'life plus fifty' to 'life plus seventy', is constitutional. The Court rejected the argument that the a First Amendment should have a role in deciding copyright cases, though the decision contains some general guidelines for defining the line between copyright and speech. The other case is *Ashdown* v. *Telegraph Group Ltd.*, decided by the Court of Appeal in the UK. Defendants in an infringement case raised a freedom of expression defence and though the Court ultimately rejected this claim, it was more willing to consider the effect freedom of expression on copyright law, at least rhetorically.

These different approaches to the role of free speech in copyright law does not necessarily refer to the bottom line of a particular discussion, i.e., whether the party who raised a free speech argument wins or loses, but to the methodology applied. The conflict between copyright law and free speech has many levels. The perspective taken here is a constitutional-methodological one. Different methodologies might result in different conclusions. It is proposed here that the explanation of the puzzle can be found in a distinction between two kinds of copyright-free speech conflicts. One is *internal* to copyright law, and the other is *external* to it. Roughly speaking, the American view of the conflict is internal, and the emerging European approach is external. The reason for the different approaches is rooted in the underlying rationale of copyright law on each continent.

The following sections are each devoted to American law and European law. Each reviews the rough consensus as to the understanding of copyright law in each jurisdiction and the status of free speech in either jurisdiction: the First Amendment and Article 10 of the ECHR. Next, the judicial response each jurisdiction provided to the *conflict argument*, i.e., the argument that there is a conflict between copyright law and free speech, is outlined through a short discussion of *Eldred* and *Ashdown*. The conclusion unties the puzzle presented here.

---

[2]   I will use 'free speech' (which is the American term) and 'freedom of expression' (the European term) interchangeably.

II. The American Experience: Denying the Conflict

II.1. COPYRIGHT LAW AS AN INSTRUMENTAL REGIME

American copyright law is anchored in the Constitution and is widely interpreted as a utilitarian regime. The Constitution grants Congress the power to 'promote the Progress of Science ..., by securing for limited Times to Authors ... the exclusive Right to their ... Writings'.[3] Copyright is generally understood to be a legal artefact, and not a natural right. Thomas Jefferson insisted that this is the best understanding of intellectual property.[4] Congress held a close view,[5] and the Supreme Court agreed. *Mazer* v. *Stein* is a typical and an oft-quoted summary of the utilitarian view:

> 'The economic philosophy behind the clause empowering Congress to grant patents and copyrights is the conviction that encouragement of individual effort by personal gain is the best way to advance public welfare through the talents of authors and inventors in "Science and useful Arts" '.[6]

The American copyright scheme is quite clear: there is a goal to be accomplished, and its nature is a public interest. The means to achieve the public goal is according rights to individuals. Copyright is thus an instrument, the justification of which depends on, and is derived from, the public goal. The rights of the individual are, accordingly, secondary to the public goal. The emphasis on the public is pervasive throughout the history of American copyright law. Courts emphasised that there is a hierarchy in which the public goal ranks higher than the rights: 'The copyright law, like the patent statutes, makes reward to the owner a secondary consideration';[7] '[t]he limited grant is a means by which an important public purpose may be achieved'.[8] Or:

> 'The limited scope of the copyright holder's statutory monopoly, like the limited copyright duration required by the Constitution, reflects a balance of competing claims upon the public interest: Creative work is to be encouraged and rewarded, but private motivation must ultimately serve the cause of promoting broad public availability of literature, music and other arts'.[9]

---

[3]   US Constitution, Article I, §8 clause 8.
[4]   See discussion in *Graham* v. *John Deere Company of Kansas City*, 383 U.S. 1, 8-9 [1966].
[5]   See e.g., H.R. No. 2222, 60th Congress, 2nd Session.
[6]   347 U.S. 201, 219 [1954] (internal quotation marks omitted).
[7]   *Ibid.*
[8]   *Sony Corp. of America* v. *Universal City Studios*, 464 U.S. 417 [1984].
[9]   *Twentieth Century Music Corp.* v. *Aiken*, 422 U.S. 151, 156 [1975].

Congress held a similar view.[10] This scheme rests on some economic observations.[11] The rights are understood as incentives to authors, without which they might not create intellectual works.

Under this scheme, the debate focuses on the meaning of the public goal: One answer emanates from the economic analysis and views the goal as maximizing welfare. This analysis carries important insights and in some instances is a helpful tool. The law, under this view, is busy protecting copyright and strengthening it. But from this point forward it is just a short route to view copyright law through only one pair of lenses: that of the market. Copyright law is interpreted along lines of cost/benefit and when this happens some values find it hard to survive on this playground. The public interest in free speech is one of these excluded players.

Another answer reads the public goal as having a political dimension and shapes the right accorded to authors accordingly. Various scholars attempted to articulate this political goal. L. Ray Patterson and Stanley Lindberg celebrate the *users* of knowledge and their demand for sufficient information and knowledge.[12] They insist that we should be guided by the goal of copyright law, which is understood as maximizing the public's interest in promoting the progress of knowledge. The emphasis, accordingly, is not only on the *creation* of knowledge, but on its *use* as well. The use requires that works are created, but also that they are disseminated and that access thereto is guaranteed.

This view is deeply rooted in a political view of democracy. Knowledge (which is the original meaning of the constitutional phrase 'science'),[13] is valuable, for it serves other values that we, in a democratic society, cherish. More and better knowledge enables us, collectively, to make better decisions about our community. Better knowledge means that deliberation and discourse are improved. This, in turn serves democratic values such as self-government and equal participation. Knowledge is for *all* to have, rather than to be concentrated in the hands of few.[14]

---

[10] The House Report on the 1909 Copyright Act explained that copyright law is 'Not primarily for the benefit of the author, but primarily for the benefit of the public'. – H.R. 2222, 60th Congress, 2nd Session, 7.

[11] See W.M. Landes & R.A. Posner, 'An Economic Analysis of Copyright Law', in *Journal of Legal Studies* 18 (1989) 325.

[12] L.R. Patterson & S.W. Lindberg, *The Nature of Copyright: A Law of User's Rights*, Athena, Ga. (1991).

[13] E.C. Walterscheid, 'To Promote the Progress of Science and Useful Arts: The Background and Origin of The Intellectual Property Clause of the United States Constitution', in *Journal of Intellectual Property Law* 2 (1994) 1, 51.

[14] Few scholars advocated a democratic understanding of copyright law, though there are important differences between them. See N. Elkin-Koren, 'Cyberlaw and Social Change: A Democratic Approach to Copyright Law in Cyberspace', in *Cardozo Arts & Entertainment Law Journal* 14 (1996) 215; N.W. Netanel, 'Copyright and a Democratic Civil Society', in *Yale Law Journal* 106 (1996) 283; Y. Benkler, 'Free as the Air to Common Use: First Amendment Constraints on Enclosure of the Public Domain', in *New York University Law Review* 74 (1999) 354.

II.2. THE FIRST AMENDMENT

The First Amendment prohibits government from restricting free speech.[15] Two points are important for our discussion. One is that despite its language the Amendment is not understood to be an absolute prohibition.[16] It is read as embodying a moral principle, and much of the jurisprudence regarding it is an attempt to articulate this principle.[17] The second point is the methodology applied to free speech matters. Contemporary jurisprudence is not one that balances free speech considerations against other interests, but rather applies a categorical approach.[18] It is first asked whether the expression at stake is *covered* by the Amendment.[19] Obscenity for example is not covered.[20] If it is covered, the speech at stake is classified. Political speech is accorded the highest level of protection, whereas commercial speech (currently) receives a somewhat lower level of protection and so on.[21] The nature of the restriction is also examined: whether it is content-based or content-neutral. The medium is also relevant: Print deserves different treatment than broadcast, cable another kind, the Internet yet another.[22] All theses factors are translated into the level of scrutiny courts apply.

This methodology is important for our purposes, for copyright – if seen as an

---

[15] US Constitution, Amendment I: 'Congress shall make no law ... abridging the freedom of speech, or of the press'.

[16] Justice Hugo Black's views that it is an absolute prohibition did not gain support. See *New York Times* v. *Sullivan*, 376 U.S. 254, 292 [1964] (Black, J., concurring); and *Beauharniais* v. *Illinois*, 343 U.S. 250, 254 [1952] (rejection of the view).

[17] See R. Dworkin, *Freedom's Law – The Moral Reading of the Constitution*, Cambridge, Mass. (1996), 72; and, generally F. Schauer, *Free Speech: A Philosophical Enquiry*, Cambridge, UK (1982), 89.

[18] 'Balancing' has acquired a rather specific meaning in American constitutional law and refers to *ad hoc* balancing. A different kind of balancing is definitional. See M.B. Nimmer, 'The Right to Speak from Times to TIME: First Amendment Theory Applied to Libel and Misapplied to Privacy', in *California Law Review* 56 (1968) 935, 942. For a critical discussion of balancing in US law, see T.A. Aleinikoff, 'Constitutional Law in the Age of Balancing', in *Yale Law Journal* 96 (1987) 943.

[19] 'Coverage' and its companion term, 'protection', are of F. Schauer, *op. cit.* in footnote 17, at 89.

[20] The debate then turns on the definition of 'obscenity'. See *Roth* v. *United States*, 354 U.S. 476 [1957] and *Miller* v. *California*, 413 U.S. 12 [1973].

[21] Compare, e.g., the high level of scrutiny applied to political speech in the Pentagon Papers case, to the four-part test applied in commercial speech cases, see *Central Hudson Gas and Elect. Corp.* v. *Public Service Communication*, 447 U.S. 557 [1980].

[22] Compare *Miami Herald Publishing Co.* v. *Tornillo*, 418 U.S. 241 [1974] (print) to *Red Lion Broadcasting Co.* v. *FCC*, 395 U.S. 367 [1969] (radio); *Denver Area Educational Telecommunications Consortium* v. *FCC*, 116 S. Ct. 2374 [1996] (cable); *ACLU* v. *Reno*, 521 U.S. 844 [1997] (Internet).

interference with free speech – should be examined under it.[23] The categorical methodology does not weigh the free speech rights of one party against the copyright rights of the other party. That would be balancing approach, and not the law in the US, at least not the declared law.

II.3. The Response to the Conflict Argument[24]

How did the American legal system react to the claim that under certain circumstances there might be a conflict between copyright law and the First Amendment? The argument was first raised in three law review articles in 1970.[25] They responded to two cases in which the copyright-free speech collision seemed to be frontal. *Time Inc.* v. *Bernard Geis Associates*,[26] addressed the use of the famous – and copyrighted – Zapruder film which captured the assassination of President John F. Kennedy. Defendant drew sketches based on frames from the film in a book about the investigation. The court refused to prohibit the use of the images. In *Rosemont Enterprises* v. *Random House Inc.*,[27] the court refused to allow Howard Hughes to assert copyright (through a corporation he controlled) so as to block a biographer from using certain raw materials in a biography about Hughes. In both cases the copyright owners' claims were rejected on the grounds of the fair use defence. The First Amendment was not explicitly mentioned in either case.

In the early 1970s the conflict argument found its way to courts. The initial judicial response was to reject it outright. In *McGraw-Hill*, for example, a district court in New York explained that 'Defendant's First Amendment argument, in so far as it is distinguishable from their claim of fair use, can be dismissed as flying in the face of established law'.[28] Other cases in which the argument was raised rejected the relevance of the First Amendment to copyright law, adopting an originalist mode of interpretation. They relied on an argument from the history of

---

[23] Netanel and Benkler separately argued that a rigorous intermediate scrutiny should be applied to the CTEA. The *Eldred* court, however, refused. See N.W. Netanel, 'Locating Copyright within the First Amendment Skein', in *Stanford Law Review* 54 (2001) 1; Y. Benkler, 'Through the Looking Glass: Alice and the Constitutional Foundations of the Public Domain', in *Law and Contemporary Problems* 66 (2003) 173; and *Eldred*, at 788-789.

[24] For an analysis of the judicial response of US courts to the conflict argument see M.D. Birnhack, 'The Copyright Law and Free Speech Affair: Making-Up and Breaking-Up', in *IDEA: The Journal of Law and Technology* 43 (2003) 233.

[25] M.B. Nimmer, 'Does Copyright Abridge the First Amendment Guarantees of Free Speech and Press?', in UCLA Law Review 17 (1970) 1180; P. Goldstein, 'Copyright and the First Amendment', in *Columbia Law Review* 70 (1970) 983; L.S. Sobel, 'Copyright and the First Amendment: A Gathering Storm?', in *Copyright Law Symposium (ASCAP)* 19 (1971) 43.

[26] 293 F.Supp. 130 [SDNY 1968].

[27] 366 F.2d 303 [2nd Cir. 1966].

[28] *McGraw-Hill Inc.* v. *Worth Publishers*, 335 F.Supp. 415, 422 [SDNY 1971].

the Constitution, its text and structure. The message was simple: there is no conflict because of the constitutional co-existence of both the First Amendment and copyright law.

The argument about history is that the *framers* did not perceive any conflict. The framers of the copyright clause were almost the same people who amended the Constitution to include the First Amendment. They also enacted the first American Copyright Act. Unfortunately, little is known about the particular circumstances of the enactment of the copyright clause.[29] The judicial conclusion that followed was that there *is* no conflict, which means that copyright law can restrict the First Amendment's command. The appeal to the framers' intention is apparent in *Harper & Row Publishers* v. *Nation Enterprises*: In our haste to disseminate news, it should not be forgotten that the *framers intended* copyright itself to be the engine of free expression.[30]

The argument also appeals to what the framers *did* rather than to what they intended. They enacted a prohibition on abridging speech and a few years later, a limitation on speech; the two regimes being born into American law as coexistent. The coexistence, we are then told, is 'built-in' in the Constitution. It is the constitutional structure that dictates the coexistence, and thus, copyright is a permitted restriction of the First Amendment and we should dismiss any argument that proclaims the superiority of either over the other.[31] The effective meaning of such an approach is that copyright law is immunized from the First Amendment.

Later on a more sophisticated judicial answer developed as to the question of the relationship between copyright law and the First Amendment. *Harper & Row* is the current definitive position of the Supreme Court, and it is, in short, that this question need not bother us. This approach was adopted by the *Eldred* court, though it opened some new channels for future situations. The contemporary judicial response is willing to assume that there is a conflict, but only for the sake of the discussion, a discussion that routinely ends in rejecting the conflict argument. The judicial response does not end the discussion with the Constitutional text and an originalist interpretation. It argues that copyright law and the First Amendment share the same goal, namely the promotion of knowledge and the maintenance of a robust public sphere, but divide the areas of responsibility as to the achievement of the goal. Elsewhere I called this explanation the *shared goal argument*. It ties the two allegedly conflicting areas of law together, at their most important point: their goal. *Harper & Row* (stating that 'copyright [is] the engine of free expression') is the clearest statement of this approach. It invokes a theme of

---

[29] See B. W. Bugbee, *Genesis of American Patent and Copyright Law*, Washington (1967), 117, 129.

[30] 471 U.S. 539, 558 [1985]. Emphasis added.

[31] See e.g., *Dallas Cowboys Cheerleaders, Inc.* v. *Scoreboard Posters, Inc.*, 600 F. 2d 1184, 1187 [5th Cir. 1979], in which the Court of Appeals dismissed a First Amendment-based argument by turning to the 'judgment of the Constitution'.

joint venture, a beneficial cooperation. One (copyright) pulls the other (free speech), and together they progress.[32]

The *shared-goal argument* is accompanied with the *division of labour* argument, which designates separate areas of responsibility for the First Amendment and copyright law and thus creates a division between them. Consider for example the following comment, by the Court of Appeals in the Eleventh Circuit: 'Where the First Amendment removes obstacles to the free flow of ideas, copyright law adds positive incentives to encourage that flow'.[33] Under the labour division, copyright law is responsible for the production of speech and the First Amendment is responsible for protecting that production. This division results in placing the two areas of law in a linear order. First copyright creates speech, and then the First Amendment protects speech from abridgements.

Another important element of the judicial response to the argument that there is a conflict between copyright and speech turns to the fair use defence and the idea/expression dichotomy (copyright law protects only the latter), which are familiar to copyright students.[34] These copyright mechanisms are designated a role as dissolving the conflict. Consider *Harper & Row*'s view, recently reaffirmed in *Eldred*:

'In view of the First Amendment protections *already embodied in the Copyright Act's* distinction between copyrightable expression and uncopyrightable facts and ideas, and the latitude for scholarship and comment traditionally afforded by fair use, we see no warrant for expanding the doctrine of fair use to create what amounts to a public figure exception to copyright'.[35]

Many courts found recourse in the dichotomy, following the lead of Professor Melville Nimmer, who found the most efficient machinery in the resolution of the conflict is the dichotomy:[36]

'[T]he idea-expression line represents an acceptable definitional balance as between copyright and free speech interests. In some degree it encroaches upon freedom of speech in that it abridges right to reproduce the 'expression' of others, but this is justified by the greater public good in the copyright encouragement of creative works. In some degree, it encroaches

---

[32] Recall the Constitutional grant of power to Congress, which is 'to promote the *progress* of science'. Progress is a historically loaded term and is relevant to the interpretation of copyright law. See M.D. Birnhack, 'The Idea of Progress in Copyright Law', in Buffalo Intellectual Property Law Journal 1 (2001) 3.

[33] *Pacific & Southern Company Inc.* v. *Duncan*, 744 F.2d 1490, 1499 [11th Cir. 1984].

[34] See 17 U.S.C. §107 and §102(b), respectively.

[35] *Harper & Row*, at 560 (emphasis added). For a similar response, see *New Era Publications International* v. *Holt*, 873 F.2d 576, 584 (2nd Cir.).

[36] M.B. Nimmer, *op. cit.* in footnote 25, at 1192-1193.

upon the author's right to control his work in that it renders his 'ideas' per se unprotectible, but this is justified by the greater public need for free access to ideas as part of the democratic dialogue'.

The fair use defence too was designated a role in solving the conflict in several cases. *Rosemont* and *Time*, though they did not mention the First Amendment explicitly, reached a free-speech favourable result, through a liberal analysis of the fair use defence. The first case to address the conflict directly and turn to the fair use defence as its resolution was *Walt Disney* v. *Air Pirates*.[37] Defendants admitted copying Disney's cartoon characters and their names in its subversive counter-culture comic books, the *Air Pirates Funnies*.[38] Defendants argued that their cartoons were a parody and that their borrowing was entitled to the fair use defence. The district court issued a preliminary injunction and dismissed a First Amendment objection to this injunction.[39] It reasoned that 'The determination that the defence of fair use could not be successfully asserted here would seem to resolve the further contention that the First Amendment works to prevent issuance of a preliminary injunction'.[40] Interestingly, the Court of Appeals resolved the question by turning to the idea/expression dichotomy, and not on the basis of fair use. Other cases found the fair use defence to diffuse the tension between copyright law and free speech concerns, and concluded that there is no conflict.[41]

II.4. THE AMERICAN APPROACH: AN EXCLUSIVE INTERNAL VIEW

For the time being, then, copyright law in the US is immune to First Amendment scrutiny. Rephrasing this approach in constitutional terms might be helpful to better understand it. It is suggested that we distinguish between two conflicts and two points of view: an *internal* conflict and an *external* one. The *internal* conflict is the basic tension that underlies copyright law. This is the tension between copyright's goal to promote the 'progress of science' and the rights it creates in order to achieve this goal.[42] The *external* conflict addresses the relationship between copyright and free speech on a constitutional level, as two separate areas

---

[37] *Walt Disney* v. *Air Pirates*, 345 F.Supp. 108, 116 [N.D. Cal. 1972], *aff'd in part, reversed in part,* 581 F.2d 751 [9th Cir. 1978].

[38] 581 F.2d at 752-753.

[39] 345 F.Supp. at 115-116.

[40] 345 F.Supp. at 115.

[41] See for example *Wainwright Sec., Inc.,* v. *Wall Street Transcript Corp.* 558 F.2d 91, 95 [2nd Cir. 1977]; *Keep Thomson Governor Committee* v. *Citizens for Gallen Committee*, 457 F.Supp. 957 [D.NH., 1978]; *Roy Export Co.* v. *CBS*, 672 F.2d 1095, 1100 [2nd Cir. 1982]; *Triangle Publications Inc.* v. *Knight-Ridder Newspapers Inc.* 626 F.2d 1171, 1175-1176 [5th Cir. 1980]; *Association of American Medical* v. *Carey*, 482 F.Supp. 1358, 1365, n. 17 [NDNY. 1980]; *Twin Peaks Productions, Inc.* v. *Publications Int'l, Ltd.*, 778 F.Supp. 1247, 1252 [SDNY, 1991].

[42] For an extended discussion, see M.D. Birnhack, 'Copyright Law and Free Speech after *Eldred* v. *Ashcroft*', in *Southern California Law Review* 76 (2003) 1275.

of law. Each of these conflicts is familiar, but it is surprising to realize how the distinction is so often ignored or how the conflicts are confused.

Applying the internal/external distinction to the judicial response to the conflict argument provides the following picture. The conflict argument, that there is some conflict between the two regimes and hence free speech considerations should be taken into account when adjudicating copyright cases, refers to the external conflict. The early judicial response replied on the same constitutional, external level. It did so by applying an originalist and textualist interpretation. The contemporary response insists that whatever free speech interests and concerns there are, they are embodied within copyright law. The conflict was thus kept in an internal sphere of copyright law, and rephrased in familiar copyright terms. In other words, the external conflict argument was internalized: the response to the argument that copyright law and free speech collide was answered in terms of the internal conflict.

This internalization takes two forms. One is rather *mechanical*: turning to copyright devices (the fair use defence and the idea/expression dichotomy) and arguing that they already incorporate free speech concerns. Such an approach de facto confines the discussion to one legal area. The second form of internalization is *substantive*: that there is really no-conflict between copyright and free speech, for they share the same goal, have a division of labour between them, and so do not collide. The American response to the conflict argument is to internalize the external conflict in both the mechanical form and the substantive one. This approach refuses to take an external view of the conflict.

A recent example is the copyright controversy over Alice Randall's *The Wind Done Gone*, which is the 'other voice' of Margaret Mitchell's *Gone with the Wind*.[43] Randall wrote her story from the point of view of Cynara, the black daughter of the owner of the plantation, and her owner. Randall was sued by the current holder of the copyright in Mitchell's work, for copyright infringement. She raised, *inter alia*, fair use and free speech defences. In refusing to issue an injunction, the Eleventh Circuit portrayed the relationship between copyright law and the First Amendment in what was termed here the shared goal argument and opted for a substantive internalization: 'The Copyright Clause and the First Amendment, while intuitively in conflict, were drafted to work together to prevent censorship; copyright laws were enacted in part to prevent private censorship and the First Amendment was enacted to prevent public censorship'.[44] The court then added a mechanical internalization, turning to the idea/expression dichotomy and to the fair use defence.[45] However, its discussion of the latter was inspired by the First Amendment. Although the court internalized the conflict argument, it did not lose sight of the external view.

---

[43] *SunTrust Bank* v. *Houghton Mifflin Co.* 268 F.3d 1257 [11th Cir. 2001].
[44] *SunTrust Bank*, at 1263 (footnotes omitted).
[45] *SunTrust Bank*, at 1263 and 1264, respectively.

II.5. ELDRED V. ASHCROFT AND THE FUTURE OF THE CONFLICT ARGUMENT

Almost eighteen years passed since the Supreme Court last addressed the copyright law/free speech interface in *Harper & Row*, before the persistent conflict argument was heard in the Court again. Eric Eldred and his counsel, Professor Lawrence Lessig, asked the Court to declare the CTEA unconstitutional. They raised several arguments to support their case, including a First Amendment one. The Court, in an opinion written by Justice Ruth Bader Ginsburg, joined by six other justices, refused. It was willing to examine the conflict argument, but concluded that the First Amendment is irrelevant in copyright law, at least as far as traditional copyright law is at stake.[46]

The court repeated the shared goal argument, quoting *Harper & Row*. It also pointed to the internal copyright law mechanisms, such as the idea/expression dichotomy and to specific built-in exceptions in the CTEA. But the message was clear: the First Amendment is a non-issue when it comes to copyright law. Professor Eugene Volokh reads the decision (with *Harper & Row*) to create 'a copyright exception to the First Amendment, an exception that validates copyright law just like the obscenity and libel exceptions validate obscenity and libel laws'.[47] To complete the picture, it should be noted that the Court's main reason for denying the appeal was deference to Congress: the legislature operated under an explicit constitutional authorization, has acted in a similar manner – extending the duration of copyright protection – several times since the enactment of the first copyright act in 1790.[48]

The majority's opinion departs from the 33 years of traditional denial of the conflict argument in that it contains some fresh guidelines, which suggest that the no-conflict conclusion does have some limits.

Firstly, the Court explicitly refused to join the Court of Appeals' bold statement, that copyright is 'categorically immune from challenges under the First Amendment'.[49] This indicates that the external view might still be relevant to copyright law.

Secondly, the Court noted that the power of the internal copyright law mechanisms such as the fair use defence and the idea/expression dichotomy is 'generally adequate' and completed this statement with a footnote, stating that 'it is appropriate to construe copyright's internal safeguards to accommodate First

---

[46] See *Eldred*, at 788-790. For a detailed critique of the court's opinion in regard to the conflict, see M.D. Birnhack, *op. cit.* in footnote 42.

[47] E. Volokh, 'Freedom of Speech and Intellectual Property: Some Thoughts after *Eldred*, *44 Liquormart*, *Saderup* and *Bartnicki*', in *Houston Law Review* 40-4 (2003) 903.

[48] For a favourable discussion of this deference, see P.M. Schwartz and W.M. Treanor, '*Eldred* and *Lochner*: Copyright Term Extension and Intellectual Property as Constitutional Property', in *Yale Law Journal* 112 (2003) 2331.

[49] *Eldred*, at 789-790, quoting 239 F.3d at 375.

Amendment concerns'.[50] In other words, there might be situations in which copyright law's built-in mechanisms are inadequate and might not 'take care' of free speech concerns. This judicial comment calls for scholarly investigation of the limits of the copyright mechanisms.[51] It indicates that the mechanical internalization should not be taken for granted and that free speech concerns should guide the internal view of the conflict argument.

Thirdly, the Court noted that its no-conflict conclusion applies when 'Congress has not altered the traditional contours of copyright protection'.[52] What exactly are the 'traditional contours of copyright protection' is a term left undefined. There are several candidates that can be considered untraditional, such as the anti-circumvention sections of the Digital Millennium Copyright Act of 1998 (DMCA),[53] database protection and perhaps other extensions of copyright law.[54] This comment too implies that there might be situations in which the external conflict will be addressed directly, and not immediately internalized within copyright law.

These comments suggest new avenues for the constitutional discourse of copyright law, and if taken seriously, can add the much needed external view of the interaction between copyright law and the First Amendment, to the internal copyright view. It is time to turn to the European experience, which takes a different stand regarding the conflict argument.

III. The European Experience: Acknowledging the Conflict

We now cross the Ocean to ask the same set of questions in regard to the European experience. We begin by noting the prevalent understanding of

---

[50]   *Eldred*, at 789 and at note 24.

[51]   For pre-*Eldred* discussions of the limits of the fair use defence and the idea/expression dichotomy. See e.g., A.C. Yen, 'A First Amendment Perspective on the Idea/Expression Dichotomy and Copyright in a Work's "Total Concept and Feel"', in *Emory Law Journal* 38 (1989) 393; N.W. Netanel, *op. cit.* in footnote 23, at 13-23; J. Rubenfeld, 'The Freedom of Imagination: Copyright's Constitutionality' in *Yale Law Journal* 112 (2002) 1, 13-21. See parallel critiques of UK copyright law: F. Macmillan Patfield, 'Towards a Reconciliation of Free Speech and Copyright', in E. Barendt (ed.), *The Yearbook of Media and Entertainment Law 1996*, Oxford University Press (1996), 199 at 216-219, 222-223; J. Griffiths, '*Copyright Law and Censorship: The Impact of the Human Rights Act 1998*', in E. Barendt and A. Firth, *The Yearbook of Copyright and Media Law 1999*, Oxford University Press (1999), 3 at 14-20.

[52]   *Eldred*, at 789-790.

[53]   17 U.S.C. §§1201-1205. Thus far, two courts addressed the constitutionality of this portion of the DMCA, and found it passes the Constitutional threshold. See *Universal City Studios, Inc.* v. *Reimerdes*, 111 F.Supp.2d 294 [S.D.N.Y. 2000], *aff'd Universal City Studios, Inc.* v. *Corely*, 273 F.3d 429 [2d Cir. 2001]; *United States* v. *Elcom Ltd.* 203 F.Supp.2d 1111 [N.D. Cal. 2002]. Both decisions are pre-*Eldred*.

[54]   See P. Samuelson, 'The Constitutional Law of Intellectual property: After *Eldred* v. *Ashcroft*', in *Journal of the Copyright Society of the USA* 50 (2003).

copyright law in the Continent and the legal status of free speech. We then explore the response to the conflict argument. As in the American experience, we can identify two phases. The first took the internal view, but only in its weak, mechanical meaning. Recently, there are signs of an emerging new approach, which takes an explicit external view.

III.1. COPYRIGHT LAW AS A NATURAL RIGHT

It is hard to resist the intuition that no one else can tell us what to do with an object we hold. This is what we mean when we say 'this is mine'. The intuition is stronger when we created the object, and more so when it emanated form our intellect. This is the prevalent Continental-European understanding of copyright law. The theories associated with John Locke and with Hegel, though both addressed real property, are taken to explain copyright law in the Europe.

III.1.1. LABOUR AS PROPERTY

Locke's argument begins with the assertions that God has given the Earth to mankind in common; that the common ownership is the state of nature and that one owns her labour. Locke then argues that when one mixes labour with the commons, labour should not be taken from her and the product of her labour becomes her property.[55] Appropriation of the commons by one's labour is possible only as long as there is still land (Locke's main example) that is not owned by anyone: as long as there was no scarcity of land, the labour invested in a land was the means to appropriate it, for it left 'enough and as good' for others.[56] This was the Englishman's view of America of at the end of the seventeenth century.[57]

Can the labour theory explain copyright? The initial intuition is affirmative: we invest intellectual labour in creating original works. But let us list some objections: the religious anchor and the overall 'natural rights' tones of the theory might be grounds for critique. The first occupancy element of the commons, which is embedded in the theory, puts into grave doubt its applicability in a world where there is no unoccupied domain that we are willing to enclose.[58] This critique holds

---

[55] J. Locke, *Two Treatises of Government (1690) – The Second Treatise* (P. Laslett (ed.)) (1988) §§25-27, at 285-288. For an eloquent summary of Locke's theory, see W.J. Gordon, 'A Property Right in Self-Expression: Equality and Individualism in the Natural Law of Intellectual Property', in *Yale Law Journal* 102 (1993) 1533, 1544; J. Hughes, 'The Philosophy of Intellectual Property', in *Georgetown Law Journal* 77 (1988) 287, 296.

[56] Locke, at §33.

[57] Locke, at §41.

[58] For the canonical definition of the public domain, see J. Litman, 'The Public Domain', in *Emory Law Journal* 39 (1990) 965. Benkler offers a wider definition, which includes uses permitted under copyright exceptions, such as fair use. See Y. Benkler, *op. cit.* in footnote 14, at 360.

a different vision of the creative process: it is not the romantic one, but rather a sober view, that reminds us that knowledge is the product of an on going, intergenerational, cumulative process. This view is often expressed (at least in Anglo-American law) through the metaphor of building, and the metaphor of dwarfs standing on giants' shoulders.[59] The metaphors, in turn, are an expression of the idea of progress.[60] Another critique focuses on the *mixing* element of the theory. As Robert Nozick aptly asked: when spilling a can of tomato juice into the ocean 'do I thereby come to own the sea, or have I foolishly dissipated my tomato juice?'[61]

Even if we find a way around these critiques,[62] there are built-in limitations in the Lockean theory that should be noted. They ensure that owners do not harm others. The first is that 'enough and as good' should remain in the commons.[63] Wendy Gordon showed how it can safeguard a robust commons, which can provide a safe harbour for free speech concerns.[64]

Locke's labour theory explains some facets of UK copyright law, such as the interpretation of the requirement of originality.[65] It is far less apparent in continental copyright law, where the Hegelian theory occupies a greater space.

III.1.2. COPYRIGHT AS PERSONALITY

A second natural rights rationale of property (real or intellectual) turns to the ongoing relationship between a person and a resource. The most eloquent (and complex) explanation is based on G.W.F. Hegel's theory and its adaptation into American legal literature by Professor Margaret Jane Radin.[66]

Hegel's theory is based on his conception of the person.[67] Self-development of the person requires, according to this account, that a person's free will be externalized and embodied in the material world of objects. In this way, an

---

[59] For discussions of these metaphors, see E.C. Hettinger, 'Justifying Intellectual Property', in *Philosophy and Public Affairs* 18 (1989) 31, 38; and Z. Chafee, 'Reflections on the Law of Copyright: I', in *Columbia Law Review* 45 (1945) 503, 511.

[60] See M.D. Birnhack, *op. cit.*, in footnote 32.

[61] R. Nozick, *Anarchy, State and Utopia* (1974), 175.

[62] A supporting argument in favour of natural law, and quite rare in American copyright discourse, is A. Yen, 'Restoring the Natural Law: Copyright as Labor and Possession', in *Ohio State Law Journal* 51 (1990) 517.

[63] Locke, at §27.

[64] See W.J. Gordon, *op. cit.* in footnote 55. J. Hughes, *op. cit.* in footnote 55, noted also a second limitation within Lockean theory: the 'no waste' condition.

[65] See e.g., *Ladbroke (Football), Ltd.* v. *William Hill (Football), Ltd.*, [1964] All E.R. 465.

[66] M.J. Radin, 'Property and Personhood', in *Stanford Law Review* 34 (1982) 957, reprinted in M.J. Radin, *Reinterpreting Property*, University of Chicago Press (1993). Citations refer to the book.

[67] For a thorough discussion of Hegel's property theory, see J. Waldron, *The Right to Private Property*, Oxford University Press (1988), 343.

individual can develop freedom and individuality.[68] The embodiment of the personality in a material object constitutes one's identity. As Radin explains, some objects constitute personality, when in the hands of some people, at least part of the time. One's home is an example. It 'is affirmatively part of oneself'.[69] Some objects reflect our personality, such as clothes. They serve more than their utilitarian purpose. They might be a statement to the world – or a sort of statement to ourselves – about who we are, or at least who we think we are or want to be. But not all objects play such an important role in our lives and they might play different roles in different people's hands. Radin offers a distinction between *personal property* and *fungible property*.[70] A wedding ring has a different meaning to the married couple than to the jeweller.

If we accept this theory, then the different kinds of relationships we attach to different kinds of objects should be reflected in the law. How does it apply to copyright law? The Hegelian theory could not be more appropriate than when we are discussing ownership in a work *created* by a person. The starting point would be that intellectual works should be understood as personal property. But we can identify other situations as well. Works created by corporations, for example, such as the copyrighted text on shampoo tube. It would be strange to argue that the corporation's identity is developed by this reflection of its personality. So the objection to the implementation of the Hegelian-Radinian theory to copyright law is that it is difficult to identify the personal relationships that call for the personality justification,[71] and that its application is neither universal nor general.

That the natural rights theory of intellectual property is prevalent in many Continental jurisdictions, and hardly so in the US, is evident by the wide application of the doctrine of moral rights (*droit moral*).[72] Moral rights are usually distinct from pecuniary rights and are aimed at protecting the author's personhood. Examples are the right of *integrity* (preventing mutilation of the work); *attribution* (associating the artist with the work); *divulgation* (control of first publication), and *retraction* (right to retract a work).[73]

---

[68] See J. Waldron, *ibid*, at 356 and 351 respectively.
[69] M.J. Radin, *op. cit.* in footnote 66, at 37.
[70] M.J. Radin, *ibid*, at 37.
[71] See J. Hughes, *op. cit.* in footnote 55, at 339. Radin admits this problem and notes that it is difficult if not impossible to draft general rules based on subjective criteria. Thus, objective criteria are required. Radin seeks these in a concept of the 'person', and turns to Hegel for that purpose, but mentions also psychology or extrinsic moral reality. See M.J. Radin, *op. cit.* in footnote 66, at 38.
[72] See A. Françon and J.C. Ginsburg, 'Authors' Rights in France: The Moral Right of the Creator of a Commissioned Work to Compel the Commissioning Party to Complete the Work', in *Columbia – VLA Journal of the Law and the Arts* 9 (1985) 381, at 383-384; M.J. Radin, *op. cit.* in footnote 66, at 225, note 3.
[73] For an overview, see J.A.L. Sterling, *World Copyright Law*, Sweet & Maxwell (1998), at 281-284.

Moral rights have only a limited representation in US law.[74] It is required by the Berne Convention,[75] and subsequently by the WIPO Copyright Treaty (WCT).[76] Thus the doctrine is gaining power through the international instruments. Moral rights are prevalent in Europe, and are enforced rather zealously.[77] Notable articulations of the moral rights doctrine are found in French,[78] German,[79] and Italian law.[80]

III.2. FREE SPEECH: ARTICLE 10 OF THE ECHR

The level of protection of free speech in Europe differs from country to country, in its legal status and in practice. Germany, for example, included a free speech principle in its Constitution and its Federal Supreme Court practices a robust

---

[74] Following the United States' adherence to the Berne Convention in 1988, it enacted (in 1990) moral rights, but only in a limited form, see the Visual Artists Rights Act, codified as 17 U.S.C. §106A. It is limited to works of visual arts, which are narrowly defined (§101); it is limited to the life of the author (with an exception as to works which were created before the effective date of VARA (§106A(d)); it allows some exceptions as to modifications that are required for purposes of preservation and public presentation (§106A(c)), and applies only in a limited way as to works that are incorporated in a building (§113(d)). For judicial discussion of VARA, see *Carter* v. *Helmsley*, 71 F.3d 77 [2nd Cir 1995]. The General Director of WIPO, as well as the United States government were of the opinion that no changes in American law were required following the adherence to the Berne Convention, due to 'adequate practical equivalents'. See discussion in J.C. Ginsburg and J. M. Kernochan, 'One Hundred and Two Years Later: The United States Joins the Berne Convention', in *Columbia – VLA Journal of the Law and the Arts* 13 (1988), 1, 27-31. Several States enacted statutes that further protect the moral rights of authors. There are two main models for such legislation, that of California (The California Art Preservation Act, Cal. Civ. Code §987, enacted in 1979), and that of New York (Artists' Authorship Rights Act, NY Cultural Affairs Law, §14.03, enacted in 1983). In *Dastar* v. *Twentieth Century Fox*, 123 S.Ct. 2041 [2003], the Supreme Court held that Lanham Act (15 U.S.C. §1125(a)) does not prevent unaccredited copying of uncopyrighted work, thus raising even more doubts as to the adherence of the US to Berne's moral rights requirement.

[75] Article 6*bis* of the Berne Convention for the Protection of Literary and Artistic Works.

[76] WCT, Article 1, §4. For discussion of the international aspect of moral rights, see J.A.L. Sterling, *op. cit.* in footnote 73, at 292-293.

[77] See A. Dietz, 'The Moral Rights of the Author: Moral Rights and the Civil Law Countries', in *Columbia – VLA Journal of the Law and the Arts* 19 (1995) 199, 203 and cases discussed in A. Françon & J.C. Ginsburg, *op. cit.* in footnote 72.

[78] Article L. 121-1 – L. 121-9 of the Code de la Propriété Intellectuelle (codified in 1992). For discussion, see J.H. Merryman, 'The Refrigerator of Bernard Buffet', in *Hastings Law Journal* 27 (1976) 1023; A. Françon and J.C. Ginsburg, *op. cit.* in footnote 72; D. Campbell (ed.), *International Intellectual Property Law – European Jurisdictions*, John Wiley & Sons (1995), 139.

[79] Act dealing with copyright and related rights, (9 September 1965, as amended, 2 September 1994), §§ 12-14; J.A.L. Sterling, *op. cit.* in footnote 73; and D. Campbell (ed.), *op. cit.* in footnote 78, at 219.

[80] Act Number 633, 22 April 1941, Article 20-21, 24, 142; D. Campbell (ed.), *op. cit.* in footnote 78, at 324.

interpretation thereof.[81] Other countries vary in the degree of protection they guarantee.[82] Now these countries are bound, to different extents, to the ECHR, which includes an explicit protection of free expression. This, however, does not necessarily mean that the free speech laws are harmonized, for the member states enjoy a margin of appreciation in their interpretation and enforcement of human rights.[83]

Article 10 of the ECHR states the right in a universal form ('everyone has the right'), and elaborates what the right consists of ('freedom to hold opinions and to receive and impart information and ideas without interference by public authority and regardless of frontiers'), it then adds a general qualification:

'The exercise of these freedoms, since it carries with it duties and responsibilities, may be subject to such formalities, conditions, restrictions or penalties as are *prescribed by law* and are *necessary in a democratic society*, in the interests of national security, territorial integrity or public safety, for the prevention of disorder or crime, for the protection of health or morals, *for the protection of* the reputation or *rights of others*, for preventing the disclosure of information received in confidence, or for maintaining the authority and impartiality of the judiciary'.

Many things can be said about this interesting structure, especially in comparison to the word-stingy First Amendment.[84] The article explicitly takes a non-absolutist, pro-balancing approach.[85] European courts added another requirement, that of proportionality, i.e., that the restriction on speech is proportionate to

---

[81] See Article 5 of the 1949 Basic Law of the Federal Republic of Germany, and discussion, by U. Karpen, 'Freedom of Expression and National Security: The Experience of Germany', in S. Coliver, P. Hoffman, J. Fitzpatrick and S. Bowen (eds.), *Secrecy and Liberty: National Security, Freedom of Expression and Access to Information*, Martinus Nijhoff Publishers (1999), 289.

[82] France, for example, incorporated Article 11 of the 1789 Declaration of the Rights of Man and of the Citizen in the preamble of its 1958 Constitution, and French courts affirmed the constitutional status of the right. See R. Errera, 'France: National Security, Secret-Défense and Freedom of Expression', in S. Coliver, P. Hoffman, J. Fitzpatrick, and S. Bowen (eds.), *Secrecy and Liberty: National Security, Freedom of Expression and Access to Information*, Martinus Nijhoff Publishers (1999), at 269-270. For the situation in the UK, see *infra*, section III.B.

[83] For the complex situation of judicial review see J.H.H. Weiler, *The Constitution of Europe*, Cambridge University Press (1999), 102-107. For the doctrine of the 'margin of appreciation' see e.g., *Bowman* v. *United Kingdom* [1998] 26 E.H.R.R. 1; and, 'The Margin of Appreciation Doctrine', in H.Ch. Yourow (ed.), *The Dynamics of European Human Rights Jurisprudence*, Martinus Nijhoff Publishers (1996).

[84] For a comparison of article 10 to the First Amendment, see Ch. McCrudden, 'The Impact on Freedom of Speech', in B.S. Markesinis, (ed.), *The Impact of the Human Rights Bill on English Law*, Oxford University Press (1998), 85, at 99-103.

[85] See *Bladet Tromsø* v. *Norway*, 29 E.H.R.R. 125 [1999].

the legitimate aim pursued.[86] Restriction of speech is allowed only if it passes several barriers.[87] Does copyright law pass these barriers? It is prescribed by law, is necessary in a democratic society, whatever theory we adopt, and is for the protection of the rights of others. Is it a 'necessary' and proportional restriction of speech?

III.3. THE RESPONSE TO THE CONFLICT ARGUMENT

It seems that until recently the conflict argument was not directly addressed in European judicial decisions (including those of national courts). It also deserved little attention in the literature.[88] The reasons are complex and require separate investigation. Professor P. Bernt Hugenholtz points to the 'mystique' of natural rights as one reason and reminds us that property enjoys a constitutional status in Europe.[89] Once copyright (and other forms of intellectual property) is understood as a particular instance of property it is unlikely that free speech would be considered a problem. Furthermore, as Hugenholtz explains, the judiciary had a rather weak power *vis-à-vis* the legislature, in comparison to the power of judicial review enjoyed by the US judiciary. A third reason he notes is the reluctance to apply human rights in 'horizontal relationships', i.e., in the private sphere.[90] Human rights are usually understood as a protection of the

---

[86] See *Bowman* v. *United Kingdom* [1998] 26 E.H.R.R. 1, at 13; M. Supperstone & J. Coppel, 'Judicial Review after the Human Rights Act', in *European Human Rights Law Review* 3 (1999) 301, 312.

[87] See P. Mahoney & L. Early, 'Freedom of Expression and National Security: Judicial and Policy Approaches Under the European Convention on Human Rights and other Council of Europe Instruments', in S. Coliver, P. Hoffman, J. Fitzpatrick, and S. Bowen (eds.), *Secrecy and Liberty: National Security, Freedom of Expression and Access to Information*, Martinus Nijhoff Publishers (1999), at 109 and 113, and the discussion in *Hertel* v. *Switzerland*, 28 E.H.R.R. 534 [1998].

[88] Notable exceptions are H. Cohen Jehoram, 'Freedom of Expression in Copyright Law', in *European Intellectual Property Review* 6(1) (1984) 3; M. Sayal, 'Copyright and Freedom of the Media: A Balancing Exercise', in *Entertainment Law review* 6(7) (1995) 263; F. Macmillan Patfield, *op. cit.* in footnote 51; M. Spence, 'Intellectual Property and the Problem of Parody', in Law Quarterly Review 114 (1998) 594, at 617; J. Griffiths, *op. cit.* in footnote 51; P.B. Hugenholtz, 'Copyright and Freedom of Expression in Europe', in R. Dreyfuss Cooper, D. Leenheer Zimmerman and H. First (eds.), *Expanding the Boundaries of Intellectual Property: Innovation Policy for the Knowledge Society*, Oxford University Press (2001), 343; P.B. Hugenholtz, 'Copyright and Freedom of Expression in Europe', in N. Elkin-Koren, N.W. Netanel (eds.), *The Commodification of Information*, Kluwer Law International (2002), 239.

[89] P.B. Hugenholtz, *ibid*, at 241. Property is protected in Article 1 of the First Protocol of the ECHR, guaranteeing the right to peaceful enjoyment of possessions, was interpreted as a right to property. See F.G. Jacobs & R.C.A. White, *The European Convention on Human Rights*, Oxford University Press (2nd ed. 1996) at 246-259.

[90] P.B. Hugenholtz, *op. cit.* in footnote 88, at 241-242.

individual *vis-á-vis* the state, not other individuals (though it has been applied in the 'private' sphere.)[91]

As a result, in the terms applied here, no explicit external view of the relationship between copyright law and free speech was taken. The relationship was internalized into copyright law. Lucie Guibault surveyed the response to the conflict argument in sixteen countries, eleven of which are European, and found that:

> '[s]tatutory limitations on the exercise of exclusive rights are already the result of the balance of interests, carefully drawn by the legislator to encourage both creation and dissemination of new material. The protections of fundamental freedoms, of public interest matters, and of public domain material forms an integral part of the balance and, as a consequence, these notions should not be invoked a second time when interpreting statutory copyright limitations'.[92]

This approach rings a bell: it is equivalent to the mechanical internalization of the conflict argument, i.e., turning to internal mechanisms of copyright law, namely the idea/expression dichotomy and the fair use defence. Indeed, we can note long lists of limitations built within European copyright statutes. France and Belgium have explicit parody exceptions.[93] Most countries have exceptions that allow the use of copyrighted material in news reporting,[94] classroom use,[95] and personal use.[96] The Berne convention (as updated in the Paris Act), and hence TRIPS and

---

[91] E.g., *Tolstoy Miloslavsky* v. *UK* [1995] 20 EHRR 442.

[92] See L. Guibault, 'Limitations Found Outside of Copyright Law', General Report ALAI Study Days, Cambridge (1998), available at http://www.ivir.nl/publications/guibault/VUL5BOVT.-doc, at 1.

[93] See in France, Article L. 122-5, 4° of the Code de la Propriété Intellectuelle (allowing parody, pastiche and caricature), and discussion in D. Campbell (ed.), *op. cit.* in footnote 78, at 139. Belgian Copyright Act, Article 22 §1, 6°.

[94] See e.g., in Austria (D. Campbell (ed.), *op. cit.* in footnote 78, at 26-27); in France: Article L. 122-5, 3° (allowing critical comments, press reviews and public speeches, on the condition that the author's name is mentioned); in the Netherlands: Article 15 §1 of the Auteurswet 1912, English translation available at http://www.ivir.nl/final-uk1.html. In Portugal: Portuguese Code of Copyrights and Connected Rights, Article 7 (news reports, public debates, speeches), see D. Campbell (ed.), *op. cit.* in footnote 78, at 420.

[95] See e.g., in the Netherlands: Copyright Act, Article 16; in Portugal, Portuguese Code of Copyrights and Connected Rights, Article 75.

[96] See e.g., in France, Article L. 122-5, 1° (allowing private representation in family circle) and 2° (allowing private use); in Austria (D. Campbell (ed.), *op. cit.* in footnote 78, at 26); in the Netherlands: Copyright Act, Article 16b.

the WCT too, allow exceptions only under the 'three step test',[97] and so does the EC Directive, which enumerates a closed list of exceptions.[98]

The mechanical internalization means that free speech concerns are eliminated as an independent factor in the discussion. It thus differs from the substantive internalization, which can come only through identifying a congruence and unification of the goals of the two separate legal regimes. That was the *shared goal argument*. It is absent in the European approach.

But there are indications that a new paradigm is emerging. Guibault noted in her study that 'While [the deference to the legislature's (mechanical) internalization] is certainly true in principle, several factors may now justify having a look at other bodies of law in support of the intellectual property bargain'.[99]

A few national courts in Europe explicitly acknowledged the constitutional role of freedom of speech, such as Article 10 of ECHR, in the context of copyright law. One notable case is a Dutch opinion, discussing the 'missing pages' of Anne Frank's diary. Apparently, the worldwide publication of the diary was short of five pages, which Mr. Otto Frank, Anne's father, had torn out and deposited in the hands of a friend, Mr. Cor Suijk. Two Dutch newspapers, *Het Parool* and *De Volkskrant* obtained the pages and published them. The Anne Frank Fund, the current owner of the copyright to the diary, sued the newspapers, claiming copyright infringement. The first instance refused to order an injunction, expressing a stronger position of freedom of expression over copyright law. The Court of Appeals overturned the decision.[100] It based its ruling on the fact that the five pages were unpublished, and on its interpretation of Article 10 of the ECHR. The court announced that free speech concerns might overcome copyright claims, but, then, found – factually – that the speech in this case was commercial, due to its connection to (then) forthcoming biographies of Anne Frank.[101]

The judgment about the commercial nature of the newspapers' publication is strange, to say the least, but for our purposes here, what is interesting, is the way in which the court defined the legal situation. It was an *external* view: copyright (interpreted on the background assumption of a proprietary view) vs. free speech,

---

[97] See Article 9(2) of the Berne Convention. Under this test, an exception is allowed if it is in 'certain special cases', that it 'does not in conflict with a normal exploitation of the work', and 'does not unreasonably prejudice the legitimate interests of the author'. For discussion of the exceptions and limitations of copyright, see S. Ricketson, 'WIPO Study on Limitations and Exceptions of Copyright and Related Rights in the Digital Environment', WIPO (2003), available at http://www.wipo.org/documents/en/meetings/2003/sccr/pdf/sccr_9_7.pdf. Article 9(1) of TRIPS incorporates, *inter alia*, Article 9(2) of Berne, and Articl 13 of TRIPS is a specific 'three step test'. Article 1(4) of the WCT also incorporates Berne's Article 9(2), and it too has a specific three step test, in Article 10.

[98] See Article 5(5) of the Information Society Directive.

[99] See L. Guibault, *op. cit.* in footnote 92.

[100] *Anne Frank Fond* v. *B.V. Het Parool* (decision of the Gerechtshof Amsterdam, of 8 July 1999).

[101] *Ibid.* at 12-13.

where the source is found to be outside the realm of copyright law. Free speech concerns were not forced into copyright law, but gained an independent position.

Another Dutch case turned on what can be rephrased in American legal terms as the right of publicity, but the Dutch Supreme Court discussed it under the heading of copyright law.[102] Section 21 of the Dutch Copyright Act allows individuals to prevent the use of their portrait. The plaintiff's picture, taken in a gay club in Amsterdam, was used – without his consent – in an advertisement in a gay magazine. The court ruled against the defendants. It rejected also a free expression defence the defendant magazine raised. But interestingly, the rejection was not an outright one (that free expression is irrelevant, like the American early response to the conflict argument), or that there are built-in mechanisms within the Copyright Act that take care of free expression concerns. The Supreme Court juxtaposed the individual's privacy right with the free expression interest, i.e., it portrayed the situation as an external conflict. The court then simply declared the privacy interest to outweigh the free expression interest.[103]

There were more cases of the like in other countries.[104] The reasoning of a 1997 Austrian case illustrates the arguments made here.[105] A magazine published an open letter written by the son of the Bundespresident to his mother, following a political but personal family saga.[106] This took place a short while before re-elections. The magazine added a caricature, referring to the political and personal situation of the President. The caricature was first published a few days earlier in a different newspaper and the magazine's publication thereof was unauthorized. The defendants tried to justify their taking by clinging to a specific exception that the Austrian Copyright Act allows, namely, that when copyrighted works become

---

[102] *M. v. IT*, S. Ct., 2 May 1997, reported in [1997] 11 EIPR, at D-281.

[103] In yet another case, the Court of Appeal of the Hague declared Article 10 to govern, and that under the particular circumstances of the case, 'the copyright counts for less'. See 99/1040 *Church of Spiritual Technology* v. *SataWeb B.V.* [4 September 2003]. Defendant in this case published sections of a copyrighted book of the Church of Scientology in order to criticize the Church.

[104] See P.B. Hugenholtz, *op. cit.* in footnote 88. The constitutional setting is clear in Germany, where both freedom of expression enjoys a constitutional anchor (Article 5), and copyright is deemed to be 'property', which in turn enjoys (a limited) constitutional protections (Article 14). In *Germania 3*, BVerfGH 825/98 (29 June 2000), the Federal Constitutional Court decided that a play writer, Heiner Muller, who quoted 17 pages of one of Bertolt Brecht's plays in his own 75 page long play, did not infringe Brecht's copyright, since the extensive quote was contextualized so that it is critical of the original work. The Court ruled that freedom of expression (and more specifically, the artistic freedom protected in Article 5(3) of the Basic Law), should influence the interpretation of copyright law. In the terms applied here, the Court internalized the constitutional dimension into the internal copyright dimension, without losing site thereof.

[105] 4 Ob 361/97 (Supreme Court, December 1997), [1998] G.R.U.R. Int. 896.

[106] The political context of the case is addressed in the court's decision only in a subtle manner. For a fuller account of the background, see a report on the case in [1998] 20 EIPR (7), at N-110.

public in the course of public events they can be reproduced.[107] The court rejected this argument, on the basis that the caricature itself was not the public event and was used by the defendants merely as an illustration. Defendants than raised another claim: that of free expression. The court explicitly acknowledged the external conflict between copyright law and free expression.[108] Immediately thereafter, the court declared that the public-events exception to copyright takes account of free expression concerns. In the terms offered here, this is a mechanical internalization of the conflict argument. But the court then turned to examine the argument itself and did so under the framework of Article 10(2) of the ECHR. In this section of the decision, the court rejected defendants' claim that the low economic value of the caricature trumps the copyright. The interesting element here, for the sake of our discussion, is the methodology which the court applied: it took both the internal view and the external one without denying the relevance of free speech considerations to copyright law. A court situated in the US, one might assume, would refuse to take the external view at all and would limit its view to the internal sphere of copyright law.

French copyright law is considered the most favourable to authors. It is thus a telling situation that the French legal system not only recognized the relevance of Article 10 in the context of copyright law, but it was the decisive factor in the *Utrillo* decision.[109]

The cases just discussed took an external view of the conflict, but found copyright law to be a legitimate restriction of free speech. Accordingly, we can conclude that following the growing recognition of the role of free speech through its articulation in Article 10 of the ECHR there are signs that the conflict argument might shift to an external mode. A recent important UK case illustrates this methodological shift.

III.4. *ASHDOWN* V. *TELEGRAPH GROUP LTD.*: THE UK APPROACH[110]

In October 2000, the Human Rights Act 1998 (HRA) came into force in the UK, incorporating several important sections of the ECHR into domestic law, among

---

[107] See Federal Act on Copyright in Works of Literature and Art and on Related Rights, §42(c).
[108] See *supra* footnote 105, at 898. The court imposed this proposition on the defendant: 'defendant knows that the fundamental right of free information is in tension with the copyright'.
[109] See discussion of the case in P.B. Hugenholtz, *op. cit.* in footnote 88, at 11.
[110] An important caveat is in place: although I will be referring to few European cases, the main European example is that of the UK. Copyright law in the UK is not a perfect representative of copyright law in other European jurisdictions. In fact, it can be said that it is even closer to the US law, since it provided the historical source of US copyright law, and shares much of its philosophy. See e.g., B. Ringer, 'Two Hundred Years of American Copyright Law', in *200 Years of English & American Patent, Trademark & Copyright Law*, University of Chicago Press (1977), 117, at 125. However, US copyright law diverged from its source in the past two centuries in many respects. The interpretation of the requirement of originality is one clear

them Article 10.[111] This is a major change in British constitutional law, in that it explicitly includes the protection of human rights in a statute.[112] This is not to say that prior to 2000 freedom of expression was not protected. Courts created and developed a powerful principle of freedom of expression and held it was in accordance with the ECHR.[113] Now, however, the formal change is likely to bring about material changes. The enactment of the HRA is much broader than the issue of freedom of expression, and courts started to interpret it and determine its practical affect. Copyright law has already deserved a judicial discussion under the new regime, in a case decided by the Court of Appeal in 2001, *Ashdown*.[114]

The case involved a factual pattern not unfamiliar to that discussed in the US case of *Harper & Row*. Defendant newspaper got hold of a secret minute, not yet published at the time, written by plaintiff, a prominent political figure and then the leader of the Liberal Democrats. It published parts of the leaked document and was subsequently sued for copyright infringement. The newspaper raised, *inter alia*, a free speech defence, explicitly referring to Article 10. The first instance deferred to the legislature:

'The balance between the rights of the owner of the copyright and those of the public has been struck by the legislative organ of the democratic state itself, in the legislation it has enacted. There is no room for any further defences outside the code which establishes the particular species of intellectual property in question'.[115]

The court pointed to 42 exceptions and defences, in which copying is allowed. It

---

cont.

example where UK law adheres to a Lockean view, and settles for skill and labour, while US law explicitly rejected 'sweat of the brow' as sufficient. Compare the UK case of *Ladbroke, op. cit.* in footnote 65, to the US case of *Feist Publications, Inc.* v. *Rural Telephone Service Company, Inc.*, 499 U.S. 340, 345 [1991]. Other differences are for example the protection of moral rights, and the far more limited exceptions that UK law allows, in comparison to US law. Furthermore, UK law is subject to European law, such as the European Convention on Human Rights (ECHR), and it will move farther away from US law once the Information Society Directive is implemented. See Directive 2001/29/EC of the European Parliament and of the Council of 22 May 2001 on the harmonization of certain aspects of copyright and related rights in the information society, [2001] OJ L 167 (the 'Information Society Directive').

[111] See Human Rights Act, 1998, Sections 1, 3, and also Section 12, regarding remedies.

[112] See *R.* v. *Shayler* [2002] UKHL 11 (HL), at ¶33.

[113] E.g., *Attorney General* v. *Guardian Newspapers Ltd* [1990] 1 AC 109, 283-284; *Derbyshire, County Council* v. *Times Newspapers Ltd* [1993] AC 534, 551 (HL); *R.* v. *Secretary of State for the Home Department, ex parte Simms* [2000] 2 AC 115 (HL).

[114] [2001] E.M.L.R. 44 (CA) (*Ashdown II*). For analysis of the court's opinion see M.D. Birnhack, 'Acknowledging the Conflict between Copyright Law and Freedom of Expression under the Human Rights Act', in *Entertainment Law Review* (2003) 24; J. Griffiths, 'Copyright Law after Ashdown – Time to Deal Fairly with the Public', in *Intellectual Property Quarterly* (2002) 240.

[115] *Ashdown* v. *Telegraph Group* Ltd. [2001] Ch. 685, 696 (*Ashdown I*).

then proceeded to examine the relevant copyright exceptions and found against the newspaper. In the terms applied here, this is a clear case of mechanical internalization and a refusal to discuss the external conflict.

The Court of Appeal dismissed the newspaper's appeal, but applied a different methodology as to the relationship between copyright law and freedom of speech. It pointed to the idea/expression dichotomy and the fair dealing defence, but added a crucial comment:

> '[R]are circumstances can arise where the right of freedom of expression will come into conflict with the protection afforded by the Copyright Act, notwithstanding the express exceptions to be found in the Act. In these circumstances, we consider that the court is bound, insofar as it is able, to apply the Act in a manner that accommodates the right of freedom of expression. This will make it necessary for the court to look closely at the facts of individual cases (as indeed it must whenever a "fair dealing" defence is raised). We do not foresee this leading to a flood of litigation'.[116]

Thereafter the Court examined the particular defences, but dismissed them.[117] In the terms applied here, however, this is a clear acknowledgment that the internalization of the conflict argument might occasionally be inadequate and then the external conflict should be seriously considered.

What then, is the constitutional meaning of *Ashdown*? It is submitted that *Ashdown* reflects an important shift in the judicial discourse of the conflict between copyright law and freedom of expression in the UK and this is an indication of the emerging European response to the conflict argument. Prior to *Ashdown*, freedom of expression was hardly mentioned in UK copyright law and was generally thought of as irrelevant beyond the internal copyright mechanisms such as the fair dealing defence.[118] There are many explanations for this approach, but now that freedom of expression is gaining a new legal status, the legal setting changed: it is no longer a conflict between a statutory right (copyright) and a general principle of common law (free expression). Rather, it is a conflict between a statutory right (copyright) and a constitutional principle, anchored in a binding text of a higher normative level.[119]

This major constitutional change shifts the conflict discourse from one which was limited to the internal sphere of copyright law, to a much richer one, which is

---

[116] See *Ashdown II*, at ¶45.

[117] The Court's treatment of the defences attracted criticism. See M.D. Birnhack, *op. cit.* in footnote 114, at 33, and J. Griffiths, *op. cit.* in footnote 114.

[118] A rare exception is a short comment in an important fair dealing case. See *Hubbard* v. *Vosper* [1972] 2 Q.B. 84, at 94.

[119] Lord Steyn argued in a law review article that rights entrenched in a Bill of Rights should be accorded a higher normative status. See 'The New Legal Landscape', in *European Human Rights Law Review* 6 (2000) 549, at 550.

willing to examine the external interaction as well. It is still yet to be seen whether this is just a rhetorical shift, and in practice the conflict argument will still be internalized, but acknowledging the conflict is a crucial step in the right direction.

IV. Conclusion

Our discussion of the American and European responses to the conflict argument – the argument that there is a conflict between copyright law and free speech and that it should be addressed – taught us that there are two main models with which to grasp the argument. One was an internal view, which eliminates the articulation of the conflict as one between two separate areas of law, and *de facto* internalizes the conflict, so it is discussed in terms of copyright law alone. The internalization takes one of two forms: the first is weak, and is performed by focusing on copyright doctrines, which are said to 'take care' of whatever free speech concerns there might be. This is a mechanical internalization. We identified it both in the US and in Europe. The second form in which the discussion is narrowed to copyright law alone is a substantive internalization. It is accomplished through the *shared-goal argument* that ties the two areas of law into one whole at their most fundamental link: their purpose. This stronger form of internalization of the conflict argument appears only in the American version thereof.

The other model to grasp the conflict argument is external: it is understood to be a conflict between two separate legal regimes. One is the body of law that constitutes copyright law and the other is the body of law that constitutes free speech jurisprudence. The American approach systematically refused to acknowledge such a conflict and insisted on its internalization. The European approach is not as hostile to this model as the American courts are and there is an emerging presence of this approach.

The task of this chapter was to explain how American law, with its strong free speech tradition and a weaker copyright law basis ignores the external conflict, while European law, with a weaker legal free speech tradition and a tradition of strong protection of copyright law is willing to acknowledge the conflict argument. It should be emphasized that the fact that a conflict is identified at the beginning of a discussion does not mean that it is irresolvable. It does not mean that free speech 'wins' and that copyright law is unconstitutional or redundant. But before we can turn to resolve a conflict, it is crucial that we properly grasp it: this is why the approach to the conflict argument is important.

We can now explain the puzzle observed at the beginning of this chapter. American law refuses to acknowledge the external conflict because it internalizes free speech concerns in both the mechanical and the substantive ways. The substantive internalization is possible only once copyright law is understood as an instrumental legal artefact to achieve some other goal. Only when copyright law is understood to have a goal, can one plausibly claim that free speech concerns are incorporated in copyright law. This is the path taken in *Eldred*, where the Court internalized the conflict argument, but pointed to some signs, as to the circumstances in which it might be willing to examine the external conflict as well.

On the other hand, a European emerging approach, which articulates the conflict argument as external, is possible only because copyright law is understood on a different basis. In the absence of an officially declared goal, the shared goal argument cannot be made. The conflict can be internalized only in a mechanical way: free speech concerns require and justify creating exceptions to copyright law, so to protect free speech concerns. The *Ashdown* case illustrates that both the internal and the external avenues can be taken.

Chapter 4

Recapturing Liberated Information – The Relationship Between the United Kingdom's Freedom of Information Act 2000 and Private Law Restraints on Disclosure

*Jonathan Griffiths**

I.   Introduction

Increasingly, it is understood that the 'right to know' plays an essential part in any democratic society. Access to information is, in some circumstances, a human right.[1] Citizens have been granted a variety of specific and general rights of access to information.[2] In the United Kingdom, general access legislation, in the form of the Freedom of Information Act 2000 ('FOIA 2000'), has recently been enacted.[3] The scope of this Act is controversial. It has, for example, been widely suggested that there are too many exemptions to the right of access to information under the Act.[4] There is, however, a feature of the FOIA 2000 that has generated little commentary; yet is very likely to detract significantly from the effectiveness of the access regime that it establishes. This is the Act's failure to regulate the potential conflict between the right of access to information and the continued ability of

---

*   Lecturer in Law, Department of Law, Queen Mary, University of London.
[1]   See, for example, *Gaskin* v. *United Kingdom* [1989] 12 E.H.R.R. 36; *Guerra* v. *Italy* [1998] 26 E.H.R.R. 357.
[2]   In the United Kingdom, for example, rights of access to specific types of information have been provided by the Environmental Information Regulations 1992 (environmental information) and the Data Protection Act 1998 (personal data).
[3]   Although various, largely procedural, provisions of the FOIA 2000 are already in force, the right of access which it establishes is unlikely to be fully in force until the end of 2005. The act does not apply to public authorities falling within the jurisdiction of the Scottish Parliament, which has passed its own freedom of information legislation (Freedom of Information (Scotland) Act 2002).
[4]   See, for example, G. Robertson & A. Nicol, *Robertson & Nicol on Media Law*, Sweet & Maxwell (4th ed., 2002) pp. 602-609; D. Feldman, *Civil Liberties and Human Rights in England and Wales*, Oxford University Press (2nd ed., 2002), pp. 783-5.

P.L.C. Torremans (ed.), Copyright and Human Rights, 63–85
© *2004 Kluwer Law International. Printed in the Netherlands.*

individuals or bodies to employ *private law* rights to resist, or to sanction, disclosure.[5] In this chapter, the extent to which rights established under the laws of defamation, confidentiality and copyright can be used to prevent the disclosure of information requested under FOIA 2000 is examined.

The chapter begins with an outline of the structure of the Act and an introduction to the different ways in which disclosure of information could be hampered through reliance on the laws of defamation, confidentiality and copyright. It then proceeds to show how freedom of information laws in a number of other common law jurisdictions (Australia, New Zealand, Canada and Ireland) contain immunities from liability that serve to minimize potential conflict between these competing bodies of law. The central argument advanced in this chapter is that the absence of comparable immunities in the FOIA 2000 is likely to diminish the effectiveness of the right of access to information in the United Kingdom.

II. Access to Information Under FOIA 2000 – an Introduction

FOIA 2000 provides a right of access to information held by over 50,000 public authorities.[6] These include departments of central government, local authorities, and a wide range of lesser bodies (from the Adjudicator for the Inland Revenue and Customs and Excise and the Administration of Radioactive Substances Advisory Committee to the Zoos Forum).[7] Under the Act, public authorities are obliged to provide access to 'information recorded in any form'[8] without significant formality,[9] without inquiry into the applicant's motives and at subsidized cost. The right of access applies to any information 'held' by a public authority – and thus extends to information which, while originally created or held by third parties, has fallen into a public authority's hands.[10] Applicants for information under FOIA 2000 are entitled to express a preferred means of communication from a list set out in the Act. This list includes the communication of copies of the requested information, the provision of applicants with a reasonable opportunity to inspect a record and the furnishing of a digest or

---

[5] There are also numerous potential conflicts between the right introduced by the FOIA 2000 and statutory obligations to maintain confidentiality. In order to minimize such potential conflicts, a wide-ranging power to amend or repeal enactments prohibiting disclosure of information is included within the FOIA 2000 (Section 75)

[6] For a more detailed analysis of the rights granted under FOIA 2000, see J. Wadham, J. Griffiths & B. Rigby, *Blackstone's Guide to the Freedom of Information Act 2000*, Blackstone Press / Oxford University Press (2001).

[7] FOIA 2000 Sections 3-7, Sch. 1.

[8] *Ibid.*, Section 84.

[9] *Ibid.*, Section 8.

[10] *Ibid.*, Sections 1, 3(2).

summary. Where the applicant's preference is reasonable, the public authority must comply with it.[11]

As with all freedom of information regimes, the right of access under the FOIA 2000 is subject to a number of exemptions – that is, legislative provisions which, in specified circumstances, permit public authorities to refuse to communicate information to an applicant. Some exemptions are designated 'absolute exemptions' and are effective regardless of any conflicting public interest in disclosure of the information to which they relate.[12] The majority of exemptions are, however, only effective where a public authority can demonstrate that the public interest in maintaining confidentiality outweighs the public interest in disclosure.[13] Where an exemption applies to requested information, a public authority is entitled to refuse to disclose that information. However, under the FOIA 2000, it is not obliged to do so.[14] Responsibility for determining whether or not disclosure should be made rests with the public authority itself.

Unlike freedom of information legislation in many other jurisdictions, the FOIA 2000 makes no provision for 'reverse FOI' – that is, for a procedure under which third parties have a right to challenge disclosures harmful to their interests.[15] In the absence of such a 'reverse FOI' procedure, third parties wishing to take proceedings to prevent, or to seek remedies for, disclosure of information by a public authority will be obliged to employ existing private law causes of action, such as defamation, breach of confidence and infringement of copyright.[16] A third party concerned about a threatened disclosure under FOIA 2000 may seek

---

[11] *Ibid.*, Section 11.

[12] *Ibid.*, Section 2(3). See, for example, Section 21 (Information reasonably accessible by other means), Section 23 (Information supplied by, or concerning, certain security bodies) and Section 32 (Information contained in court records).

[13] *Ibid.*, Section 2(2). See, for example, Section 30(1) (Information held for the purpose of criminal investigations), Section 35(1) (Information relating to the formulation or development of government policy) and Section 37(1) (Information relating to communications with Her Majesty, with other members of the Royal Family or with the Royal Household).

[14] In other jurisdictions, some exemptions are mandatory (*cf.*, for example, Ireland's Freedom of Information Act 1997, Sections 22, 26, 27, 28 and 32). In the United Kingdom, the authority may, of course, be obliged to maintain the confidentiality of certain information by other laws, for example, the Official Secrets Act 1989 or the law of contempt of court.

[15] Such procedures exist in other jurisdictions – see, for example, the Australian Freedom of Information Act 1982, Section 27 and the Canadian Access to Information Act 1982, Section 28. Under a code of practice issued under Section 45, FOIA 2000, public authorities are obliged to consult third parties whose rights or interests would be affected by disclosure (see *Code of Practice on the discharge of public authorities' functions under Part I of FOIA 2000 – dealing with requests for information*, November 2002, paragraphs 31-40).

[16] Judicial review of an authority's decision to disclose information would also seem to be possible. Nevertheless, the restricted form of review and limited orders available in judicial review may mean that third parties prefer to rely upon their private law rights in challenging decisions to disclose.

an interim injunction to prevent that disclosure. If the information in question has already been disclosed, he or she may seek damages and an injunction preventing future disclosure.

Responsibility for enforcing the legislation's right of access lies with the Information Commissioner,[17] who also supervises the regime established under the Data Protection Act 1998. On complaint by an applicant, the Commissioner has the power to investigate whether a public authority's reliance upon an exemption can be justified. If not, she can order disclosure of the requested information.[18] A third party who considers that a public authority is about to (or already has) disclosed information wrongfully has no right to seek redress from the Information Commissioner. While some of the provisions of the FOIA 2000 are already in force at the time of writing, the right to request access to information under Section1 (1) of the Act will not be fully in force until the beginning of 2005.[19]

III. Potential private law claims arising from disclosure

It has been suggested above that challenges to disclosure of information under the FOIA 2000 may be made under the laws of defamation, breach of confidence or copyright.[20] In this section, the likely nature of such challenges is briefly outlined. More detailed analysis of the conditions of liability within each of these forms of action is provided later in the chapter.[21]

In order to appreciate how proceedings for defamation could be brought to prevent, or penalize,[22] disclosure, it is helpful to examine a hypothetical disclosure

---

[17] See FOIA 2000, Sections 47-56.

[18] *Ibid.* Sections 50-52. Although see the limitation on this power imposed by Section 53. Also, note that the Commissioner cannot make compensation orders.

[19] For example, certain public authorities are currently subject to the obligation to publish a publication scheme established under Section 16, FOIA 2000 (see, *Annual report on bringing fully into force those provisions of the FOIA 2000 which are not yet fully in force*, Lord Chancellor's Department, November 2002, H.C. 6).

[20] While defamation, breach of confidence and copyright are perhaps the most likely causes of action to be employed in resisting disclosure, others may also be relevant (e.g. the torts of misfeasance in public office or negligence or an action for infringement of database right under the Copyright and Rights in Databases Regulations 1997 (SI 1997/3032)). An individual seeking to prevent disclosure of *personal* information, will be able to rely upon his or her rights under the Data Protection Act 1998 or upon rights to privacy developed within the law of breach of confidence (see, for example, *Campbell* v. *MGN Ltd* [2002] EMLR 30). Disputes arising in relation to such information are not, however, my primary focus in this paper because they are comprehensively regulated by the expressly coordinated provisions of FOIA 2000 and the Data Protection Act 1998.

[21] See section 4 below.

[22] A claimant seeking an interim injunction in libel proceedings faces particular difficulties. These arise from the 'rule against prior restraint', under which a court will not normally grant an interim injunction if a defendant intends to rely on a defence of justification (*Bonnard* v. *Perryman* [1891] 2 Ch 269; *Holley* v. *Smyth* [1998] 2 WLR 742).

under the Act. Consider, for example, a case in which A, a local resident, has sent a letter to her local authority. The letter is defamatory of B plc. Under the Act, C, a journalist, applies to the local authority, requesting disclosure of the information in the letter. The local authority may refuse to disclose this information. In resisting disclosure, it may, for example, cite Section 43 (2), exempting public authorities from the duty to release information where disclosure 'would be likely to prejudice the commercial interests of any person' (B plc in this example). Despite the potential applicability of this exemption, however, the public authority may disclose the information. It may do this because it is unaware that the information in the letter is defamatory or because it considers that the public interest in disclosure outweighs the public interest in continued non-disclosure.[23] On receipt of the requested information, C may decide to publish the defamatory information to the world at large.

Potential claims for defamation may arise at a number of points on these hypothetical facts. Could the public authority, for example, be liable for defamation for disclosing information in response to a request under the Act?[24] In seeking an answer to this question, is it necessary to distinguish between information to which access could have been refused under one of FOIA 2000's exemptions and information that the public authority was obliged to disclose because it was not covered by any of the FOIA 2000's exemptions? Could A, who initially supplied the defamatory information, also incur liability as a result of the public authority's disclosure? Is C, the recipient of defamatory information disclosed under the procedure established under the Act entitled to publish it further without incurring liability?

Similar questions arise in relation to breach of confidence. Consider, for example, a situation in which X plc provides information to a public authority for a specific statutory purpose.[25] Y, a member of a pressure group, requests access to this information under the FOIA 2000. In response to Y's request, the public authority may be entitled to argue that the information is exempt from the duty to disclose under Section 41 of the Act ('Information provided in confidence').[26] However, the public authority is not obliged to rely on the exemption. It may

---

[23] Section 43(2) is a qualified exemption

[24] A claimant can only succeed in defamation where a defamatory statement has been *published*, i.e. has been communicated to some person other than the claimant. Disclosure under FOIA 2000 will constitute 'publication' for this purpose.

[25] For example, in compliance with obligations under legislation passed to ensure the safety of pharmaceutical products.

[26] '(1) Information is exempt information if:
　　(a) it was obtained by the public authority from any other person (including another public authority); and
　　(b) the disclosure of the information to the public (otherwise than under this Act) by the public authority holding it would constitute a breach of confidence actionable by that or any other person'.

overlook its potential applicability and disclose the information requested in any event. Alternatively, because the scope of an implied obligation of confidentiality is often uncertain, the public authority may be unsure whether the information is covered by Section 41 or not, and may decide to disclose it. Again, disclosure of the information by the public authority under FOIA 2000 may be the first in a chain of disclosures. Y may decide to share what she has discovered with other members of her pressure group. Ultimately, the information could be published in the media. Would X plc be entitled to bring proceedings against the public authority for disclosure of the information under the Act? What if the authority had acted in the *bona fide* belief that disclosure would not constitute a breach of confidence? Once the information is released under the Act, can it be considered to have entered 'the public domain' and, as a result, would Y and others be entitled to re-publish it without restriction?

When information is requested under FOIA 2000, issues may also arise under copyright law. As noted above, an applicant under the legislation is entitled to request disclosure of information in a variety of ways. Where he or she is provided with an opportunity to inspect a record containing requested information, copyright is unlikely to be infringed.[27] However, where information is reproduced in the course of disclosure – for example, where copies are provided to an applicant – potential infringement undoubtedly occurs. Could the owner of the copyright in the recorded information rely on his her copyright interest in order to prevent disclosure of the information under FOIA 2000 and/or to prevent its subsequent publication? Could a public authority's disclosure of information under the Act constitute 'authorization' of infringement by an applicant who re-publishes disclosed information? Furthermore, would a public authority itself be entitled to rely on a copyright interest in refusing disclosure or further dissemination of requested information?

These are important questions. If private law actions can be maintained in the situations outlined above, the 'right to know' provided under the FOIA 2000 may lose much of its force. An understanding of the risk presented by the civil law in such circumstances has led other common law states to provide answers to some of the questions raised above within their freedom of information laws.

IV. Statutory Immunity in Other Jurisdictions

In such common law states, public authorities, and others involved in the

---

[27] There will be no infringement where an applicant inspects, for example, a letter, memorandum or photograph, because the provision of information in this manner will not constitute any of the infringing acts listed under Section 16 of the CDPA 1988. However, it is quite possible that gaining access to information recorded digitally in a computer could fall within the definition of 'reproduction' because a transient copy of the record in question will inevitably be produced when access to the record is granted (see CDPA 1988, Section 17(2)).

disclosure of information under freedom of information legislation, are, in certain circumstances, granted immunity from liability for defamation, breach of confidence and infringement of copyright. In this section, the relevant provisions in Australia, New Zealand, Canada and Ireland are analyzed.

IV.1. AUSTRALIA

In Australia, freedom of information legislation has been introduced at both federal and state levels.[28] In this chapter, the federal statute, the Freedom of Information Act 1982 (Cth), is considered. Section 91(1) of that Act provides immunities against liability for certain specific causes of action – defamation, breach of confidence and infringement of copyright – arising from disclosure of 'documents' [29] under the Act:[30]

> 'Where access has been given to a document and:
> (a) the access was required by this Act to be given. . .; or
> (b) the access was authorized by a Minister, or by an officer having authority. . .to make decisions in respect of requests, in the *bona fide* belief that the access was required by this Act to be given;
> no action for defamation, breach of confidence or infringement of copyright lies against the Commonwealth, an agency, a Minister or an officer by reason of the authorizing or giving of the access,
> and no action for defamation or breach of confidence in respect of any publication involved in, or resulting from, the giving of the access lies against the author of the document or any other person by reason of that author or other person having supplied the document to an agency or Minister'.

The beneficiaries of the immunity are the public authority itself and the author and supplier of the information in question. There is no immunity from liability provided to an applicant who receives disclosed information or to anyone making subsequent disclosures of information released under the statute. Indeed, Section 91(2) specifies that disclosure of information by a public authority under the Act does not constitute 'authorization or approval' of subsequent publication of disclosed information by the person to whom access is given for the purposes of

---

[28] At state level, access to information is provided under the Freedom of Information Act 1989 (New South Wales), the FOIA 1992 (Queensland), the FOIA 1991 (South Australia), the FOIA 1982 (Victoria) and the FOIA 1992 (Western Australia).

[29] The Freedom of Information Act 1982 (Cth) provides access to 'documents' rather than to 'information' (as in the FOIA 2000). *Cf.* the Irish Freedom of Information Act 1997, which provides a right of access to 'records'.

[30] Note also that the FOIA 1982 (Cth) also provides immunity from criminal prosecution arising as a result of the grant of access to information under the Act (Section 92).

the laws of defamation, breach of confidence and copyright.[31] As can be seen, immunity is enjoyed where the Act requires access to be granted; that is, where information is not covered by any of the exemptions provided under the federal statute.[32] Immunity also arises where access was granted to a document by a properly authorized person in the '*bona fide* belief that the access was required' under the Act.[33] Thus, for example, where an authorized officer of a government agency considers, in good faith, that a requested document is not covered by any of the statute's exemptions and, as a result, discloses it, neither that person nor the author or supplier of the document in question will be liable for defamation, breach of confidence or infringement of copyright.[34]

IV.2. NEW ZEALAND

In New Zealand, a right of access to information is provided under the Official Information Act 1982. The relevant immunities are contained in Section 48:

'(1) Where any official information is made available in good faith pursuant to this Act:
(a) No proceedings, civil or criminal, shall lie against the Crown or any other person in respect of the making available of that information or for any consequences that flow from the making available of that information; and
(b) No proceedings, civil or criminal, in respect of any publication involved

---

[31] 'The giving of access to a document (including an exempt document) in consequence of a request shall not be taken to constitute an authorization or approval:
    (a) for the purposes of the law relating to defamation or breach of confidence – of the publication of the document or its contents by the person to whom access is given;
    (b) for the purposes of the law of copyright – of the doing, by the person to whom access is given, of any act comprised within the copyright in:
        (i) any literary, dramatic, musical or artistic work;
        (ii) any sound recording, cinematograph film, television broadcast or sound broadcast; or
        (iii) a published edition of a literary, dramatic, musical or artistic work; contained in the document'.
(Freedom of Information Act 1982 (Cth), Section 91(2))

[32] Part IV of the statute contains a list of documents exempt from the obligation to disclose.

[33] Section 23 of the FOIA (Cth) 1982 explains who the persons authorized to decide on the disclosure of documents are. Thus, for example, Section 23(1) provides that, in relation to most government agencies, 'a decision in respect of a request made to an agency may be made, on behalf of the agency, by the responsible Minister or the principal officer of the agency or … by an officer of the agency acting within the scope of authority exercisable by him in accordance with arrangements approved by the responsible Minister or the principal officer of the agency'.

[34] Rather oddly, it is the state of belief of the responsible person within the public authority which determines whether or not the immunity applies to an author or supplier of information (as well as to the public authority itself).

in or resulting from, the making available of that information shall lie against the author of the information or any other person by reason of that author or other person having supplied the information to a Department or Minister of the Crown or organization'.

As can be seen, immunity is not restricted to particular causes of action under the Official Information Act 1982, but covers any civil or criminal proceedings arising as a result of disclosure of information under the legislation.[35] However, in other respects, Section 48 has a very similar scope to the corresponding provision in the Australian federal statute. Immunity is granted to those responsible for the disclosure of information under the Act and to the supplier (but not the author) of the information disclosed.[36] No immunity is granted to the applicant or to anyone making a subsequent disclosure. Indeed, as under the Australian Act, it is specified (in Section 48 (2)) that disclosure of information under the Act is not to be taken as authorization or approval of publication of the disclosed information by the recipient.[37] Again, the immunity will only apply where information is made available in good faith pursuant to the Act.

IV.3. CANADA

As in Australia, there are freedom of information regimes at both federal and state levels in Canada. In this section, consideration is restricted to the federal statute – the Access to Information Act 1985. The immunity contained in this statute is much terser than the comparable provisions in Australia and New Zealand:

'Notwithstanding any other Act of Parliament, no civil or criminal proceedings lie against the head of any government institution , or against any person acting on behalf or under the direction of the head of a government institution, for the disclosure in good faith of any record or any part of a record pursuant to this Act or for any consequences that flow from

---

[35] When it first came into force, the provision only provided immunity against liability for the same specific causes of action covered by the Australian statute. However, it was amended by Section 21 of the Official Information Amendment Act 1987. See I. Eagles *et al.*, *Freedom of Information in New Zealand* Auckland, Oxford University Press (1992), pp. 613-5.

[36] The provision refers to the 'Crown' because the 1982 Act applies only to bodies forming part of New Zealand's central government. Access to information held by local authorities is available under the Local Government Official Information and Meetings Act 1987.

[37] 'The making available of, or the giving of access to, any official information in consequence of a request made under this Act shall not be taken, for the purposes of the law relating to defamation or breach of confidence or infringement of copyright, to constitute an authorization or approval of the publication of the document or of its contents by the person to whom the information is made available or the access is given'.

such disclosure, or for the failure to give any notice required under this Act if reasonable care is taken to give the required notice'.[38]

As in the case of New Zealand's Official Information Act, this immunity is not restricted to particular causes of action. However, in contrast with those having effect in Australia and New Zealand, it extends only to the public authority itself and does not, therefore, cover the author or supplier of information.[39] Again, as in Australia and New Zealand, an official disclosing information under the access legislation will be entitled to benefit from the immunity where he or she discloses information 'in good faith'.

IV.4. IRELAND

The Irish Freedom of Information Act 1997 also contains immunities that are comparable to those discussed above. These are to be found in Section 45 of the statute. They apply to any 'civil or criminal proceedings' and are enjoyed by the public authority and the author or supplier of a disclosed document. As is the case in Australia and New Zealand, it is expressly provided that the grant of access by a public body is not to be taken as authorization or approval of subsequent publication for the purposes of defamation, breach of confidence or copyright law.[40] It is, however, in relation to the conditions to be satisfied before the immunity can be enjoyed that the Irish provision differs most notably from those discussed above. Under Section 45 immunity arises where the public authority's grant of access constitutes:

'an act that was required or authorized by, and complied with the provisions of, this Act or was reasonably believed by the head concerned to have been so required or authorized and to comply with the provisions of this Act'.[41]

Again, therefore any disclosure that is required under the Act is immune. However, where disclosure is not required under the Act (i.e. because an exemption would have permitted the public body to refuse to disclose the information in question), a public body discloser will only be protected where he or she had a reasonable belief that disclosure was required. Good faith alone is insufficient.

---

[38] Access to Information Act 1985, Section 74.

[39] Also, unlike the equivalent provisions in Australia and New Zealand, Section 74 does not state whether or not disclosure under the Act could constitute authorization or approval of subsequent publication or disclosure of the information.

[40] Freedom of Information Act 1997, Section 45(4).

[41] The reference to 'the head' in this provision is a reference to the head of a public body covered by the legislation.

IV.5. COMMON PRINCIPLES

It can be seen that, despite differences of detail, the common law jurisdictions considered above have arrived at similar solutions to the issues under consideration here. There is general agreement that public authorities should be offered some protection against private law liability for disclosure of information under freedom of information legislation. This protection generally extends to disclosures which need not have been made because the requested information in question was covered by an exemption from the duty to disclose. Most of the jurisdictions considered above also provide protection to those who supply information that is subsequently disclosed and to the authors of that information. In none of the jurisdictions, however, does immunity extend to an applicant for information or to a person who subsequently obtains disclosed information.[42]

This common position inevitably compromises the rights of third parties in relation to information held by public authorities. It is, therefore, important to consider how it can be justified. If the immunities from liability described above are to be justified on the ground that they support the rights of those benefiting from them, the right of freedom of expression would appear to be most relevant. However, it seems unlikely that the common approach has arisen as a result of such rights-based reasoning. Public authorities are the primary beneficiaries of the immunities under consideration here. Governmental bodies, however, are not generally considered to enjoy rights of freedom of expression and any rights enjoyed by lesser public authorities must be very significantly circumscribed by their corporate status and public functions.[43] Equally, it seems unlikely that an individual officer of a public authority carrying out his or her function in disclosing information under the legislation can be said to be exercising his or her right of freedom of expression in doing so.

The true justification for the immunities discussed above appears to be entirely instrumental. In the absence of immunity, a public authority would be likely to find itself in a very difficult situation. On one hand, it would be subject to obligations of disclosure under freedom of information legislation. On the other, it would be subject to civil claims for disclosing potentially exempt information. Faced with the need to make delicate judgments with potentially onerous consequences for misjudgement, a rational public authority would be likely to follow the least risky course open to it. As failure to comply with the obligation to disclose information under freedom of information legislation does not generally result in financial penalties, an authority faced with this dilemma is likely to err on the side of non-disclosure. Thus, if immunities are not provided to public

---

[42] This position is justified as a 'fair balance of the competing public and private interests involved' by I. Eagles *et al.*, *Freedom of Information in New Zealand*, Auckland, Oxford University Press (1992), p. 618.

[43] See, for example, *Derbyshire C.C.* v. *Times Newspapers* [1993] A.C. 534.

authorities, it is likely that less information will be disclosed. The effect of immunity for supplies and authors of information is likely to be less pronounced. However, it is certainly possible that the flow of information into a public authority's hands could be reduced if authors and suppliers of information were aware that they could incur liability as a result of subsequent disclosure of the information by a public authority.

What, however, can be the justification for refusing to grant immunity to an applicant who receives information under freedom of information legislation? Indeed, at first sight, it would appear to be easier to construct an argument for immunity based upon the right to freedom of expression for an applicant than for the primary beneficiary of the immunity. However, the grant of immunity to an applicant (and to a subsequent recipient) of information would be tantamount to the denial of all third party rights in information coming into a public authority's hands. Such an unbalanced result is hard to justify where, in any event, an applicant's rights to freedom of expression are already guaranteed by mechanisms within the laws of the jurisdiction concerned – for example, by defences within the law of defamation, breach of confidence or copyright. By contrast with the position of public authorities, there are no easily identifiable instrumental reasons for granting immunity to the recipient of information. Indeed, the existence of such an immunity could produce undesirable consequences. The knowledge that information obtained under freedom of information legislation is free from obligations applying more generally to the disclosure of information, may tempt applicants to make speculative requests for information in the hope that a public authority will overlook the potential applicability of any relevant exemptions.

Thus, it can be seen that there are justifications for the common approach adopted to this issue in Australia, New Zealand, Canada and Ireland. These justifications are related to the purpose of the legislation, that is, to the promotion of maximum disclosure of information by public authorities. It is now necessary to move on to consider the extent to which the models and lessons provided by these jurisdictions are reflected in the United Kingdom's FOIA 2000.

V. The Freedom of Information Act 2000 – Relationship With Rights Under Civil Law

Surprisingly, a rather different approach has been taken in this jurisdiction. The Freedom of Information Act 2000 contains only one provision granting immunity (Section 79) and this applies solely to defamation:

> 'Where any information communicated by a public authority to a person ('the applicant') under section 1 was supplied to the public authority by a third person, the publication to the applicant of any defamatory matter contained in the information shall be privileged unless the publication is shown to have been made with malice'.

As a result of this limited approach to immunity, the question of whether or not a disclosure under FOIA 2000 could result in civil liability can only be answered following a close examination of the conditions of liability pertaining in each relevant body of civil law. In this section, therefore, potential liability for defamation, breach of confidence and infringement for copyright law are considered closely in turn.

V.1. DEFAMATION

Under English law, defamation is:

'[T]he publication of a statement which reflects on a person's reputation and tends to lower him in the estimation of right-thinking members of society generally or tends to make them shun or avoid him'.[44]

As a result of Section 79, a public authority will not be liable in defamation for communicating information 'supplied to the public authority by a third person' unless the public authority makes the disclosure with 'malice'. In effect, the provision creates a form of statutory qualified privilege. 'Malice' has a technical meaning in defamation law. A publication will be malicious where a defendant uses a privileged occasion[45] for an improper purpose. For example, a public authority's disclosure of defamatory information would be malicious if the authority's agent knew that the information was false and was exempt from the duty to disclose under FOIA 2000 but chose to disclose the information in any event through a desire to damage a third party.[46]

Unlike the provisions in other common law jurisdictions discussed above, Section 79 does not state clearly that it covers both disclosures required under the Act and potentially exempt disclosures. It speaks simply of the communication of information 'by a public authority to a person...under section 1'. On the face of it, the wording of this provision suggests an intention to cover both forms of disclosure. Furthermore, if the provision had been intended to apply only to disclosures reiquired under the Act, there would have been no reason to exempt malicious disclosures from the scope of Section 79. It is not easy to see how such disclosures could ever be malicious. In any event, where a disclosure is required under the Act, a defence of statutory authorization would seem to apply to any claim of defamation.

Section 79 can thus be assumed to cover both 'correct' and 'incorrect' disclosures. Indeed, the primary function of the provision must be to insulate

---

[44] W.V.H. Rogers (ed.), *Winfield and Jolowicz on Tort*, London, Sweet & Maxwell (17th ed., 2002), p. 404.
[45] Here, the disclosure of information in response to an application under the FOIA 2000.
[46] For consideration of the concept of malice in this context, see *Horrocks* v. *Lowe* [1975] 1 AC 135.

public authorities against liability for mistaken disclosures. Public authorities (and persons acting on their behalf) will not be liable in defamation if they disclose information supplied by a third party in the *bona fide* belief that they are obliged to do so under the Act. Although differently expressed, the position is similar to that in Australia, Canada and New Zealand. The immunity is more generous than that provided under the Irish Freedom of Information Act.[47] However, in one respect, it should be noted that Section 79 is significantly more limited than its overseas counterparts. It applies only to information supplied to it by third parties and not to information generated within the public authority itself. Thus, for example, Section 79 would not apply to internal minutes or departmental reports released under FOIA 2000. If sued in defamation for the publication of defamatory information within such documents, a public authority would have to fall back upon existing defences within the law of defamation.[48]

Authors and suppliers of information have no immunity from liability for defamation under FOIA 2000. This does not, however, mean that they will necessarily be liable where a public authority discloses defamatory information. Under the law of defamation, re-publication of a defamatory statement through the voluntary act of another will generally break the chain of causation from the initial publisher of that statement.[49] However, where the maker of a defamatory statement could reasonably have foreseen that the statement would probably be repeated, he or she could be liable for the subsequent re-publication.[50] It is possible that, in certain circumstances, the supplier of information to a public authority could reasonably foresee that the information supplied would probably be released in response to a request under FOIA 2000. However, such circumstances seem unlikely to arise often in practice.

In common with the overseas FOI laws investigated above, no immunity against liability for defamation is provided for applicants for information under the Act. If an applicant (or subsequent recipient) faced a claim for defamation as a result of his or her further dissemination of disclosed information, he or she could only avoid liability by relying upon the defences generally available under the law of defamation. In the case of a media defendant, the development of the defence of qualified privilege arising from the decision of the House of Lords in *Reynolds* v. *Times Newspapers Ltd* may offer protection for 'public interest' disclosures.[51] Unlike most of the overseas laws discussed above, the FOIA 2000 is silent on the

---

[47] In *Horrocks* v. *Lowe* [1975] A.C. 135, a defamatory statement was made with 'gross and unreasoning prejudice'. However, because the defendant believed everything that he said, the statement was not malicious.
[48] It seems unlikely that the authority would be able to claim common law qualified privilege for a disclosure because it will be difficult to argue that it had a *duty* to reveal information that was potentially exempt from disclosure.
[49] *Weld-Blundell* v. *Stephens* [1920] A.C. 945.
[50] *Slipper* v. *B.B.C.* [1991] 1 QB 283; *McManus* v. *Beckham* [2002] EMLR 40.
[51] [2001] 2 A.C. 127.

question of whether or not disclosure by a public authority can be deemed to constitute authorization or approval of an applicant's publication of disclosed information for the purpose of the law of defamation.[52] In the absence of such immunity, a public authority could be liable for authorizing re-publication. This is, however, rather unlikely to occur in practice. Nevertheless, as discussed above, it could also be liable for re-publication where it is reasonably foreseeable that disclosed information would probably be re-published. In the absence of a clear warning against re-publication at the time of disclosure, the likelihood that re-publication will follow a successful request for information under FOIA 2000 would seem to be quite high.

V.2. BREACH OF CONFIDENCE

No immunity against liability for breach of confidence is provided in the FOIA 2000. Accordingly, it is necessary to consider the equitable doctrine itself when asking whether disclosure under the Act could lead to liability. In Megarry J.'s often-quoted words:

> '[T]hree elements are normally required if. . .a case of breach of confidence is to succeed. First, the information itself, in the words of Lord Greene MR. . .must 'have the necessary quality of confidence about it'. Secondly, that information must have been imparted in circumstances importing an obligation of confidence. Thirdly, there must be an unauthorized use of that information to the detriment of the party communicating it'.[53]

Under FOIA 2000, public authorities are exempt from the duty to communicate information where doing so would constitute a breach of confidence owed to a third party.[54] As a consequence of this exemption, if a public authority discloses information in breach of an obligation of confidence owed to a third party, it will not be able to rely upon a defence of statutory authorization. In such circumstances, it would be forced back upon arguments arising within the action for breach of confidence itself. It may, for example, claim that the information in question was not provided to the authority under an obligation of confidence or

---

[52] Liability for authorizing a publication can arise in the law of defamation. See discussion P. Milmo and W.V.H. Rogers (eds.), *Gatley on Libel and Slander*, Sweet and Maxwell (9th ed., 1998), 8.28.

[53] *Coco* v. *A. N. Clark (Engineers) Ltd* [1969] RPC 41.

[54] See note 26 above. Note that this exemption only applies where communication of information would breach an obligation of confidence owed to some person or body other than the public authority receiving the request under the FOIA 2000 (see Section 41(1)(a)).

that the authority was entitled to disclose the information 'in the public interest'.[55] This latter claim is, however, likely to be of only limited effectiveness in protecting a public authority from liability for disclosure of confidential information. While the scope of the 'public interest defence' is uncertain,[56] it has been delimited in terms that are undeniably narrower than the concept of 'public interest' underpinning freedom of information legislation.[57] Such legislation is premised upon a belief that information held by public authorities should be available to the public unless there is a good reason for secrecy to be maintained. The 'public interest' defence to breach of confidence is not, however, based upon such a generous presumption.[58] It will not, for example, justify publication to the world at large where more limited disclosure would suffice.[59] It has also been suggested that the defence will only apply where disclosure is required in the public interest.[60] To the extent that this remains the case,[61] it is clearly based upon a presumption that information should remain confidential unless a very strong reason for disclosure can be established. As such, public authorities which release confidential information of private significance only or make disclosures through inadvertence will not be protected from liability.

An author or supplier of information disclosed by a public authority may, in certain circumstances, be liable in breach of confidence for disclosing information *to*

---

[55] For examples of the use of the 'public interest' claim, see *Initial Services* v. *Putterill* [1968] 1 QB 396; *Lion Laboratories* v. *Evans* [1985] QB 526; *W.* v. *Egdell* [1990] 2 WLR 47. Where this 'defence' applies to particular information, a public authority will (unless the information is covered by another exemption under FOIA 2000) be *obliged* to communicate it because disclosure could not constitute an actionable breach of confidence (as required under Section 41).

[56] See *Hyde Park Residence Ltd* v. *Yelland* [2001] Ch 143 (C.A.). Recent developments following the coming into force of the Human Rights Act 1998 have tended to render its scope even more uncertain. For a notable example, see *A* v. *B plc* [2002] E.M.L.R. 21 (C.A.).

[57] *Cf.* Lord Falconer of Thoroton, Hansard HL, 17 October 2000, col. 928.

[58] This is particularly so in the case of private claimants. Public bodies seeking to rely upon the equitable duty of confidence will themselves have to establish a public interest in maintaining confidentiality (see *A-G* v. *Guardian Newspapers Ltd (No.2)* [1990] 1 AC 109.

[59] See, e.g., *A-G* v. *Guardian Newspapers Ltd (No.2)* [1990] 1 AC 109 at 282-3 per Lord Goff: *Francome* v. *Mirror Group Newspapers Ltd* [1984] 1 WLR 892.

[60] See, e.g., J. Toulson and C. Phipps, *Confidentiality*, London, Sweet & Maxwell (1996) p.80: '[T]he true principle is not (as dicta in some cases suggest) that the court will permit a breach of confidence whenever it considers that disclosure would serve the public interest more than non-disclosure, but rather that no obligation of confidence exists in contract or in equity, in so far as the subject matter concerns a serious risk of public harm (including but not limited to cases of "iniquity") and the alleged obligation would prevent disclosure appropriate to prevent such harm'.

[61] Following developments in 'privacy' cases such as *A* v. *B plc* [2002] E.M.L.R. 21 (C.A.) and *Campbell* v. *M.G.N. Ltd* [2003] E.M.L.R. 2 (C.A.).

a public authority.[62] The author or supplier of information will, however, be unlikely to incur liability as a result of a subsequent disclosure of the information *by* a public authority. While the law of breach of confidence is not as well-developed on this point as defamation law,[63] it would seem unlikely that the independent act of the public authority in disclosing information in response to a request under FOIA 2000 would result in liability for the original author or supplier of that information.

The question of whether or not an applicant for information under the FOIA could be liable for breach of confidence as a result of his or her further disclosure of disclosed information is interesting. Once implicated in the public authority's breach of confidence by knowledge of the breach, the applicant would appear to be vulnerable to such an action. Third party recipients of information who become aware of its confidential status are normally themselves also bound by an obligation of confidence.[64] However, where an applicant is unaware of the confidential status of disclosed information, he or she would not incur liability for disclosure of that information.[65] In addition, as in the case of the public authority itself, an applicant or subsequent recipient of disclosed information may, where applicable, be entitled to rely on the 'public interest' defence.[66] The argument that, once information has been disclosed by a public authority under the FOIA 2000, it forms part of the 'public domain', and therefore cannot form the basis of an action for breach of confidence, seems unlikely to succeed. Courts have shown themselves willing to restrain disclosure of information having only relative confidentiality.[67] Where a public authority has disclosed information in breach of confidence, a court is unlikely to be deterred from preventing further disclosure because there has already been some disclosure of that information.

---

[62] He or she may, however, be able to rely upon the defence of statutory authorization (for example, where there is a statutory obligation to supply information to the public authority) or upon the 'public interest' defence discussed above. In considering the application of the 'public interest' defence to breach of confidence, courts have tended to look favourably upon disclosures to an appropriate public body.

[63] See text accompanying note 51 above.

[64] *A-G* v. *Guardian Newspapers Ltd (No.2)* [1990] AC 109 at 260 (per Lord Keith).

[65] See *Thomas* v. *Pearce* [2000] FSR 718.

[66] For example, where disclosed information reveals wrongful conduct on the part of the person to whom the obligation of confidence is owed.

[67] See, e.g., *Franchi* v. *Franchi* [1969] RPC 149. Compare the position of the recipient of information justifiably disclosed in breach of confidence under New Zealand's Official Information Act 1982 (I. Eagles *et al.*, *Freedom of Information in New Zealand*, Auckland, Oxford University Press (1992), p. 617). As a result of Section 41, it would not appear to be possible to release information justifiably in breach of confidence under FOIA 2000 (save where it is covered by the 'public interest' or other defence within that cause of action).

V.3. COPYRIGHT

As noted above,[68] the circumstances in which disclosure of information under the Act can give rise to liability for infringement of copyright are more limited than in the case of defamation and breach of confidence. For example, while spoken, private communications may incur liability in defamation or breach of confidence, such communications cannot infringe copyright. However, the provision of copies of requested information (which is likely to be the most frequently employed mechanism for disclosure) may, *prima facie*, constitute an infringement of copyright. Whether the copying and disclosure of information protected by copyright will in fact infringe copyright in any particular case is an issue that is more closely considered below.

Where disclosure of copyright-protected information is mandatory under the FOIA 2000 (i.e. where there is no applicable exemption), a public authority will be protected against any action for copyright infringement. This protection derives from two sources. First, the defence of statutory authority applying generally in the law of tort would appear to cover the disclosure.[69] Secondly, section 50 of the Copyright Designs and Patents Act may also provide protection. This provides that:

'(1) Where the doing of a particular act is specifically authorized by an Act of Parliament, whenever passed, then, unless the Act provides otherwise, the doing of that act does not infringe copyright'.

These defences will, however, only be effective where disclosure is authorized (at common law) or where it is 'specifically authorized' (under Section 50). Where a public authority releases information that is covered by an exemption from the duty of disclosure, it would not appear to be possible to describe its disclosure as authorized or 'specifically authorized' by the statute.[70] In such circumstances,

---

[68] See section 2 above.

[69] For discussion of the application of this defence in copyright law, see H. Laddie, P. Prescott & M. Vitoria, *The Modern Law of Copyright and Designs*, London, Butterworths (3rd ed., 2000), 20.47.

[70] This may also be true where a public authority could reasonably have disclosed information in a manner that would not infringe copyright (for example, by allowing an applicant a reasonable opportunity to inspect records containing the information). Indeed, a copyright owner may be tempted to argue that, as a result of Section 44(1) of the FOIA 2000, infringement of copyright can *never* be authorized under that Act. Section 44(1) provides that:
'Information is exempt information if its disclosure (otherwise than under this Act), by the public authority holding it:
(a) is prohibited by or under any enactment ...'
In reliance upon this provision, a copyright owner may argue that the CDPA 1988 is an enactment prohibiting disclosure of information and, therefore, that a public authority is *never* obliged to make any disclosure infringing copyright. As a result, it could be argued, disclosures of information involving infringement of copyright can never be regarded as authorized or

therefore, a public authority would appear to be vulnerable to liability for copyright infringement[71] unless it can bring itself within the scope of any of the other defences to copyright infringement. It is likely to face considerable difficulty in doing so because the statutory 'permitted acts' within the CDPA 1988 are closely tailored to specifically articulated legitimate uses of a copyright work. It is difficult to see how 'mistaken' disclosure of information by a public authority under FOIA 2000 can fall within any such statutory permitted act. The common law defence of 'public interest' is even more uncertain in scope in copyright law than it is in breach of confidence[72] and, in any event, will not apply to inadvertent disclosures.

As in the case of public authorities, the FOIA 2000 contains no immunity from an action for copyright infringement for an author or supplier of information disclosed under the Act. Is it possible, therefore, that such a person could be liable for 'authorizing' an authority's subsequent disclosure of information protected by copyright. The authority's subsequent disclosure will not, of course, infringe copyright where disclosure is required under the Act. Equally, in such a case, it would not be possible for the supplier or author of the information in question to incur liability for authorizing an infringement. An infringement is a necessary precondition for authorization liability to arise. However, where a public authority discloses potentially exempt information, a supplier or author could be liable where he or she could be regarded as granting or purporting to grant a right to commit copyright infringement in disclosing the information.[73] In practice, it seems very unlikely that a supplier or author of information would ever be regarded as having authority to grant such a right when supplying or creating such information. Simple knowledge that information may be disclosed in

---

cont.

'specifically authorized' by FOIA 2000. However, the difficulty with this argument is that, if it were accepted, the purpose of the FOIA 2000 would be frustrated entirely. This could surely not be justified (*cf.* M. McDonagh, *Freedom of Information Law in Ireland*, Dublin, Round Hall (1998), p. 74). The Act contains ample protection for the commercial interests of third parties and it is not satisfactory for copyright owners to argue that public authorities could disclose requested information without infringing copyright – for example, by providing a summary or digest. It is questionable whether 'information' disclosed in such a form would be the same 'information' as that requested by an applicant. In any event, the FOIA 2000 clearly reveals an intention that an applicant should, wherever practicable, be able to obtain disclosure in his or her chosen form. As acceptance of this argument would tend to frustrate the purpose of the FOIA 2000, it is suggested that courts will be likely to interpret Section 44(1) in such a way that a copyright interest is not regarded as prohibiting 'disclosure' (as opposed to reproduction, performance in public etc.) and therefore that the CDPA 1988 is not considered to fall within the scope of Section 44(1).

71 Where a 'substantial part' is reproduced (see CDPA 1988, Section 16(3)(a)).
72 See *Hyde Park Residence Ltd* v. *Yelland* [2001] Ch 143 (C.A.); *Ashdown* v. *Telegraph Group plc* [2002] Ch 149 (C.A.).
73 *CBS Songs* v. *Amstrad* [1988] 2 All ER 484.

response to a request under FOIA 2000 would not be sufficient to give rise to liability for authorizing copyright infringement.

What then of the applicant who receives information disclosed under the Act? In most cases, simple receipt of information is unlikely to infringe copyright. However, where a recipient wishes to reproduce and further disseminate disclosed information, he or she may incur liability. Neither the common law defence of statutory authorization, nor Section 50 CDPA 1988, will protect an applicant or subsequent recipient in such circumstances. The duty to disclose information under FOIA 2000 cannot provide the basis of a claim to statutory authorization because that duty applies solely to public authorities. It would appear, therefore, that copyright owners could seek to prevent further dissemination of disclosed information protected by copyright whether or not that information was 'correctly' disclosed by a public authority.[74] This is problematic. It may be considered acceptable for a copyright owner to rely upon its interest to prevent the reproduction of information that need not have been disclosed by a public authority. However, it is surely not acceptable for a copyright owner to have a power to prevent all further dissemination of information properly disclosed under FOIA 2000. While the continued application of rights in defamation and breach of confidence following disclosure will be restricted to cases in which a third party's interest in reputation or confidentiality is jeopardized, there is no such restriction under copyright law. Whenever disclosed information is clothed in copyright, a potential infringement will arise. Particularly where a copyright owner's motivation in bringing proceedings in such circumstances is to impede the flow of information (as opposed, say, to protect the commercial value of the information in question), a threat to the underlying purpose of FOIA 2000 would appear to arise. As a result, it is possible that courts would be willing to develop the common law 'public interest' defence to ensure that the right of access to information is not frustrated.[75]

Because FOIA 2000 does not contain a provision stating that disclosure of information by a public authority cannot be deemed to authorize or approve further publication by an applicant, copyright owners may also be able to argue that, in disclosing information, public authorities can incur liability for authorizing an applicant's subsequent copyright infringement. Again, such an argument could be made whether or not the public authority's initial disclosure was 'correct' or not. The chances of success of such a claim will depend upon the

---

[74] In some cases, the copyright owner could even be the public authority itself. See J.A. Kidwell 'Open Records Law and Copyright' in *Wisconsin Law Review* (1989) 1021. The applicant or subsequent recipient may, of course, be entitled to rely upon the statutory 'permitted acts' within the CDPA 1988. For example, in some cases, disclosure may be justifiable under Section 30(2) CDPA, which permits fair dealing with copyright works for the purpose of reporting current events.

[75] *Cf.* the Court of Appeal's application of the public interest defence to ensure that copyright law does not contravene the European Convention on Human Rights in *Ashdown* v. *Telegraph Group plc.* [2002] Ch 149.

manner in which the authority discloses the information in question. If disclosure is accompanied by a suitably worded disclaimer, it seems unlikely that the authority could be regarded as granting, or purporting to grant, the right to commit an infringing act to the applicant.

VI. Potential Problems Arising as a Result of the Limited Statutory Immunity Granted Under FOIA 2000

As has been demonstrated above, the FOIA 2000 allows considerable scope for the continued use of private law actions to impede disclosure of information. In this respect, it differs significantly from comparable legislation in other common law jurisdictions. In this section, some of the problems arising as a result of the decision to introduce only limited statutory immunity are explored.

VI.1. PROBLEMS FOR PUBLIC AUTHORITIES

Public authorities are not generally protected against 'unnecessary' or 'mistaken' disclosures under FOIA 2000. Limited protection against liability for defamation is available. However, no protection at all is available in the case of breach of confidence or infringement of copyright. An authority is therefore at risk even if it acts in good faith or on a reasonable belief that it is obliged to disclose requested information. This absence of protection places a public authority in an awkward position. On one hand, it is subject to statutory duties to disclose under FOIA 2000.If it fails to disclose information that ought to be disclosed, the Information Commissioner can enforce compliance with the Act. On the other hand, if it wrongly assesses the scope of an exemption or fails to appreciate the status of information in its hands, it may face civil proceedings for breach of confidence or infringement of copyright. Its position is rendered even less attractive by the difficulty of predicting the exact scope of the FOIA's exemptions and of the relevant causes of action in civil law.

These difficulties do not only present a problem for public authorities. They also create a real threat to the effective operation of the freedom of information regime introduced under FOIA 2000. As has previously been indicated, when faced with the dilemma outlined above, a public authority is very likely to opt for a conservative approach to information disclosure. The consequences of breaching the private law rights of third parties (awards of damages and orders for legal costs) are considerably more onerous than those of failing to comply with the requirements of the Act.[76] FOIA 2000 was introduced to improve the accountability and quality of administration. Adoption of a conservative

---

[76] The enforcement powers of the Information Commissioner are set out in FOIA 2000, Sections 50-56.

approach to disclosure will reduce the likelihood that this aim will be achieved and will increase the administrative burden on the Information Commissioner. In addition to liability arising from its own disclosure of information in response to a request under FOIA 2000, a public authority also faces potential liability for authorizing or approving subsequent disclosures by applicants or subsequent recipients. Faced with the risk of such liability, an authority is likely to seek to protect itself by developing disclosure forms that strongly discourage further dissemination of information communicated under FOIA 2000. Such documents are likely themselves to tend to 'chill' public debate; thus further frustrating the rationale for of freedom of information legislation.

VI.2. PROBLEMS FOR AUTHORS/SUPPLIERS

Authors and suppliers of information are less vulnerable to civil action under FOIA 2000. As noted above, a public authority's disclosure of information is unlikely to lead to liability for the original supplier or author of that information in very many cases. Nevertheless, other jurisdictions have considered it worthwhile to provide immunity for suppliers and authors. Presumably, in doing so, they have been motivated by the fear that, in the absence of such immunity, the communication of information to public authorities is likely to be reduced. It is difficult to imagine that the fear of liability for authorizing defamation, breach of confidence or infringement of copyright would have a very significant impact upon the flow of information to public authorities. Nevertheless, to the extent that it would, the absence of immunity in FOIA 2000 will tend to interfere with the public interest in free communication of information.

VI.3. PROBLEMS FOR APPLICANTS

As has been demonstrated above, those to whom information is disclosed under FOIA 2000 may face civil proceedings for further dissemination of that information. In this respect, the Act does not differ from its common law counterparts. Nevertheless, the absence of immunity for public authorities that is characteristic of the FOIA 2000 may also have adverse consequences for recipients of disclosed information. It has been noted above that, in order to avoid potential liability for authorizing an applicant's wrong, public authorities are likely disclose information under cover of strongly-worded disclaimers. Such notices may have a 'chilling' effect on the further dissemination of disclosed information – even where further dissemination is lawful.

VII. Conclusion

What then does the approach to immunity adopted in the FOIA 2000 tell us about the prevailing attitude towards the law of information disclosure in this jurisdiction? It seems possible to draw a number of tentative conclusions. First, tenderness towards private law rights (to reputation, confidentiality and property in creative works) appears to mark the regime introduced under the FOIA 2000. This is in keeping with a historical tendency for law-makers in this jurisdiction to favour individual first-generation liberties over positive rights such as the right of access to information. The recent incorporation of the European Convention on Human Rights could be argued to reinforce this preference for individual liberties and is likely to have made those responsible for the FOIA 2000 particularly wary of introducing a regime that interferes substantially with third party rights.

Secondly, the absence of immunities reflects governmental ambivalence about the desirability of freedom of information legislation. As noted above, the risk of civil proceedings is likely to cause public authorities to adopt a conservative approach to information disclosure. The United Kingdom government is unlikely to regard this as particularly problematic. There is ample evidence to demonstrate its lukewarm commitment to freedom of information. This evidence ranges from the delays in bringing a Bill before Parliament and the postponement of the Act's coming into force to the extensive range of exemptions available to public authorities and the existence of a ministerial power to override decisions of the Information Commissioner.[77]

Finally, however, it is also possible to suggest that the situation described in this paper is representative of the increasingly complex and inconsistent body of 'information law' in this jurisdiction. There are now a huge number of measures governing the circumstances in which information can, or must, be disclosed. Despite the impact of the Human Rights Act 1998, these measures are often overlapping and inconsistent.[78] The fact that the aims of the FOIA 2000 can be frustrated through reliance on competing private law rights is typical of a continued tendency to allow the features of particular causes of action, rather than underlying principle, to determine the contours of our information law. Section 75 of the FOIA 2000 grants a power to the Secretary of State to amend or repeal any enactment 'capable of preventing the disclosure of information' under the Act.[79] The time may, however, have come for a much more radical review of all our laws governing disclosure of information.

---

[77] See FOIA 2000, Section 53.

[78] See, for example, uncertainty caused by the largely unpredicted consequences of the Data Protection and Database Directives (*Campbell* v. *M.G.N. Ltd* [2003] E.M.L.R. 2 (C.A.) *and British Horseracing Board Ltd* v. *William Hill Organisation Ltd* [2001] R.P.C. 31 respectively), by the re-shaping of the law of confidentiality to protect personal privacy (*A* v. *B plc* [2002] E.M.L.R. 21 (C.A.) and *Campbell* v. *M.G.N. Ltd* [2003] E.M.L.R. 2 (C.A.) and by the overlapping forms of protection offered by breach of confidence and copyright (*Hyde Park Residence Ltd* v. *Yelland* [2001] Ch 143 (C.A.)).

[79] A review of such enactments has been conducted and a number have been identified as suitable for repeal or amendment, see *Annual report on bringing fully into force those provisions of the FOIA 2000 which are not yet fully in force* (Lord Chancellor's Department, November 2002, H.C. 6).

Chapter 5

Fair Dealing and Freedom of Expression

*Patrick Masiyakurima**

I.   Introduction

Tensions between copyright owners and users permeate almost every aspect of UK copyright law. This polarization is fuelled by several factors including the wide ambit of domestic copyright protection, the wave of international copyright harmonization measures with their broad rights and narrow exceptions and the proliferation of revolutionary copying technologies. Courts deploy various statutory and common law controls when reconciling the rights stemming from copyright ownership with other public interests. Owing to the systemic weaknesses of most of these mechanisms, a proper application of the fair dealing defence balances the interests of copyright owners and users because it permits the unauthorized appropriation of protected expressions.

This article examines the interaction of fair dealing and freedom of expression in UK copyright law.[1] The article is divided into three parts. The first part provides a contextual framework for the discussion of fair dealing and freedom of expression while the second part outlines the benefits of fair dealing to freedom of expression. Given that most fair dealing cases fail because the copyright work was used unfairly, the third and chief part of the article investigates the free speech effects of the factors that affect a 'fairness' inquiry. The article concludes with a brief assessment of some of the main reforms that are proposed in this area.

An important *caveat* must be made to the analysis in this article. Most of the cases cited here were decided before the enactment of the Human Rights Act 1998. However, some of these authorities are still persuasive because they recognized the importance of freedom of expression in copyright law[2] and may provide some useful insight into the general interpretation of the fair dealing provisions. In any

---

*   Lecturer in Law, University of Aberdeen. A draft of this article was presented at an 'International One Day Conference on Rights in Information'. I would like to thank the participants at that conference, David Vaver and Heather Lardy for their helpful comments. The usual disclaimers apply.
[1]   Where appropriate, materials from other jurisdictions will also be referred to in the article.
[2]   *Pro Sieben Media AG* v. *Carlton UK Television Ltd* [1999] 1 WLR 605 (CA) 612; *Newspaper Licensing Authority* v. *Marks & Spencer* [2000] 3 WLR 1256 (CA) 1268; *Kennard* v. *Lewis* [1983] FSR 346, 347; *PCR* v. *Dow Jones Telerate* [1998] FSR 170, 186.

P.L.C. Torremans (ed.), Copyright and Human Rights, 87–108
© *2004 Kluwer Law International. Printed in the Netherlands.*

event, the post 1998 judgment in *Ashdown* v. *Telegraph Group Ltd*[3] does not depart significantly from the earlier cases. Thus, subject to a cautious interpretation, the 'old' cases illuminate the issues discussed here.

II. Copyright and Freedom of Expression

Freedom of expression safeguards a person's right to impart and receive information and it has three interdependent rationales. Firstly, it allows individuals to gather the information necessary for making various choices as part of the democratic process.[4] Secondly, the analysis generated by readily available information may foster the discovery of truth.[5] Lastly, freedom of expression may be an end in itself because it promotes self-actualization.[6] Although copyright is sometimes congruent with the aims of freedom of expression, it is principally concerned with protecting the expression of ideas in various cultural media. It is this protection of ideas which may impede freedom of expression. Several themes cut across any discussion of the conflicts between copyright and freedom of expression and it is to a consideration of these themes that we now turn.

Sometimes, copyright's incentives promote freedom of expression by stimulating the creation of new expressions.[7] However, meaningful access to these expressions is proscribed by the gradual metamorphosis of copyright from a set of incentives designed to induce creativity into a rigid 'property' system with myriad benefits and narrow exceptions.[8] The economics of copyright affects freedom of expression at two distinct stages of a copyright work's life. Given that publishing decisions are usually routine commercial matters, publishers may abandon or limit the extensive dissemination of important but financially unattractive expressions.[9] There is therefore a serious risk that important information may never reach the public. Upon publication, the incentives granted to authors may create artificial monopolies in expressions and price impecunious users out of the market of

---

[3]   *Ashdown* v. *Telegraph Group Ltd* [2001] 3 WLR 1368 (CA).
[4]   A. Meiklejohn, 'The First Amendment is an Absolute', in *Supreme Court Review* (1961) 245.
[5]   E. Barendt, *Freedom of Speech*, Oxford University Press (1985).
[6]   F. Schauer, *Free Speech: A Philosophical Enquiry*, Cambridge University Press (1982), chapters 4-5; *Whitney* v. *California* 274 US 357 [1927] 375.
[7]   W.M. Landes and R.A. Posner, 'An Economic Analysis of Copyright Law', in *Journal of Legal Studies* 18 (1989) 325; *Harper & Row* v. *Nation Enterprises*, 471 US 539 [1985], 558; *cf.* A. Plant, 'The Economic Aspects of Copyright in Books', in *Economica*, New Series, Volume 1, Issue 2, (1934) 167; S. Breyer, 'The Uneasy Case for Copyright: A Study of Copyright in Books, Photocopies, and Computer Programs', in *Harvard Law Review* 84 (1970) 281.
[8]   D. Vaver, 'Intellectual Property: The State of the Art', in *LQR* 116 (*Law Quarterly Review*) (2000) 621.
[9]   *Malcolm* v. *The Chancellor, Masters and Scholars of the University of Oxford T/A Oxford University Press* [1994] EMLR 17.

ideas.[10] Where access to a work is possible, copyright's extensive rights disable valuable unauthorized uses of copyright materials. Although publishers play a pivotal role in the publication and exploitation of copyright works, courts and legislatures are generally oblivious to the dangers publishers pose to the public interest. One possible explanation for this position is that while individuals generally vindicate their fundamental freedoms against public bodies, copyright typically pits privately owned publishers against private users. Consequently, courts may not uphold freedom of expression as vigorously as in cases involving direct actions by the government or other public bodies.[11] Additionally, owing to the relative little weight attached to commercial speech,[12] judges are reluctant to condone the misappropriation of a competitor's intellectual capital under the banner of freedom of expression. This reluctance to advance freedom of expression in copyright cases is unfortunate because it ignores the risks posed to creativity and access to copyright works by the gradual convergence of different media and the resulting concentrated ownership of copyright works by a few publishers.

Despite pervading most discussions on copyright, utilitarianism is not sacrosanct. Other arguments including those championing the non-pecuniary benefits of authorship also vie for prominence.[13] For instance, copyright may be regarded as a vehicle for preserving an author's 'personality'[14] as encapsulated in her work.[15] The 'personality' basis of copyright is coterminous with the self-actualization rationale for freedom of expression and is of major importance to burgeoning authors who may lack the means or the opportunity to rectify distortions to their expressions. Copyright safeguards the authenticity of artistic expressions by granting authors various moral rights which may be used to attribute speech or to veto significant unauthorized changes to copyright works. Moral rights also yield collateral free speech benefits to the public because they guarantee the genuineness of the expressions that reach the public and preserve

---

[10] P. Goldstein, 'Copyright and the First Amendment', in *Columbia Law Review* 70 (1970) 983, 989; N.W. Netanel 'Copyright and a Democratic Civil Society', in *Yale Law Journal* 106 (1996) 283, 292.

[11] R. Abel, *Speech and Respect*, Sweet & Maxwell (1994), 48-58.

[12] E. Barendt, *Freedom of Speech*, Oxford University Press (1985).

[13] J. Hughes, 'The Philosophy of Intellectual Property', in *Georgetown Law Review* 77 (1988) 287, 330.

[14] M.J. Radin, 'Property and Personhood', in *Stanford Law Review* 34 (1982) 958.

[15] F. Pollaud-Dulian, 'Le Droit Moral En France, a travers la jurisprudence récente', in *RIDA* 145 (*Revue Internationale du Droit d'Auteur*) (1990) 126, 127; R. Sarraute, 'Current Theory on the Moral Right of Authors and Artists under French Law', in *American Journal of Comparative Law* 16 (1968) 465; J.H. Merryman, 'The Moral Right of Maurice Utrillo', in *American Journal of Comparative Law* 43 (1995) 445; A. Dietz, 'The Artist's Right of Integrity under Copyright Law – A Comparative Approach', in *IIC* 25 (*International Review of Industrial Property and Copyright Law*) (1994) 177.

our cultural heritage from unwarranted distortions.[16] However, an overprotection of authors' rights may encumber freedom of expression by restricting the extensive dissemination of useful information through sympathetic adaptations of copyright works.[17] Additionally, overprotecting authors' rights subtracts from the corpus of cultural materials available for the self-actualization of subsequent authors and users.[18] Copyright therefore attracts praise and opprobrium in almost equal measure because while it promotes the self-development of authors it restricts meaningful public access to authors' expressions.

Authors faced with unauthorized disclosures of their intimate personal details may protect their privacy indirectly through a copyright claim.[19] The interaction of copyright and privacy has diametrically opposed effects on freedom of expression. Firstly, access to private copyright works aids freedom of expression by making new or restricted information available for public consumption. However, this argument ignores the possibility that some authors may genuinely desire to secure a personal zone in which they can delimit the recipients of their expressions. At another level, authors may impede freedom of expression by censoring disclosures of potentially embarrassing information through litigation.[20] This anti-dissemination effect of copyright is firmly rooted in its early links with censorship.[21] Thirdly, where unauthorized disclosures interfere with an author's plans to publish the same materials, the exercise of copyright may delay the publication of important current information. There is also the additional risk that a change in the author or publisher's circumstances may prevent the publication of the information. Ownership of most copyright works by companies adds a different dimension to the preceding arguments because privacy loses most of its lustre if inanimate corporate persons rely on it.[22]

Ordinarily, the use of interlocutory injunctions in civil cases reduces the risks, costs and delays associated with full-scale litigation.[23] However, the significant risk of error[24] arising from hasty decisions and limited opportunities for cross-

---

[16] C. Graber and G. Teubner, 'Art and Money: Constitutional Rights in the Private Sphere?', in *Oxford Journal of Legal Studies* 18 (1998) 61.

[17] P. Goldstein, 'Adaptation Rights and Moral Rights in the United Kingdom, the United States and the Federal Republic of Germany', in *IIC* 14 (1983) 43.

[18] Z. Chafee, 'Reflections on the Law of Copyright', in *Columbia Law Review* 45 (1945) 501.

[19] T. De Turris, 'Copyright Protection of Privacy Interests in Unpublished Works', in *Annual Survey of American Law* (1994) 277.

[20] *Commonwealth* v. *John Fairfax & Sons Ltd* [1981] 55 ALJR 45; *Hyde Park* v. *Yelland* [2000] RPC 604

[21] B. Kaplan, *An Unhurried View of Copyright*, Columbia (1967).

[22] *Australian Broadcasting Corporation* v. *Lenah Game Meats Pty Ltd* [2002] 76 ALJR 1, paragraph 26.

[23] A.A.S. Zuckerman, 'Interlocutory remedies in quest of procedural fairness', in *Modern Law Review* 56 (1993) 325.

[24] *Douglas* v. *Hello! Ltd* [2001] 2 WLR 992 (CA), 1019 (Brooke LJ).

examination poses serious challenges to freedom of expression in copyright cases. Although judges may restrain the chilling effects of interlocutory injunctions by refusing to grant these remedies in cases involving freedom of expression[25] or by relying on Section 12(4) of the Human Rights Act 1998, the application of these safety valves has been largely conservative.[26] True, interlocutory injunctions are only provisional and their drawbacks may be exterminated by a subsequent trial on the merits but in many cases, these injunctions finalize the dispute between the parties.[27] It is therefore conceivable that prohibitive costs and the uncertainty of success at the trial may be used to coerce defendants to settle their claims unfavourably.[28] Settlements of this kind reduce the opportunities for a judicial delimitation of the boundaries of the public interest in copyright cases.

Where copyright conflicts with the public interest, courts attempt to strike a delicate balance between maintaining public access to protected expressions and securing the economic benefits of copyright ownership. This balancing exercise reflects the general qualification of fundamental rights by other competing interests. Courts rely on several statutory and common law measures when reconciling copyright with the public interest. The following brief assessment of these techniques reveals their inadequate protection of freedom of expression.

Originality circumscribes the reach of copyright by requiring a modicum of creativity in copyright works. Users may therefore freely access and appropriate the 'unoriginal' parts of a work. However, unlike in the USA[29] and continental Europe,[30] originality in the UK is not principally concerned with creativity. Instead, it only requires that a work be not copied from another work, that it 'originates' from its author and that it involves a scintilla of effort in its creation.[31] Consequently, humdrum works such as past examination papers[32] and football coupons[33] attract the same copyright protection as magisterial literary and musical works. This over inclusiveness limits what users can legitimately appropriate from a copyright work. True, the EU's gradual tightening of the test of originality[34]

---

[25] *Hubbard* v. *Vosper* [1972] 2 WLR 397; *Consorzio del Prosciutto di Parma* v. *Marks & Spencer Plc* [1991] 351, 358-359; *cf. Commonwealth of Australia* v. *John Fairfax & Sons Ltd* [1981] 55 ALJR 45, 58.

[26] *Ashdown* v. *Telegraph Group Ltd* [2001] 2 All ER 370; *Imutran* v. *Uncaged Campaigns Ltd* [2002] FSR 2.

[27] *Associated Newspapers Group Plc* v. *News Group Ltd and Ors* [1986] RPC 515, 516.

[28] *Williams* v. *Spautz* [1992] 174 CLR 509 (Deane J).

[29] *Feist Publications Inc* v. *Rural Telephone Service Co* 111 US 1282 [1989].

[30] See e.g. Article L.112-4 of the French Intellectual Property Code, Law No. 92-597 of 1 July 1992.

[31] *Ladbroke (Football) Ltd* v. *William Hill (Football) Ltd* [1964] 1 WLR 273, 291(HL).

[32] *University of London Press* v. *University Tutorial Press* [1916] 2 Ch 601.

[33] *Football League Ltd* v. *Littlewoods Pools Ltd* [1959] 1 Ch 637.

[34] E.g. Article 3(1) of the Database Directive and Article 3(3) of the Computer Programs Directive; D.J. Gervais, 'A Comparative Analysis of the Notion of Originality in Copyright Law', in *Journal of the Copyright Society of the USA* 49 (2002) 949.

offers additional protection to users but in its current form, originality is neutered by judicial reticence in determining aesthetic merit[35] and the use of copyright to prevent misappropriation of valuable information.[36] Conversely, it may be posited that the low test of originality seriously promotes freedom of expression by allowing authors of different abilities to express themselves meaningfully. However, the low test of originality fences off large *quanta* of basic information and dissipates the raw materials for future creativity.

The idea/expression dichotomy promotes freedom of expression by allowing users to exploit the underlying ideas in copyright works freely.[37] However, the usefulness of this principle is circumscribed by the unmapped boundaries between ideas and their expression.[38] The absence of a clear test for distinguishing ideas from their expression is especially evident in works where ideas and their expression are interstitially linked.[39] Moreover, to prevent the misappropriation of valuable expressions, courts usually interpret 'expressions of ideas' widely.[40] Even if this distinction obtains, the idea/expression dichotomy is unhelpful to defendants who must use an author's exact expressions[41] to minimize significant distortions to the author's views or for the purposes of efficiency. Nebulous principles such as the idea/expression dichotomy have negligible benefits in copyright cases implicating vital public interests and betray the major short-comings of copyright's internal balancing processes.

In theory, copyright's temporal limits guarantees eventual unfettered public access to protected expressions.[42] However, progressive domestic and interna-tional extensions of the copyright term[43] severely dilute or postpone the

---

[35] *Bleisten* v. *Donaldson Lithographing Co* 188 US 239 [1903] 251.

[36] *Designers Guild Ltd* v. *Russell Williams (Textiles) Ltd* [2001] 1 All ER 700 (Lord Bingham of Cornhill).

[37] M.B. Nimmer, 'Does Copyright Abridge the First Amendment Guarantees of Free Speech and Press?', in *UCLA Law Review* 17 (1970) 1180, 1189; *Feist Publications, Inc* v. *Rural Telephone Service Co* 111 US 1282 [1989], 349-350; *Harper & Row* v. *Nation Enterprises*, 471 US 539 [1985], 558.

[38] *Nichols* v. *Universal Pictures* 45 F 2D 119 [1930].

[39] E.C. Hettinger, 'Justifying Intellectual Property', in *Philosophy & Public Affairs* 18 (1989) 31, 32; *Kenrick* v. *Lawrence* [1890] 25 QB 99; *Designers Guild Ltd* v. *Russell Williams (Textiles) Ltd* [2001] 1 All ER 700.

[40] *Harman Pictures* v. *Osborne* [1967] 2 All ER 324; *Elanco Products* v. *Mandops (Agrochemichal Specialists)* [1980] RPC 213 (CA); *Designers Guild Ltd* v. *Russell Williams (Textiles) Ltd* [2001] 1 All ER 700 (HL).

[41] *Ashdown* v. *Telegraph Group Ltd* [2001] 3 WLR 1368 (CA).

[42] S. Ricketson, 'The Copyright Term', in *IIC* (1992) 753, 754; K. Puri, 'The Term of Copyright Protection – Is It Too Long in the Wake of New Technologies?', in *EIPR* 12 (*European Intellectual Property Review*) (1990) 14; T. Limpberg, 'Duration of Copyright Protection', in *RIDA* 103 (1980) 53.

[43] E.g. Term Directive 93/98 EEC; Copyright Term Extension Act, S 505 PL 105-298 11 Stat 2827 (US); *Eldred* v. *Ashcroft* [2003] 65 USPQ 2d 1225.

enrichment of the public domain by copyright expressions. Even if the copyright term is carefully calibrated, its benefits may be of little assistance to users who wish to exploit current information. Other significant practical and theoretical problems are generated by the *post-mortem auctoris* protection of copyright works. Firstly, a deceased author's heirs may abuse their copyright and censor expressions that are critical of the dead author.[44] Secondly, it is difficult to decipher the free-speech interests that are protected after the author's death. While copyright protection during and after an author's life may preserve the authenticity of the author's personal expressions, there are no credible explanations for limiting this protection to the current 70 years after an author's death. In any event, a deceased author's successors in title may authorize critical interferences with the work and destroy the authenticity of its expressions. These difficulties reduce the availability of meaningful tools for promoting the public interest in the copyright arena.

Compulsory licensing may reduce copyright's anti-dissemination effects by sanctioning the circulation of information held by monopolistic organizations. However, the delays and costs associated with complex copyright litigation may dissuade impecunious users from relying on this remedy. Even if users have the patience and the financial muscle to vindicate their rights, a determined copyright owner may rely on the full panoply of interlocutory procedures and appeals to delay the publication of current information. Additionally, courts use compulsory licensing sparingly because it alters the parties bargaining power and may reduce the royalties paid to copyright owners significantly. Apart from these difficulties, the application of this remedy to unexploited and unpublished personal materials is contentious. Arguably, given that compulsory licenses are designed to combat waste, these licenses reduce the potential waste arising from failing to access personal works containing new and important information. Conversely, compulsory licensing may force individuals to speak to unfamiliar or unwanted audiences and may infringe an author's privacy. Thus, despite its usefulness in advancing competition in the copyright sector, compulsory licensing has little practical relevance in cases that do not raise competition issues.

The public interest defence[45] promotes freedom of expression by securing the availability of restricted or unpublished materials. Although this defence is prominent in breach of confidence claims, its usefulness in copyright cases is severely compromised by enervating doubts about its theoretical soundness and its proper boundaries.[46] Generally, courts interpret the public interest defence narrowly because if successful, the defence sanctions free exploitation of copyright works. Moreover, courts may be anxious to maintain a copyright owner's privacy

---

[44] *Morang & Co* v. *Le Sueur* [1911] 45 SCR 95 (Canada).
[45] Section 171(3) of the Copyright, Designs and Patents Act 1988.
[46] *Hyde Park* v. *Yelland* [2001] 3 WLR 1172 (CA); *cf. Ashdown* v. *Telegraph Group Ltd* [2001] 3 WLR 1368 (CA).

especially in cases involving the unauthorized disclosure of personal information. All these uncertainties may impede freedom of expression by precluding users from relying on the defence when exploiting copyright works. The weaknesses of the public interest defence and other tools for balancing copyright and the public interest mean that apart from developing a strong free speech defence in copyright law, fair dealing provides a realistic chance for preserving the public interest in copyright cases.

III. Fair Dealing

Fair dealing provides that in some circumstances, the unauthorized exploitation of an author's expressions will not constitute copyright infringement. This defence is aimed at advancing several public interests including aiding transformative uses of copyright works,[47] curing market failure[48] and promoting freedom of expression.[49] Notwithstanding these benefits, the fair dealing purposes in the Copyright, Designs and Patents Act face a significant onslaught from the Copyright Directive[50] which will be implemented in the UK in the near future. Article 6 of the Copyright Directive compromises the application of fair dealing in the digital environment by denying users the technical tools needed to access and copy digital works.[51] Moreover, the Directive severely restricts the recognized statutory fair dealing purposes and potentially confines fair dealing to the rich by requiring that fair compensation be paid for certain dealings with copyright works.[52] These ill-conceived restrictions ignore the growing importance of access to digital content and may curb legitimate uses of copyright materials.

Defendants may use copyright works for the purpose of criticizing or reviewing the specific works, their primary ideas or their social and moral implications.[53] Criticizing copyright works aids the democratic process and the discovery of truth by facilitating the ventilation of divergent political or cultural ideas. These benefits are extended to users of varying abilities and persuasions because courts disregard

---

[47] P.N. Leval, 'Toward a Fair Use Standard', in *Harvard Law Review* 103 (1990) 1105, 1111.

[48] W. Gordon, 'Fair Use as Market Failure: a Structural and Economic Analysis of the Betamax Case and its Predecessors', in *Columbia Law Review* 82 (1982) 1600.

[49] *Newspaper Licensing Authority* v. *Marks & Spencer* [1999] RPC 536 (HC) 546.

[50] Directive 2001/29/EC of the European Parliament and of the Council of 22 May 2001 on the Harmonization of Certain Aspects of Copyright and Related Rights in the Information Society, OJ L 167, 22 June 2001.

[51] S. Dusollier, 'Exceptions and Technological Measures in the European Copyright Directive of 2001 – An Empty Promise', in *IIC* 34 (2003) 62, 69; M. Hart, 'The Copyright in the Information Society Directive: An Overview', in *EIPR* 24 (2002) 58.

[52] See Articles 2 (a) and (b) of the Directive.

[53] Section 30 (1) of the Copyright, Designs and Patents Act 1988; *Hubbard* v. *Vosper* [1972] 2 WLR 389, 394; *Time Warner Entertainments Co* v. *Channel Four Television plc* [1994] EMLR 1, 15; *TCN Channel Nine Pty Ltd* v. *Network Ten Ltd* [2001] FCA 108.

the quality or appropriateness of the user's criticism.[54] On that basis, a Canadian case which suggested that comprehensive and effective criticism diminishes the prospects of successfully relying on fair dealing was wrongly decided.[55] Criticism also enhances self-actualization by providing opportunities for re-examining the major cultural materials that mould an individual's personality. For instance, in *Hubbard* v. *Vosper*,[56] a disaffected and disillusioned Scientologist made a blistering criticism of his former church's principal works when recanting his earlier beliefs. Despite its attractiveness, this fair dealing purpose constricts supplies of factual information because it does not excuse mere presentation of information without comment.[57] The absence of special provisions for parodies also ignores the effectiveness of this genre as a weapon of cultural criticism.[58] All these weaknesses are dwarfed into insignificance by Article 5 3(d) of the Copyright Directive which confines the application of the 'criticism or review' exception to works that have been 'lawfully made available to the public'. Granted that important political or cultural information may be gleaned from unauthorized exploitation of unpublished materials, Article 5 3(d) may censor the disclosure of this information. This shortcoming reveals the EU's obsession with creating an enabling environment for intellectual property ownership irrespective of the harm caused to the public interest.

Fair dealing for the purpose of research or private study[59] provides the ingredients for cultivation of knowledge, self-development and informed individual participation in a community's affairs. However, courts protect the financial interests of copyright owners by generally excluding dealings on behalf of third parties.[60] This approach is excusable because defendants who wish to resell copied works to third parties can obtain a licence from copyright owners.[61] A major limitation of the research or private study exception is that it circumscribes the exploitation of valuable political and cultural information by excluding

---

[54] *Pro Sieben Media AG* v. *Carlton UK Television Ltd* [1999] 1 WLR 605 (CA).
[55] *Cie Generale des Establissements Michelin* v. *CAW-Canada* [1996] 71 CPR (3rd) 348 (Fed. Ct.).
[56] [1972] 2 WLR 389.
[57] *Associated Newspapers Group plc* v. *News Group Ltd and Others* [1986] RPC 515.
[58] Although Article 5 3 (k) of the Directive recognizes the parody exception, the UK Government's Consultation Paper on implementing the Directive did not adopt this exception an that position did not change in the final implementation of the Directive through SI 2498/ 2003, the Copyright and Related Rights Regulations 2003.
[59] Section 29 of the Copyright, Designs and Patents Act 1988.
[60] *CCH Canadian Ltd* v. *Law Society of Upper Canada* [1999] 2 CPR (4th) 129 (Fed. Ct.); *Longman Group Ltd* v. *Carrington Technical Institute Board of Governors* [1991] 2 NZLR 574; *Television New Zealand Ltd* v. *Newsmonitor Services Ltd* [1994] 2 NZLR 91; *Sillitoe* v. *McGraw Hill Book Co (UK)* [1983] FSR 545; *Boudreau* v. *Lin* (1997) 75 CPR (3d) 1; *University of London Press* v. *University Tutorial Press* [1916] 2 Ch 601.
[61] *Newspaper Licensing Authority* v. *Marks & Spencer* [1999] RPC 536, 547; *Princeton University Press* v. *Michigan Document Services Inc* 99 F 3rd 1381 (6th Circ 1996); *Haines* v. *Copyright Agency Ltd* [1982] 40 ALR 264.

dealings with sound recordings, films and broadcasts.[62] These reservoirs of important information must be accessible to those researching on society's cultural development. Article 5.3(a) of the Copyright Directive compounds the ineffectiveness of the research or private study exception by confining the permitted research to scientific non-commercial research. Additionally, the directive requires private individuals who make copies from a work to pay 'fair compensation' for non-commercial copying. These extravagant requirements exalt the economic benefits of copyright ownership at the expense of the public interest and may dissuade people of modest means from accessing valuable works.

Reporting current events[63] is a pivotal fair dealing purpose and it facilitates the propagation of information necessary for political and social discourse. The free speech benefits of this exception are accentuated by the purposive interpretation of current events.[64] However, the term 'current events' is narrower than news reporting and it excludes 'information relating to past events not previously known'.[65] The exclusion of matters of purely historical interest[66] from 'current events' diminishes the sources of information which may inform society's understanding of present events. Dealings in photographs are also excluded from the current events exception.[67] This exclusion may dilute the vividness and impact of the information presented to the public[68] and removes a potential avenue for addressing the shortcomings of the idea/expression dichotomy in artistic and graphic works. Excluding dealings in photographs from current events is particularly inappropriate in digital works because the information contained in these works may consist of both text and images.

III.1 FAIRNESS

Apart from proving that the claimant's work was used for the recognized purposes, defendants must also prove that the work was dealt with fairly. Although the liberal construction of the statutory purposes of fair dealing enhances freedom of expression, the real battles between authors and users are fought over 'fairness' issues. 'Fairness' is not capable of a precise definition but the

---

[62] *Cf.* Copyright Act (Canada) 1985 (chapter 42), Section 27 (2) (a) and Copyright Act (Australia) Section 40.
[63] Section 30 (2) of the Copyright, Designs and Patents Act 1988.
[64] *British Broadcasting Corporation* v. *British Satellite Broadcasting Ltd* [1992] Ch 141; *Pro Sieben Media AG* v. *Carlton UK TV. Ltd* [1998] FSR 43, 50; *Newspaper Licensing Authority* v. *Marks & Spencer* [1999] RPC 536, 545; *PCR Limited* v. *Dow Jones Telerate Ltd* [1998] FSR 170, 185; *De Garis* v. *Neville Jeffress Pidler Pty Ltd* (1990) 18 IPR 292.
[65] *Newspaper Licensing Authority* v. *Marks & Spencer* [1999] RPC 536, 546.
[66] *Associated Newspapers Group Plc* v. *News Group Newspapers Ltd* [1986] RPC 515.
[67] See Section 30 (2) of the Copyright, Designs and Patents Act 1988.
[68] M.B. Nimmer, 'Does Copyright Abridge the First Amendment Guarantees of Free Speech and Press?', in *UCLA Law Review* 17 (1970) 1180.

accepted starting point is a passage in *Hubbard* v. *Vosper* where Lord Denning MR identified several factors that may impeach fairness and concluded that the determination of fairness is a matter of degree and impression.[69] Each case is therefore considered on its own merits but the uncertainties generated by this *ad hoc* approach to 'fairness' may dissuade users from exercising their rights and dilutes the effectiveness of fair dealing as a bulwark against copyright abuse. As will be seen from the following paragraphs, the intuitiveness of 'fairness' may achieve just results but this nebulous concept is also a cosmetic façade that conveniently hides the reluctance of judges to allow unauthorized uses of copyright works.

III.1.1. THE UNPUBLISHED NATURE OF THE INFRINGED WORK

Dealing in unpublished works may reveal unknown or restricted political and cultural information. Despite the free speech benefits arising from accessing new information, courts interpret this factor strictly and inconsistently. In *British Oxygen Co. Ltd* v. *Liquid Air Ltd*,[70] Romer J held that fair dealing does not apply to unpublished works but this rigid view was rejected in *Hubbard* v. *Vosper*.[71] However, subsequent cases generally confine fair dealing in unpublished materials to widely circulated works.[72] The prevailing view is that although fair dealing applies to unpublished works, courts are unlikely to excuse the exploitation of unpublished materials.[73] This factor attracts claimants who are anxious to protect their privacy, prevent misappropriation of their information, maintain confidences, censor the disclosure of embarrassing information or secure a private space where they can prepare their works.

Courts may protect authors' or copyright owners' privacy indirectly[74] by rejecting the fairness of dealing with unpublished works containing their intimate personal details. For instance, in *Hyde Park Residences Ltd* v. *Yelland*, the Court of Appeal protected a copyright owner's privacy when it dismissed the fairness of dealings in unpublished photographs taken at a private residence.[75] The court also made an implicit disapproval of the intense media fixation with Diana, Princess of Wales' private life. This indirect protection of privacy can be traced to the broad

---

[69] *Hubbard* v. *Vosper* [1972] 2 QB 84.
[70] [1925] Ch 383, 393.
[71] *Hubbard* v. *Vosper* [1972] 2 WLR 389 (CA) 395.
[72] *Distillers Co (Biochemicals) Ltd* v. *Times Newspapers Ltd* [1975] QB 61; *Ashdown* v. *Telegraph Group Ltd* [2001] 2 WLR 967 (HC).
[73] *Beloff* v. *Pressdram* [1973] 1 All ER 241, 262; *Ashdown* v. *Telegraph Group Ltd* [2001] 4 All ER 666 (CA); *Harper & Row, Publishers Inc* v. *Nation Enterprises* 471 US 539 [1985], 554; *Commonwealth of Australia* v. *John Fairfax and Sons Ltd* [1981] 55 ALJR 32.
[74] B. Neil, 'Privacy: a challenge for the next century', in B.S. Markesinis (ed.), *Protecting privacy*, Oxford University Press (1999) 1.
[75] *Hyde Park* v. *Yelland* [2001] 3 WLR 1172 (CA).

doctrinal connections between common law copyright and privacy[76] and it allows authors to express themselves candidly without fearing the risks associated with unauthorized disclosures of their personal views.[77] However, relying on copyright to protect privacy may limit the circulation of useful or personally embarrassing information and ideas.[78] In *Hyde Park* v. *Yelland* information casting severe doubts on Mr Fayed's character and account of the tragic events in Paris was effectively removed from widespread public scrutiny. Using copyright as a privacy tool is also inappropriate because in most cases, artificial legal persons with little discernible interest in privacy own most copyright works. Additionally, by protecting the ideas or facts in a work, privacy may go beyond the boundaries of copyright protection. Consequently, using copyright in the circumstances highlighted above may bar the publication of important and contemporary information for an unduly long time.

In *Designers Guild Ltd* v. *Russell Williams (Textiles) Ltd*, Lord Bingham of Cornhill made the following observation:

'The law of copyright rests on a very clear principle: that anyone who by his or her own skill and labour creates an original work of whatever character shall, for a limited period, enjoy an exclusive right to copy that work. No one else may for a season reap what the copyright owner has sown'.[79]

This important statement confirms the expansive use of copyright to prevent misappropriation of a competitor's valuable intangibles.[80] Misappropriation is a fluid concept which may prohibit both innocent and illegitimate copying and it inhibits freedom of expression by potentially outlawing the benefits of imitating popular expressions[81] or allowing copyright owners to censor current or important information until it is commercially convenient for them to disclose it.[82] In the fair dealing context, courts prevent misappropriation of information by routinely holding that dealings with unpublished works are unfair.[83] For example in *Ashdown* v. *Telegraph Group Limited*, the Sunday Telegraph was prevented from misappropriating a commercially valuable unpublished minute. Sometimes, curbing misappropriation may yield contentious results. In *Hyde Park* v. *Yelland*, the commercial insignificance of the infringed photographs did not prevent Mance

---

[76] *Prince Albert* v. *Strange* [1849] 41 ER 1171; L. Brandeis and S. Warren, 'The Right to Privacy', in *Harvard Law Review* 4 (1990) 193.

[77] T. De Turris, 'Copyright Protection of Privacy Interests in Unpublished Works', in *Annual Survey of American Law* (1994) 277, 288.

[78] *Salinger* v. *Random House Inc and Anor* 811 F 2d 90 [2nd 1990]; L.L. Weinreb, 'Fair's Fair: A Comment on the Fair Use Doctrine', in *Harvard Law Review* 103 (1990) 1137, 1147.

[79] [2001] 1 All ER 700 at 700.

[80] See also D. Vaver, 'Intellectual Property: The State of the Art', in *LQR* 116 (2000) 621.

[81] R.C. Denicola, 'Freedom to Copy', in *Yale Law Journal* 108 (1999) 1661, 1680.

[82] P. Goldstein, 'Copyright and the First Amendment', in *Columbia Law Review* 70 (1970) 983.

[83] E.g. *Hyde Park Residence Ltd* v. *Yelland* [2000] WLR 215, 239 (Mance LJ).

LJ from opining that fair dealing does not generally excuse misappropriation. The rejection of a fair dealing defence based on the 'unpublished nature of the infringed work' therefore allows authors and publishers to exclusively 'reap' where they have sown. However, reaping where one has sown assumes that the reaper created her expressions *ex nihilo*. The reality is that authors draw from earlier works and other contemporary events and it may be disproportionate to allow them to 'reap' what they have not exclusively sown.

Claimants with doubtful breach of confidence cases may plead alternative claims for copyright infringement hoping that the rejection of fair dealing defences would prevent widespread dissemination of leaked confidential information.[84] As Mance LJ noted in *Hyde Park Residence Ltd* v. *Yelland*, claimants may bring copyright claims to avoid the full glare of equity and the damaging effects of the public interest defence in breach of confidence cases.[85] Additionally, a claimant may fail to prove a third party's knowledge of the confidentiality of information contained in the infringed work.[86] Using copyright to maintain confidentiality has little effect on freedom of expression in cases involving ordinary commercial secrets. However, free speech interests assume great significance if confidential documents exposing controversial political information or scandals are effectively censored. For example, in *Hyde Park Residence Ltd* v. *Yelland*, the claimant relied on copyright to restrict the dissemination of important but embarrassing political information. The same result was achieved in *Ashdown* v. *Telegraph Group Ltd* where information disclosing the intriguing relationship between opposing political parties was effectively censored until the claimant published his memoirs.[87] Arguably, the 30-year rule on official papers mitigates the effects of non-disclosure of confidential government information but this rule does not cover private citizens who refuse to publish works containing vital political information. Even if the rule applies, the information would be of pure historical interest by the time of its disclosure. Using copyright as an indirect tool for maintaining confidences may therefore restrict public access to current information for an unduly long time.

Some authors use copyright to censor disclosures of personally embarrassing or important secrets. In *Distillers Co (Biochemicals) Ltd* v. *Times Newspapers Ltd Distillers*,[88] a company successfully relied on copyright to gag the dissemination of information exposing the dangers of thalidomide. Similarly, in *Commonwealth of*

---

[84]   *Beloff* v. *Pressdram Ltd* [1973] 1 All ER 241.
[85]   *Hyde Park Residence Ltd* v. *Yelland* [2000] 3 WLR 215, 238-239; See also *Lion Laboratories Ltd.* v. *Evans* [1985] QB 526.
[86]   *PCR Limited* v. *Dow Jones Telerate Ltd* [1998] FSR 170, 180.
[87]   *Ashdown* v. *Telegraph Group Ltd* [2001] 4 All ER 666 (CA).
[88]   [1975] QB 61. The case was also decided on other grounds which are not discussed here. See also *Hyde Park Residence Ltd* v. *Yelland, op. cit.*; *Salinger* v. *Random House, op. cit.*; and *Rosemont Enterprises Inc* v. *Random House Inc* 366 F 2d 303 [2nd 1966].

Australia v. *John Fairfax & Sons Ltd*,[89] Mason CJ effectively censored the disclosure of controversial political information by rejecting the fairness of dealing in unpublished works. Using copyright as a censorship tool is not always successful. In *Hubbard* v. *Vosper*[90] the claimant failed to suppress the publication of information exposing some contentious aspects of Scientology. Censorship is antithetical to freedom of expression because it may proscribe access to crucial unknown information.[91]. Unlike the confidentiality and privacy points raised earlier, claimants who use copyright as a censorship weapon are not principally motivated by the financial considerations of maintaining secrecy or the desire to protect a zone of personal autonomy. Instead, they are anxious to withdraw palpably damaging information from public consumption. Courts ignore this subtle form of censorship because it may not evoke the same feelings of outrage as state censorship.

In the *Harper & Row* case, Justice O'Connor wrote of 'the obvious benefit to author and public alike of assuring authors the leisure to develop their ideas free from fear of expropriation'.[92] Similarly, in *Ashdown* v. *Telegraph Group Ltd*, the courts did not excuse a premature publication of an *aide-memoir* prepared for the claimant's diaries by the Sunday Telegraph. Courts therefore recognize the importance of safeguarding a creative environment where expressions can be formulated and distilled before publication. Rejecting the fairness of dealing in unpublished works preserves this private space for preparation and allows authors the latitude to express themselves at their convenience. Courts tend to turn a blind eye on this temporary censorship because there is a tacit assumption that the unpublished information will be publicly available in due course. However, as *Malcolm* v. *Oxford University Press*[93] demonstrates, publishers may refuse to publish commercially risky works thereby severely restricting the dissemination of unpublished expressions. Additionally, authors may indirectly censor unpublished information permanently by reneging on their earlier undertakings to publish the information. While there is less scope for impeding free expression under this factor if the work is subsequently published, the centrality or currency of information contained in the unpublished work may diminish with the passage of time. Arguably, the subsequent publication of Lord Ashdown's diaries was an adequate and contextual dissemination of the information in the contentious minute but the delayed publication robbed the minute of its relevance to the earlier

---

[89] [1981] 55 ALJR 32.
[90] [1972] 2 WLR 389 (CA).
[91] F.M. Patfield, 'Towards a Reconciliation of Free Speech and Copyright', in E. Barendt (ed.), *The Yearbook of Media and Entertainment Law*, Volume II, Oxford University Press (1996), 199 and 215.
[92] *Harper & Row, Publishers Inc* v. *Nation Enterprises* 471 US 539 [1985], 555.
[93] *Malcolm* v. *The Chancellor, Masters and Scholars of the University of Oxford T/A Oxford University Press* [1994] EMLR 17.

debates on electoral and political reforms. A possible solution to these problems lies in forcing authors to licence the exploitation of their works but these compulsory licenses may compel authors to speak against their wishes or harm the non-pecuniary interests of authors such as the protection of reputation or personality.

III.1.2. MANNER OF OBTAINING THE INFRINGED WORK

A fair dealing defence may be vitiated by the methods used to obtain the infringed work. This factor is most relevant in cases involving unpublished materials[94] because the difficulties surrounding access to these works may tempt defendants to obtain them illegally or clandestinely. This fair dealing factor stems from the following closely related reasons. Firstly, where a claim for breach of confidence faces insuperable difficulties and the alternative copyright claim is susceptible to a fair dealing defence, claimants may rely on 'the manner of obtaining the infringed work' to limit the circulation of confidential information.[95] Secondly, courts may use 'the manner of obtaining the infringed work' to prevent the misappropriation of valuable information. Thirdly, courts may be anxious to prevent the fairness of dealing with works obtained in circumstances that involve an infringement of the author or copyright owner's privacy. Arguably, in *Hyde Park* v. *Yelland* the Court of Appeal rejected the application of fair dealing defences because it disapproved the use of illicitly obtained private information in the mass media. Lastly, it may be contrary to ordinary notions of *fairness* to hold that a work obtained and used illegally was dealt with fairly. Fairness encompasses 'honesty' and 'uprightness'[96] and these ingredients may be conspicuously absent from the methods used to access the infringed work. However, it must be noted that a fair dealing inquiry is primarily concerned with the treatment of the expressions contained in the infringed work.[97] In any event, introducing elastic notions of fairness into a fair dealing inquiry creates additional confusion in an area teeming with uncertainties.

Relying on 'the manner of obtaining information' amplifies the reasons for rejecting the fairness of dealing in unpublished works and may limit the dissemination of politically sensitive information. This dangerous outcome was achieved in *Commonwealth of Australia* v. *John Fairfax Ltd* where political information was effectively censored.[98] It is suggested that where a fair dealing defence fails on this ground, courts must allow continued publication and confine

---

[94] *Time Warner Entertainments Company LP* v. *Channel Four Television Corporation plc and Anor* [1994] EMLR 1, 10; *Beloff* v. *Pressdram* [1973] 1 All ER 241, 263.
[95] *Beloff* v. *Pressdram, op. cit.*, at 258; *Hyde Park Residence* v. *Yelland* [2000] WLR 215 (CA) 238 (Mance LJ).
[96] Oxford English Dictionary (2nd ed. 1989).
[97] *Time Warner Entertainments* v. *Channel Four Television Corporation, op. cit.*
[98] [1981] 55 ALJR 54.

the available remedies to a modest sum of damages.[99] However, great care must be taken in assessing the *quantum* of damages because damages may prevent impecunious defendants from expressing themselves. Similarly, where payment has been made to insiders for unauthorized access to the infringed work, courts must appreciate that journalists may pay for leaks to publish matters of public interest.[100] Lastly, even if a publication profits from its unauthorized access to copyright material, courts must realize that the profits generated from disseminating information to the public maintain a viable and free press.

III.1.3. AMOUNT OR QUALITY OF WORK TAKEN BY THE DEFENDANT

A fair dealing inquiry may hinge on the quantity or quality of what is taken from the infringed work.[101] The prominence of this factor principally rests on a perceived need to preserve the economic benefits accruing to authors by diminishing free-riding. For instance, in *Newspaper Licensing Authority* v. *Marks & Spencer*, Lightman J held that defendants who copy too much should seek a licence from the copyright owner.[102] Additionally, as the Court of Appeal insisted in both *Ashdown* v. *Telegraph Group Ltd* and *Hyde Park* v. *Yelland*, given that copyright does not protect ideas *per se*; lavish copying may demonstrate defendants' reluctance to formulate original expressions.[103] Despite the attractiveness of this argument, the reality is that significant departures from original expressions may be actionable.[104] In any event, ideas and expressions may be fused in informational or graphic works and a defendant may need to use a claimant's exact expressions to convey information efficiently. Even if the original expressions are capable of different presentation, alternative arrangements may dilute the poignancy of the ideas conveyed by the original work[105] or subtract from the accuracy of the information presented to the public. These anomalies are exacerbated by inadequate public access to unpublished original works which may allow dishonest authors to dispute the meaning attached to their expressions.[106]

Arguably, wholesale copying negates the purposes of copyright because it is not transformative[107] and adds little to the corpus of information and ideas. In *R* v. *James Lorimer & Co Ltd*, the Federal Court of Canada stated that little free-speech

---

[99] *Ashdown* v. *Telegraph Group Ltd* [2001] 3 WLR 1368 (CA).

[100] *Hyde Park Residence Ltd* v. *Yelland* [1999] RPC 655 (HC) 663.

[101] *Hubbard* v. *Vosper* [1972] 2 QB 84; *Associated Newspapers Group plc* v. *News Group Ltd and Others* [1986] RPC 515, 517.

[102] [1999] RPC 536 (HC).

[103] *Ashdown* v. *Telegraph Group Ltd* [2001] 3 WLR 1368 (CA).

[104] *PCR* v. *Dow Jones Telerate* [1998] FSR 170.

[105] *Hyde Park* v. *Yelland* [1999] RPC 655, 662 (reversed on appeal).

[106] P.N. Leval, 'Toward a Fair Use Standard', in *Harvard Law Review* 103 (1990) 1105, 1114.

[107] *Campbell* v. *Acuff-Rose Music Inc* 510 US 569, 579 [1994]; *Suntrust Bank* v. *Houghton Mifflin Co* 268 F 3d 1257 [2001] 1260.

benefits flowed from uncritical and wholesale copies of a government report on competition in the Canadian oil and gas industry.[108] However, the low test of originality in most common law jurisdictions ensures that not all copyright works add significant value to the body of available information. Moreover, copying all the words in an original work may serve an important social function by making authentic information publicly available. Although copying a whole copyright work is permissible[109] and *Ashdown* v. *Telegraph* recognized that freedom of expression may require a reproduction of the 'the very words spoken by another',[110] the Court of Appeal held that too much had been taken from the original minute. This decision is paradoxical because it suggests that the more substantial the part taken for free speech purposes, the less likely it is for the dealing to be fair.

An avid reliance on this factor renders the quotation of brief notes or communiqués virtually impossible. This danger is most evident in critical genres such as parodies which may require extensive quotation from original works if they are to be successful.[111] Prohibiting parodists from quoting generously from copyright works may circumscribe literary and cultural criticism. Where publication is in the public interest and accuracy is of cardinal importance, courts must give users 'reasonable latitude' in the size or quality of the selections copied for public consumption.[112]

III.1.4. COMMERCIAL COMPETITION

In *Associated Newspapers Group plc* v. *News Group Ltd*, a commercial rival's unauthorized exploitation of the Duchess of Windsor's correspondence did not benefit from the fair dealing defence.[113] More recently, the Court of Appeal held that the publication of a secret political minute competed with the market for the infringed work and was therefore unfair.[114] This approach obtains in various jurisdictions. For instance, an Australia court refused to apply the criticism or

---

[108] *R* v. *James Lorimer & Co Ltd* [1984] 1 FC 1065; *Associated Newspapers Group, op. cit.*

[109] *Hubbard* v. *Vosper* [1972] 2 QB 84, 94-5, 98 (Megaw LJ); *cf. Zamacois* v. *Douville* [1943] 2 DLR 257.

[110] [2001] 3 WLR 1368, 1381; *Fressoz and Roire* v. *France* [1999] 31 EHRR 28.

[111] B. Kaplan, *An Unhurried View of Copyright*, Columbia (1967) 69; M. Spence, 'Intellectual Property and the Problem of Parody', in *LQR* 114 (1998) 594, 610; *Campbell* v. *Acuff-Rose Music Inc* 510 US 569, 579 [1994].

[112] *Campbell* v. *Mirror Group Newspapers Ltd* [2003] 2 EMLR 39 (CA) 57; *Jersild* v. *Denmark* [1994] 19 EHRR 1, 26.

[113] [1986] RPC 515, 518 also *Hubbard* v. *Vosper* [1972] 2 WLR 389, 393; *Newspaper Licensing Agency* v. *Marks & Spencer plc* [2000] 3 WLR 1256, 1277; *Independent Television Publications Ltd* v. *Time Out Ltd* [1984] FSR 64, 75.

[114] *Ashdown* v. *Telegraph Group Ltd* [2001] 4 All ER 666 (CA).

review exception to some uses of a competitor's news broadcasts.[115] Similarly, in *Hager* v. *ECW Press Ltd*, a Canadian court dismissed the argument that lavish quotations from a competing author's work on Shania Twain qualified as fair use.[116] In the USA, commercial competition also weighs heavily against a defendant's appropriation of copyright materials.[117] Although commercial competition is central to a fair dealing inquiry, some judges recognize the importance of other public interests in copyright disputes.[118]

Like most fairness factors, the chief purpose of this factor is to prevent misappropriation of valuable information. There is nothing inherently wrong with prohibiting unfair competition but judges must realize that the very nature of fair dealing is such that it reduces the financial rewards accruing to authors because copiers do not pay royalties.[119] Lack of competition may set financial barriers to access to information and create an environment in which information monopolists may disseminate uncritical or biased content. Courts are also generally oblivious to the risks posed by the gradual convergence of different media and the resulting expansion of the 'market' for copyright works which may severely constrict legitimate copyright uses. An explanation for this oversight may lie in the misplaced idea that commercial competition does not impede freedom of expression because it deals with ordinary commercial expressions. However, the existence of hybrid information involving both commercial and political information may bridge the narrow chasm between essentially commercial and other information. For example, the commercial value of the Duchess of Windsor's private correspondence was interstitially tied to the abdication crisis. Similarly, the financial value of Lord Ashdown's minute arose from the secret and political nature of the minute. Although some commentators belittle the importance of commercial speech,[120] these views ignore the increasing commercialization and concentrated ownership of various shades of information which reduces the channels and opportunities for spreading divergent views.

---

[115] *TCN Channel Nine Pty Ltd* v. *Network Ten Pty Ltd* [2002] 118 FCR 417; *Moorhouse* v. *University of New South Wales* [1975] RPC 454; also *Television New Zealand Ltd* v. *Newsmonitor Services Ltd* [1994] 2 NZLR 91, 108.

[116] [1999] 2 FC 287.

[117] *Princeton University Press* v. *Michigan Document Services Inc* 99 F 3d 1381 (6th Circ 1996); *Harper & Row, Publishers Inc* v. *Nation Enterprises* 471 US 539 [1985].

[118] *British Broadcasting Corporation* v. *British Satellite Broadcasting Ltd* [1992] Ch 141, 158; *Pro Sieben Media AG* v. *Carlton UK Television Ltd* [1999] FSR 610.

[119] P.N. Leval, 'Toward a Fair Use Standard', in *Harvard Law Review* 103 (1990) 1105, 1125.

[120] For a survey of commercial speech see C.R. Munro, 'The value of commercial speech', in *Cambridge Law Journal* 62 (2003) 134; R. Post, 'The Constitutional Status of Commercial Speech', in *UCLA Law Review* 48 (2000) 1; F. Schauer, 'Commercial Speech and the Architecture of the First Amendment', in *Cincinnati Law Review* 56 (1987) 1181.

III.1.5. MOTIVES FOR THE DEALING

A 'fairness' inquiry may turn on the defendant's motives for copying the original work.[121] This factor buttresses 'commercial competition' and the 'amount or quality of what is taken by the defendant' because in those circumstances, defendants are usually motivated by the pecuniary benefits of copyright infringement.[122] The relevance of the defendant's motives in a fair dealing inquiry is primary influenced by judicial attitudes to misappropriation of information.[123] This factor sits uncomfortably with free speech theory because a speaker's motives are generally irrelevant to the determination of whether a case raises free speech issues or not. The soundness of this fair dealing factor is also severely compromised by the possibility that in most cases, several motives may inform a defendant's use of the infringed work. For example, in *Ashdown* v. *Telegraph Group Ltd*, the defendant was motivated by the prospect of increased circulation of its newspaper and the need to shed additional light on the close co-operation between two opposing political parties in its use of the claimant's secret minute. The problem with these seemingly unimportant fair dealing factors is that they strengthen the more serious reasons for rejecting the application of fair dealing defences and afford copyright owners the opportunity to limit the circulation of potentially embarrassing information. For instance, the aggregate effects of the motives for the defendant's dealings and other fair dealing factors persuaded the Court of Appeal to reject the fairness of using the claimant's photographs to prove the claimant's controversial theories on the death of Diana, Princess of Wales.[124] Ironically, the defendant's motives did not carry much weight in cases involving the taking of unauthorized excerpts from a controversial film[125] and a broadcast on 'chequebook journalism'.[126] Relying on the defendant's motives for infringing a copyright work may also curtail the decent profits required for disseminating information.[127]

III.1.6. COULD PURPOSE HAVE BEEN ACHIEVED BY DIFFERENT MEANS?

Although there is no test of necessity, courts may reject a fair dealing defence if a defendant fails to explore alternative means of expressing the ideas in the infringed work. For example, in *Hyde Park Residence Ltd* v. *Yelland*, the use of photographs

---

[121] *Associated Newspapers Group Plc* v. *News Group Newspapers Ltd* [1986] RPC 515, 518; *Beloff* v. *Pressdram* [1973] 1 All ER 241, 263.
[122] *Cf. Hyde Park* v. *Yelland* [2001] 3 WLR 1172 (CA).
[123] *Hubbard* v. *Vosper* [1972] 2 WLR 389, 393.
[124] *Hyde Park* v. *Yelland* [2001] 3 WLR 1172 (CA).
[125] *Pro Sieben AG* v. *Carlton UK Television Ltd* [1999] FSR 610.
[126] *Time Warner Entertainments Company LP* v. *Channel Four Television Corp Plc and Anor* [1994] EMLR 1.
[127] *Hyde Park Residence Ltd* v. *Yelland* [1999] RPC 655, 663 (HC).

obtained in breach of confidence did not qualify as fair dealing because the information conveyed by the photographs could have been expressed in words.[128] Likewise, in *Ashdown v. Telegraph Group Ltd*, it was held that the defendant did not need to use the exact words in a secret political minute to disclose the close connections between two political parties. This factor closely resembles the idea/expression dichotomy and in common with other 'fairness' factors it is designed to combat misappropriation of copyright works. The tenor of this factor is that defendants who fail to deploy different expressions when using the ideas in a copyright work are principally influenced by a desire to avoid the cost of formulating their own expressions. Obliging defendants to express information differently may invite inaccuracies and subjectivity especially where informational works are involved. In any event, the use of another's exact expressions may be an end in itself because it facilitates the availability of information.[129] Courts should therefore rely on this factor when it is clear that there are clearly efficient alternatives for expressing the same information.

IV. Conclusion

The decision in *Ashdown v. Telegraph Group Ltd* is generating considerable commentary on the relationship between copyright and freedom of expression.[130] The golden thread that runs through this literature is the growing realization that the systemic weaknesses of copyright's internal controls require a new freedom of expression defence in copyright cases. This argument has considerable force because a new defence would mitigate the deleterious effects of the Copyright Directive on the purposes of fair dealing[131] and obviate the technical difficulties arising from allocating various copyright uses to the recognized statutory exceptions. A specific free speech defence has the added advantage of allowing courts to determine freedom of expression issues outside the constraints of weak copyright doctrines.

Despite its attractiveness, an independent free-speech defence is not a magic wand that would solve the major problems plaguing the relationship between copyright and freedom of expression. The chief defect of any new copyright

---

[128] *Hyde Park Residence Ltd v. Yelland* (CA) 227.

[129] L.L. Weinreb, 'Fair's Fair: A Comment on the Fair Use Doctrine', in *Harvard Law Review* 103 (1990) 113, 1143.

[130] J. Griffiths, 'Copyright Law after Ashdown – Time to deal fairly with the public', in *IPQ* 3 (*Intellectual Property Quarterly*) (2002) 240; R. Burrell, 'Reigning in Copyright Law: is fair use the answer', in *IPQ* (2001) 361; M.D. Birnhack, 'Acknowledging the Conflict between Copyright Law and Freedom of Expression under the Human Rights Act', in *Entertainment Law Review* (2003) 24.

[131] For instance, users may rely on the new defence to circumvent Article 5 3(d) of the Copyright Directive which states that criticism or review should be limited to published works.

defence would lie in its interpretation rather than its contents. Proponents of a new free speech defence in copyright cases assume that courts would interpret the new defence purposively. However, if evidence from jurisdictions with a longer history of constitutionally enshrined fundamental freedoms is to go by, the interpretation of copyright laws is largely influenced by firmly rooted arguments in favour of maintaining the economic benefits of copyright ownership. In both the USA and Canada, courts prevent misappropriation of information by relying heavily on copyright's internal balancing processes when resolving fair use cases.[132] That approach was adopted in both *Ashdown* and *Imutran and Uncaged Campaigns Ltd*, where UK judges were anxious to prevent significant changes to the financial benefits of copyright ownership by severely curtailing the operation of Article 10 of the European Convention on Human Rights. Assuming, a new free speech defence is enacted in our copyright statutes, the resulting uncertainty generated by judges' reluctance to condone misappropriation would render the new free speech defence largely academic. It therefore means that formulating new copyright defences alone changes little if the current judicial attitudes to copyright exploitation are not neutralized.

Another possible solution lies in creatively interpreting both the fair dealing and public interest defences to safeguard various public interests including freedom of expression. This approach allows copyright policies to grow organically and creates the flexibility required for dealing with novel situations. However, purposive interpretation alone cannot expand copyright's closed list of permitted activities. For instance, unless the public interest defence is strengthened, purposive interpretation will not cure the defects of the current fair dealing purposes in relation to some dealings in photographs,[133] old news[134] or the mere presentation of information without criticism or comment.[135] The flexibility arising from interpreting the existing copyright exceptions purposively may generate uncertainty. For example, there are no rudimentary rules for determining when freedom of expression may necessitate the use of another's copyright in 'rare circumstances'. Purposive interpretation may also yield unintended results. For instance, the accuracy of the observation that 'freedom of expression should not normally carry with it the right to make free use of another's work'[136] is doubtful because ordinarily, copyright uses which qualify as fair dealing are free.

The solution to the intractable difficulties in the relationship between copyright and freedom of expression does not lie in new defences or highly nuanced

---

[132] *Harper & Row* v. *Nation Enterprises*, 471 US 539 [1985]; *Eldred* v. *Ashcroft* [2003] 65 USPQ 2d 1225; *Cie Generale des Establissements Michelin* v. *CAW-Canada* [1996] 71 CPR (3rd) 348 (Fed. Ct.); *R* v. *James Lorimer & Co Ltd* [1984] 1 FC 1065.
[133] See section 30 (2) of the Copyright, Designs and Patents Act 1988.
[134] *Associated Newspapers Group Plc* v. *News Group Newspapers Ltd* [1986] RPC 515.
[135] *Ashdown* v. *Telegraph Group Ltd* [2001] 4 All ER 666 (CA).
[136] See *Ashdown, op. cit.*, at 677.

interpretations. Instead, what is required is an understanding that misappropriation alone does not inform the existence of copyright. This shift would give fair dealing and other copyright exceptions a genuine opportunity to secure the public interest in copyright disputes.

Chapter 6

Do We have a Right to Speak with Another's Language? *Eldred* and the Duration of Copyright

*Wendy J. Gordon**

I.   Free Speech

The law embodies two contradictory sets of rights and interests pertaining to copyright and speech. On the one hand, stand authors' claims to deserve compensation and control over their works. On the other hand stand the public's claims to be free to build on and deploy the cultural works that pervade daily life.

The conflict is reflected in apparently-contradictory provisions within the Universal Declaration of Human Rights. Article 27(2) provides that 'Everyone has the right to the protection of the moral and material interests resulting from any scientific, literary or artistic production of which he is the author'. That Article seems to support copyrights, patents, and other exclusive rights in intellectual products. Yet Article 27(1) states that 'Everyone has the right freely to participate in the cultural life of the community, to enjoy the arts and to share in scientific advancement and its benefits'. An ability to participate fully sometimes requires the use of works authored by others.[1] Conceptually related to Article 27(1) are the

---

*   Professor of Law and Paul J. Liacos Scholar in Law at Boston University School of Law. She can be reached at wgordon@bu.edu. Copyright 2003 by Wendy J. Gordon. Photocopies for scholarly and classroom use permitted. The instant article draws extensively on three prior articles by Professor Gordon: 'Copyright as Tort Law's Mirror Image: 'Harms', 'Benefits', and the Uses and Limits of Analogy', in *McGeorge Law Review* 34 (2003) 533-40; 'Authors, Publishers and Public Goods: Trading Gold for Dross', in *Loyola of Los Angeles Law Review* 36 (2002) 159-97; and 'The Constitutionality of Copyright Term Extension: How Long Is Too Long? (Symposium panel with Jane Ginsburg, Arthur Miller, William Patry)', in *Cardozo Arts & Entertainment Law Journal* 18 (2000) 651, especially at 674-86. The author is indebted to the persons whose comments and assistance contributed to those articles, and to Erica Marinelli for her excellent research assistance on the instant article.
[1]   This claim is the topic of a plethora of recent scholarship. My own perspective is reflected in the various articles cited throughout. Also see, e.g., R.J. Coombe, *The Cultural Life of Intellectual Properties*, Duke University Press (1998); N.W. Netanel, 'Locating Copyright Within the First Amendment Skein', in *Stanford Law Review* 54 (2001) 1; D. Leenheer Zimmerman, 'Information As Speech, Information As Goods: Some Thoughts on Marketplaces and the

provisions of Article 19. That Article states that 'Everyone has the right to freedom of opinion and expression' including 'freedom ... to seek, receive and impart information and ideas through any media and regardless of frontiers'.

In the United States, the law reflects a similar tension. Copyright law gives authors rights to control how their expression is used, and the First Amendment to the federal Constitution provides that 'Congress shall make no law ... abridging the freedom of speech, or of the press'. Freedom of speech is hard to square with exclusive rights.

Admittedly, copyright law does not embed direct governmental censorship. Nevertheless, it can embed privately-motivated censorship[2] which government then enforces. Such restraints at government hands can be inconsistent with the public's ability to participate in its culture.[3] Copyright can be squared with the public's rights of participation and expression only if it is sharply limited in scope and duration.

Yet copyright continually grows. Following the European Union's expansion of copyright term to 'life of the author plus seventy years', the United States followed suit with the 1998 Copyright Term Extension Act (the 'CTEA').[4] In *Eldred v. Ashcroft*,[5] a legal action was brought to challenge the CTEA on the

---

cont.

Bill of Rights', in *William & Mary Law Review* 33 (1992) 665; Y. Benkler, 'Free as the Air to Common Use: First Amendment Constraint on Enclosure of the Public Domain', in *New York University Law Review* 74 (1999) 354; C.E. Baker, 'First Amendment Limits on Copyright', in *Vanderbilt Law Review* 55 (2002) 891.

[2]   W.J. Gordon, 'Toward a Jurisprudence of Benefits: The Norms of Copyright and the Problem of Private Censorship', in *University of Chicago Law Review* 57 (review essay, 1990) 1009, 1032-47.

[3]   W.J. Gordon, 'A Property Right in Self-Expression: Equality and Individualism in the Natural Law of Intellectual Property', in *Yale Law Journal* 102 (1993) 1533 at 1607 & note 400 (arguing that enforcement of intellectual property rights should be acknowledged as governmental action subject to Constitutional limitation.).

[4]   That Act actually went further than the European directive with which it sought harmonization, for the US act extended to 95 years the duration of works made for hire. As Justice Breyer noted, 'Despite appearances, the statute does *not* create a uniform American-European term with respect to the lion's share of the economically significant works that it affects – *all* works made 'for hire' and *all* existing works created prior to 1978. With respect to those works the American statute produces an extended term of 95 years while comparable European rights in 'for hire' works last for periods that vary from 50 years to 70 years to life plus 70 years. Compare 17 U.S.C.§ § 302(c), 304(a)-(b) with Council Directive 93/98/EEC of 29 October 1993 Harmonizing the Term of Protection of Copyright and Certain Related Rights, Articles 1-3, (1993) O. J. L 290 (hereinafter EU Council Directive 93/98). Neither does the statute create uniformity with respect to anonymous or pseudonymous works. Compare 17 U.S.C.§ § 302(c), 304(a)-(b) with EU Council Directive 93/98, Article 1. *Eldred v. Ashcroft*, U.S., 123 S.Ct.769 (2003), at 285 (Breyer, J., dissenting).

[5]   *Eldred v. Ashcroft*, 537 U.S. 186, 123 S. Ct. 769 (2003), rehearing denied, 123 S. Ct. 1505 (Mem. 2003).

ground that it conflicted with the US Constitution. One ground urged for unconstitutionality depended on the First Amendment's guarantee of free speech. The challenge was rejected, and the CTEA upheld. Nevertheless, the portent of Eldred for free speech in the United States is not all bad.

One could not have predicted as much from the lower court opinions in the matter. The District Court (trial court level) brushed off the First Amendment challenge as if it were trivial. Wrote that court: '[T]here are no First Amendment rights to use the copyrighted works of others'.[6] The intermediate appellate court affirmed, stating that 'copyrights are categorically immune from challenges under the First Amendment'.[7]

When the matter came to the United States Supreme Court, however, acknowledgement came: sometimes each of us does have a right to use the copyrighted works of others,[8] even if that right is 'second-class'.[9] Copyright itself has to be formed and interpreted to safeguard the public's rights of free speech.[10]

In the United States, the Court wrote, at least two doctrines provide that safeguard. The first is the so-called 'dichotomy' between expression (which can be owned) and ideas (which cannot).[11] The second is the doctrine that treats some uses of copyrighted works as 'fair' and non-infringing.[12] Given those two doctrines, the Court upheld the CTEA.

---

6   *Id.*, 537 U.S. 186 (quoting from the opinion of the District Court, *Eldred v. Reno*, 74 F.Supp.2d 1 (D.D.C.1999) at 3.)

7   *Eldred v Reno*, 239 F.3d 372 at 376 (D.C. Circuit 2001).

8   Wrote the Supreme Court, 'We recognize that the D.C. Circuit spoke too broadly when it declared copyrights "categorically immune from challenges under the First Amendment"', 537 U.S. at 789-790.

9   D. McGowan, 'Why the First Amendment Cannot Dictate Copyright Policy', in *Ohio State Law Journal* (forthcoming, 2004). McGowan is pointing to the Court's caveat: 'The First Amendment ... bears less heavily when speakers assert the right to make other people's speeches', 537 US at 789-90.

10   Thus, the Court wrote in footnote 24: '[I]t is appropriate to construe copyright's internal safeguards to accommodate First Amendment concerns. *Cf. United States* v. *X-Citement Video, Inc.*, 513 U.S. 64, 78 (1994) ("It is ... incumbent upon us to read the statute to eliminate [serious constitutional] doubts so long as such a reading is not plainly contrary to the intent of Congress")'.

11   The doctrine that copyright ownership does not extend to ideas appears in the statute at 17 USC Section 102(b). That copyright ownership does not extend to facts was made clear by *Feist Publications, Inc.* v. *Rural Telephone Service Co.* 499 U.S. 340 (1991).

12   The fair use doctrine is set out at 17 USC Section 107. Generally speaking, it permits socially desirable uses for which usual copyright market is not normatively appropriate. For discussion, see, e.g., W.J. Gordon, 'Excuse and Justification in the Law of Fair Use: Transaction Costs Have Always Been Only *Part* of the Story', in *Journal of the Copyright Society of the USA* 13 (Fiftieth Anniversary Issue 2003) 149-197; 'Reality as Artifact: From *Feist* to Fair Use', in *Law and Contemporary Problems* 55 (1992) 93-107; 'Fair Use as Market Failure: A Structural and Economic Analysis of the '*Betamax* Case and its Predecessors', in *Columbia Law Review* 82 (1982) 1600-1657.

One applauds the Supreme Court's recognition that the idea/expression dichotomy and the fair use are constitutionally mandated. At the same time, one can certainly disagree with the Court's assessment that with these doctrines in place, copyright poses no danger to free expression. Both fair use and the idea/expression dichotomy are notoriously unpredictable, and creative experimentation can be chilled by uncertainty as to liability. Moreover, to imagine that idea/expression dichotomy can accommodate a wide range of expressive concerns is to overstate its capacity: creative artists who need to use predecessor's work have sharply questioned 'copyright's notion that ideas and facts are anterior to their particular expressions'.[13] Ideas and facts are *not* inevitably 'separable, yielding to paraphrase, transmissible without either disfigurement or infringement'.[14]

Therefore, even if the idea/expression dichotomy and the fair use doctrine are expanded, the long duration of copyright remains a danger to the public's participation in its culture. The long copyright term also poses a danger to copyright's ability to serve the public's welfare interests, for a grant far in the future gives an author little incentive (remember that the author decides whether or not to write *today*).This should be compared with the significant costs that the far-future grant can impose on audiences and second authors (who will continue to decide whether or not to purchase or adapt a work *in the future*). Yet the *Eldred* court refused to admit the danger posed.

Perhaps an accommodation can be reached from the other side: Perhaps the author has no justifiable claims of right that would grant her a copyright that extended into the life of her great-grandchildren.

In what follows, I employ both instrumentalist welfare norms and norms of moral right to explore whether a life-plus seventy copyright term makes sense. I begin with illustrating the welfare loss.

II. The Naturally Circumscribed Rights of the Author, and the Public's Welfare Interest

Let me begin by making things more concrete. What does it mean to have a copyright duration of life plus seventy? It is hard for us to project into the future, since so many of its changes are unimaginable now. So instead, let us project into the past.

Imagine that the 'life plus seventy' rule had been enacted at the turn of the last century, and turn your mind's eye to a talented, fictional somebody born in 1900. Imagine that this individual immigrates to the United States a child, learns an

---

[13] Paul Saint-Amour, *The Copywrights: Intellectual Property and the Literary Imagination*, Cornell University Press (2003), at 189 (discussing James Joyce's view of copyright law, as expressed in *Ulysses*).

[14] *Ibid.*

immense amount growing up in New York City, comes to maturity, and becomes a songwriter and lyricist. Her many brilliant songs during the Roaring Twenties are said to capture the spirit and age of the City. Let us now say that in 1931, at the age of thirty-one, she writes something that captures the transition between the period of prosperity she had long celebrated, and the economic anxiety that followed the 1929 Wall Street crash. The song is played everywhere, and every artist wants his or her voice to be heard singing this particular song. This vogue goes on for a few years, but, as with most popular music, after a while the song stops being so popular.

However, for the long copyright term to have any impact, the song would need to become the kind of classic whose market never dries up completely. So let us assume this is the case. The song has become a 'standard'. Recordings continue to sell, bands continue to 'cover' the song, and the song continues to reside in the public imagination. Anyone hearing even a few bars of the tune will recognize it. And let us assume that the song has an influence in the music community. As with literature and the visual arts, individual pieces of music can significantly alter the course of the art form, and so it is with our musical work.

So, an individual who arrived in New York near the start of the last century, and lived the immigrant New York experience that so many of our families shared, forged a great piece of music, which was released in 1931 and remains of interest years later. Imagine, now, that this individual dies at the age of seventy in 1970. She leaves middle-aged sons and daughters, along with grandchildren in their twenties.

Under a life plus seventy rule, the copyright of that piece of 1931 music would not expire until the year 2040.[15] At that point, the composer's grandchildren would be in their nineties, if they were alive at all, and those grandchildren would have adult grandchildren and great-grandchildren of their own. Therefore, a cultural and musical fixture, which was created under a series of influences from the very early twentieth century, and which in turn influenced the growth and development of the twentieth century, will have copyright protection through a good part of the twenty-first.

During the last twenty years or so of that term – an amount equal to what is added by the Bono extension – it is likely that the composer will have personally known none of the surviving royalty recipients. Yet, should a new composer want

---

[15] The example in the text simplifies by imagining that something like the Bono Act had been applicable at the time the 1931 song was created. Under the actual Sonny Bono Copyright Term Extension Act, 'life plus seventy' only applies to works created on or after January 1, 1978. See 17 U.S.C. § 302(a). There are special rules for works for hire and some other works, see *id.* § § 302(b)-(c), and the Act also gives special treatment to works that were created earlier than 1978. See *id.* § 303. Thus, for works are already in their renewal terms when the Bono Act became effective, the copyright term is '95 years from the date copyright was originally secured'. *Id.* § 304(b).

to adapt the famous song to reflect on a twenty-first-century period of financial tumult and transition, the new composer could not do so without permission from at least one of those copyright owners. Similarly, someone who in 2031 wants to make a multi-media CD-ROM showing the history of mid-twentieth-century music could not include this and other music from the period without seeking permission from remote holders of copyrights all over the world. Some of the people who hold the copyrights in these century-old songs will no longer be identifiable through ordinary methods of search. The CTEA makes us face the question of whether all this is a good idea.

III. Illustrating the Welfare Loss

There are two aspects of importance in understanding the welfare loss: discounting, and the effect of a unitary copyright term on disparate works.

III.1. DISCOUNTING

The notion that we 'discount' benefits we will receive far in the future is a familiar one. Thus, Lord Macaulay used the notion when in the nineteenth century he opposed a particular copyright extension. 'For the sake of the good we must submit to the evil', argued Lord Macaulay of copyright, 'But the evil ought not to last a day longer than is necessary for the purpose of securing the good'.[16] What is 'necessary' must be judged from the perspective of what is necessary to induce the lazy author to get up earlier in the morning to work. Will he be so encouraged because he expects a far-distant advantage might accrue to his heirs? Macaulay thought not:

> 'We all know how faintly we are affected by the prospect of very distant advantages, even when they are advantages which we may reasonably hope that we shall ourselves enjoy. But an advantage that is to be enjoyed more than half a century after we are dead, by somebody, we know not by whom, perhaps by somebody unborn, by somebody utterly unconnected with us, is really no motive at all to action'.[17]

It is equally hard to imagine that a long copyright term would add a significant amount to the sum a publisher will offer today for an assignment of the copyright. Consider the following example.

Let us imagine an author who anticipates that a writing of hers would bring

---

[16] T. Macaulay, *Speech Before the House of Commons (Feb. 5, 1841)*, in Lady Trevelyan (ed.), *The Works of Lord Macaulay* 8 (1906) 203-204 [hereinafter Macaulay Speech of 1841], available at http://www.kuro5hin.org/story/2002/4/25/1345/03329.

[17] *Ibid.* at 200.

$1,000 in gross revenue every year from the moment of creation until copyright ends (this assumption is very generous to supporters of the CTEA, for ordinarily revenues are extremely hard to predict, and strongly decrease over time as works fall out of fashion). Assume the author is sixty in 2002, and that actuarial tables tell her she can expect to live another twenty-five years, to 2027.[18] If in 2002 she were deciding whether to write this new book, under the pre-CTEA copyright law she would expect her copyrights to expire in 2077. Assuming a five percent rate of interest and no inflation, the present value of seventy-five years of receiving $1,000 yearly would be $19,490.[19] Under a pre-CTEA copyright term, a publisher would therefore anticipate receiving up to $19,490 from the new work she contemplates. Of course, in offering to buy the copyright, the publisher would offer the author less than that, to cover risk, publishing and distribution costs, and the publisher's own profit share. Let us say the publisher would offer half, or $9,745.

Now let us examine what happens under the CTEA's grant of an additional twenty years. What is the present value of the additional income stream, assuming that $1,000 continued to be earned every year between 2077 and 2097? It is $320, raising the 2002 present value from $19,490 to $19,810.[20] It is thus possible that with a long term, a publisher will anticipate receiving $320 more. If the publisher offers half of that to the author, the resulting increase in authorial incentive is $160. That is a very small sum indeed compared to the whole. It is likely to have small or zero marginal incentive effect, an effect which (even if it exists) is gained at the disproportionate expense of the public.[21]

---

[18] The example in text is premised on a sixty-year-old author. A younger author would anticipate having a longer term. This 'life plus' structure of the law is potentially counterproductive: as Macaulay argued, a term hinging on the life of the author gives the longest period of legal protection to 'juvenile' works, and the shortest period to 'mature' works. Yet works 'written in maturity' tend to be more valuable. If it is thought necessary to give more incentive, terms should be defined by a certain term, rather than by a 'life plus' formula. See Thomas Macaulay *Speech Before the House of Commons (Apr. 6, 1842)*, in Lady Trevelyan (ed.), *The Works of Lord Macaulay* 8 (1906) 210-16. Also available at the website identified in footnote 16.

[19] Affidavit of Hal R. Varian paragraph 5-9, *Eldred v.Reno*, 239 F.3d 372 (D.C.Cir. 2001) (No.99-5430) [hereinafter Varian Affidavit], available at http://cyber.law.harvard.edu/eldredvreno/varian.pdf.

[20] See Varian Affidavit at paragraph 5-9, *Eldred* (No.99-5430).

[21] See Stan Liebowitz, *infra*, at Figure 2 and accompanying explanation. Thomas Macaulay argued that '[a] monopoly of sixty years produces twice as much evil as a monopoly of thirty years, and thrice as much evil as a monopoly of twenty years'. Macaulay Speech of 1841, *supra*, note 16, at 200. This is mathematically correct if by 'evil' he meant the costs to the public without regard to the offsetting benefits that copyright also brings. Taking both into account, however, Macaulay underestimated. The offsetting benefits are higher, and the costs lower, in the first years of a monopoly than in its later years. The deadweight loss caused by increases in monopoly duration grows at a far faster rate than the incentive effect does. See Stan Liebowitz and my discussion of his thesis *infra* Part IV. A monopoly of sixty years imposes more than twice as much deadweight loss (exclusive of the impact of discounting) as does a monopoly of thirty years.

III.2. EFFECT OF UNITARY TERM ON DISPARATE WORKS

As Stanley Liebowitz has shown, the cost of monopoly increases at a far faster rate than the incentive effect does.[22] This is not just because of the familiar discounting arguments. The following takes into account the loss attributable to unnecessary copyright protection in a way that should make it easy to see the costs of long copyright terms.

Let us backtrack to basics. Different creative works require different incentives. Some works would have come into being without any copyright at all; some would have come into being with a promise of five years of copyright protection; some would have come into being with a promise of ten years of protection; and so on. Only when a work would have come into existence without the need of a particular monopoly provision, should that provision be counted as generating a deadweight loss. This applies to provisions about duration as well. Every year that copyright lasts, more and more works fall into the category of works that did not need a copyright term this long to be produced. Every year of added duration brings additions to the group of works as to which copyright generates deadweight loss,[23] and subtractions from the group as to which copyright provides a social benefit.

Consider, for example, a copyright duration of five years. Assume there is a work for which the author needed the full five-year term to be induced to produce the work. Let us assume the work in question is an interpretive translation of *Beowulf*[24] called *Beowulf Transmuted*. For *Beowulf Transmuted*, a five-year copyright term generates no loss: if the book is valuable, its value is a gain attributable to that five-year copyright.[25] However high in price and small in quantity the copies of *Beowulf Transmuted* might be, they are a pure gain compared to an alternative state of shorter copyright in which this version of Beowulf did not exist. This is not true as to works that would have come into being with a term of less than five years: for a work that needed only three years of copyright to come into being, a five-year term generates two years of deadweight loss.

What happens in year six? We are dealing with a book, *Beowulf Transmuted*, whose author would have written it so long as she anticipated copyright protection would last five years. If copyright ended at five years, in year six the book would be in existence, and could be reproduced and sold competitively. Per-copy price would go down and the quantity in circulation would rise.

---

[22] See Stan Liebowitz, *supra*, note 21, at Figure 2 and accompanying explanation.

[23] *Ibid.* In this and succeeding paragraphs of the instant section, my analysis is heavily indebted to that of Stan Liebowitz.

[24] Michael Alexander (ed.), *Beowulf*, Penguin Books (1995).

[25] The work's existence is also attributable to many other contributing causes, such as the translator's efforts, dictionaries she may have employed, and, of course, the sources of the first *Beowulf*. When I speak of the work's being 'attributable to' copyright, I mean only that copyright is one of its many causes-in-fact.

By contrast, if copyright continued in the sixth year, the book would be sold at a higher price to fewer people. Under copyright, it would thus generate less benefit than it could in the absence of copyright. The decrease is 'deadweight loss' attributable to the extra year of protection. In assessing the value of a sixth year of copyright, then, an economist would put *Beowulf Transmuted* into the category of works for which copyright generates a loss – although for the fifth year of the copyright's duration, the book had belonged in the category of works for which copyright generated a social benefit.[26]

Every year, more and more works make the transition from the plus to the minus category. The same book for which copyright generated no deadweight loss in year Y (because its author needed as incentive a copyright whose term continued through that year), may generate deadweight loss the next year. When the Court upheld the term of 'life plus seventy', every book and film that would have come into existence even without the extra twenty years fell into the category of contributing to deadweight loss.

III.2.1. *A Graphical Analysis May Help to Illustrate*

The expectation that authors will discount to present value is a common-sense part of the explanation of why copyright terms should be limited rather than perpetual. Interestingly, however, a long copyright term can produce a net loss for society even if authors are indifferent as between immediate and future rewards. Economist Stan Liebowitz has developed a fascinating illustration to this effect. He shows that under some assumptions, copyright could produce a net social loss even if authors did not respond less favourably to distant rewards than to immediate ones.[27] In the illustration, all works are assumed to last for ten years. Without copyright, the value of a work to society is assumed to be $100 per year. Under copyright, since the price is higher and fewer copies are disseminated, the value of the work to society is assumed to be $60 per year. Assume that without copyright 100 copies will be produced. The copyright term can be from zero to ten years long, and for every year of copyright that the law promises, authors are assumed to respond by bringing forth six additional works.

Although the assumptions are quite constraining, most of us will nevertheless be surprised by the result: *less* value is generated under a nine or ten year copyright term than under no copyright at all. On the following graphs, the duration of the copyright term is measured (in years) on the horizontal axis. The vertical axis measures the monetary value of the works created under each designated

---

[26] See the mathematical example and charts, *supra*, note 18, for an illustration of the mechanism.

[27] E-mail from Stan Liebowitz, Professor of Managerial Economics, University of Texas at Dallas (Autumn 2002) (on file with author). Incidentally, although I make use of Professor Liebowitz's illustration with his permission, I subject it to uses of my own, and responsibility for any errors rest with me.

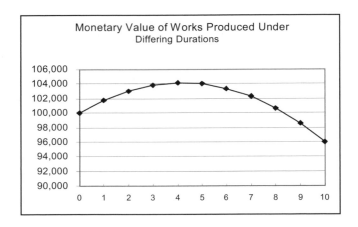

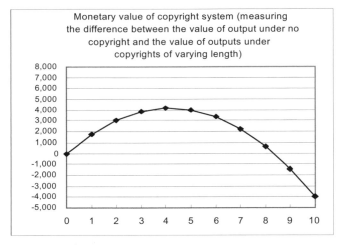

copyright term. The first chart measures the gross output of works: the value of works under no copyright, and the value of works under copyright terms of from one to ten years. The second chart shows how these various copyrights compare with a regime of no copyright at all. In a sense, the second chart measures the monetary value, under the assumed facts, of the various copyright systems.

The following examples will illustrate the method of calculation. Note that discounting plays no role, nor are administrative costs of the copyright system included.

- *Under no copyright*: With zero copyright, 100 works are produced which are worth $100 yearly and last ten years. Their value over the ten years (without discounting) is thus $100,000.
- *Under a regime giving one year of copyright protection*: With one year of

copyright, six more works are produced, totalling 106 works. The first year of these works' existence is under copyright, so each generates $60 in value ($6,360 for all). The next nine years they are in the public domain, so, without discounting, over that period each of the 106 generate $900 ($95,400 for all). Summing the value during the ten years that the works last, the 106 works have a value of $101,760 (this appears on the first chart above). This is an increase of $1,760 over a system of no copyright (this figure appears on the second chart).

– *Under a regime giving nine years of copyright protection*: With nine years of copyright protection promised, authors produce (9 × 6) or fifty-four more works than they would without copyright. Under a nine-year term, therefore, 154 works would be in existence. For each of the nine years under copyright, they generate $60 each, for a total of $83,160. In their last year, the 154 generate $100 of value each, or $15,400 for all. The total value of the works produced under a regime of nine years of copyright protection is $98,560. The copyright system now has produced a loss as compared with a system of no copyright.

– *With a ten-year term*, the loss grows larger. Under a ten-year term, 160 works would be in existence and would yield a total value of $96,000 – a loss of $4,000 in comparison with the $100,000 generated with no copyright at all.

What drives the social loss in the illustration is copyright's unitary term. CTEA proponents are not alone in assuming that extending a copyright term will sometimes bring forth more works. Such an assumption necessarily implies that different works or classes of works (novels versus movies, perhaps) respond to different incentives. A unitary term by definition is unable to respond to different works' needs with varying periods of protection. In a world where different works respond to different terms, a unitary term will therefore generate deadweight loss.

IV. Perspectives from Policy and Rights

My role in this section is not to talk about the constitutionality of the CTEA. Rather, I am going to look at the statute through the lens of two kinds of policies. One set of policies might be grouped under the title, 'authors' rights'. The other set might be called 'instrumentalist'. They provide two quite different evaluative perspectives.

The authors' rights advocate usually views copyright as resting on some characteristic tie between the author and her work, which justifies giving ownership to the author, regardless of its societal effects. Thus, authors' rights approaches focus on the individual producer, and tend to look backwards: A work has been produced – now how should the law treat it? The answer of the authors' rights advocate typically is that the creator of the work deserves ownership in it.

By contrast, an instrumentalist policy focuses on economic incentives or other societal effects of granting copyright. Instrumentalism is concerned with the producer, too, but views her as one person among many who may be affected by a change in law. Instrumentalism looks forward, rather than back. Its proponents ask: How best can the law encourage authors to produce new work in the future, and do so in such a way that the value of new works so induced exceeds the costs of the system?[28] The answer to that question is not always ownership.

The US Constitution empowers the federal legislature to grant copyrights and patents in a Clause that is instrumentalist in wording. Congress is given its power 'to promote the Progress of Science and the useful Arts'.[29] Yet, when James Madison defended the Clause in the Federalist Papers, he did so on the grounds that granting copyrights and patents was one of the few places where the public interest coincided with private claims of right.[30] This convergence of private and public perspectives – analogous to authors' rights and instrumentalism – occurs often. Our law tends to be most stable and least contested when such convergence occurs.

One area where the two kinds of policies would likely converge is in the giving of copyright in the first instance.[31] To extend the term of copyright from zero years to ten years, for instance, would greatly increase the incentives of authors, and simultaneously honour their ties to their work. And the resulting incentives would outweigh the monopoly restraints on access that copyright also brings. Therefore, both perspectives would give a 'thumbs up' if the question were increasing a copyright term from zero years to ten. Increasing the term of copyright from ten years to, let's say, thirty years or fifty years might also gain support from instrumentalists, as well as authors' rights advocates.

But when the question instead is extending copyright from life-of-the-author plus fifty to life-of-the-author plus seventy, one would think that the authors' rights and instrumentalist approaches might pull away from each other. A simple view of authors' rights seems to say: All Power to the Poet – increase the copyright term as much as you can. By contrast, an instrumentalist is likely to doubt that incentives will be significantly enhanced by the extra twenty years of copyright term. It provides twenty more years of making works expensive and difficult to

---

[28] See S. Liebowitz, 'Copyright Law, Photocopying and Price Discrimination', in R. Zerbe (ed.), *Research in Law and Economics 8* (1986) 181-200 (exploring the trade-off between duration, incentives, and monopoly restraints).

[29] US Constitution Article I, § 8, clause 8.

[30] 'The public good', he wrote, 'fully coincides ... with the claims of individuals'. J. Madison, 'The Federalist No. 43', in J.E. Cooke (ed.), *The Federalist,* Wesleyan University Press (1961), at 309 [hereinafter Madison]. Let us leave outside our scope whether Madison was correct in thinking that the common law would have given authors valid claims to control the copying of their published work.

[31] See W.J. Gordon, 'An Inquiry into the Merits of Copyright: The Challenges of Consistency, Consent and Encouragement Theory', in *Stanford Law Review* 41 (1989) 1343, 1365-1366.

access, without giving a compensating gain in incentives.[32] As Lord Macaulay said of a piece of legislation that would have increased copyright term to a length less than that granted by the Bono Act, 'it leaves the advantages nearly what they are at present, and increases the disadvantages at least four fold'.[33] Someone who believes the goal of law is the instrumental one of being 'beneficial for mankind'[34] is thus highly unlikely to favour the extension.

So one would hardly expect convergence here. One might assume that persons flying an authors' rights flag would favour the Bono extension of copyright term, while those wearing instrumentalist colours would oppose it.

The theory of the various instrumentalist positions – at least those classified as economic or utilitarian – are fairly well understood. Still needed, however, is a deeper understanding of the authors' rights claim. Too often, such claims are presented as a sort of unreasoned impulse that leaves the important questions unanswered.

For example, we might all agree it is laudable to 'reward authors'. But how much reward is appropriate? For another example, some authors' rights advocates speak of 'giving every cow its calf'. But unlike calves and kids, a new intangible can have many mothers and look like none of them. So how should the cow-calf relationship be defined? Or sometimes authors' rights advocates take refuge in the notion that 'reaping without sowing' is an evil that should be prohibited.[35] But to oppose 'reaping without sowing' is profoundly antisocial. From Ben Kaplan[36] 'and John Dawson[37] back through time, students of society have realized that we all obtain benefits that we did not earn, simply by being born into human society. To learn is to reap more than we sow.[38] If we could not use the tools that make up our culture without the permission of the descendants of whoever initially created that culture, many bad results would follow. One result, I think, is that we would end up with a feeling that we do not really belong to the same community, which

---

[32] See Stan Liebowitz, *supra*, note 28.

[33] Macaulay, *supra*, note 16, at 733.

[34] *Ibid.* at 732. The law of England at the time of Macaulay's speech gave copyright for the duration of the author's life or twenty-eight years, whichever was longer. The bill he opposed would have extended copyright to life of the author and sixty years. See *ibid.* at 731. Macaulay himself apparently favoured copyright for life, or forty-two years, whichever was longer.

[35] The most famous American case prohibiting reaping without sowing appears in *International News Service* v. *Associated Press*, 248 U.S. 215, 239 (1918) (upholding a right to sue for misappropriation of news). For a fuller discussion, using restitution law as an analogy to limit 'reap and sow' claims, see W.J. Gordon, 'On Owning Information: Intellectual Property and the Restitutionary Impulse', in *Virginia Law Review* 78 (1992) 149, 149-166, 178-180.

[36] See B. Kaplan, *An Unhurried View of Copyright*, Columbia University Press (1967).

[37] See J.P. Dawson, 'The Self-Serving Intermeddler', in *Harvard Law Review* 87 (1974) 1409.

[38] As Justice Benjamin Kaplan noted, 'if man has any "natural" rights, not the least must be a right to imitate his fellows ... "[P]rogress" ... depends on generous indulgence of copying'. B. Kaplan, *supra*, note 36, at 2.

could have some bad effects for legitimacy, willingness to obey the law, and general civility. Reaping without sowing is hardly something that deserves broad condemnation.

Therefore, I will illustrate what I think to be the best form that an author's claim of right can take. Oddly enough, in the end, I find that authors' rights advocates should condemn the new extension. They should join the instrumentalists in opposing it.

There are many views of authors' rights. The most popular links authors' rights to the natural rights of property, as explicated in John Locke's second treatise.[39] Current thinkers, including myself, are not the only ones who find Locke congenial – so did the Framers. John Locke was one of the most influential of the philosophers read by the group who wrote our Constitution – including the Copyright and Patent Clause.[40]

Locke's second treatise says that originally we all owned the earth in common. He explains this common ownership by reference to God's gift and God's intent. For secular readers of today, the explanation lies in a belief in equality that was still questioned in Locke's time. In fact, fostering an increase in equality was integral to Locke's main goal:[41] he wrote in opposition to the divine right of kings.[42] Locke sought to justify a right to government that serves the people's interest by reference to this original common ownership of the earth. Therefore, he posited that in a state of nature we would all be equally entitled to the fruits of the earth, whether they are fish in the sea or nuts and apples in the forest.

Now, to understand how Locke's property theory fits with his theory of government, we need to recall the arguments of Sir Robert Filmer, another philosopher of the period. Filmer supported the divine right of kings.[43]

Filmer belittled the notion of common ownership. He argued that if everybody owned the earth the common, then no one person could ever take even a walnut from a walnut tree, without getting the consent of everyone else. That would be an insuperable barrier to ever creating private property. Therefore, Filmer concluded that the only way for private property to come into being – this institution that his contemporaries saw all around them and thought so beneficial – was to have a king. A king does not have to create a consensus of the whole every time somebody gets hungry and wants to eat a walnut. A king can declare who owns what.

---

[39] For discussion of the John Locke's natural rights theories, and their application to copyright law, see W.J. Gordon, 'Property Right in Self-Expression', in *Yale Law Journal* 102 (1993) 1533, relying on John Locke, *Two Treatises of Government* (P. Laslett (ed.)), Cambridge University Press (2nd ed., 1967), 287-88 (based on the original 3rd ed. 1698, corrected by Locke) (book II).

[40] See W.J. Gordon, *supra*, note 39, at 1539.

[41] See *ibid.* at 1542.

[42] The work he was primarily aiming to refute was Filmer's *Patriarcha*. Sir Robert Filmer, *Patriarcha and Other Political Works*, (P. Laslett (ed.)), Basil Blackwell (1949).

[43] *Ibid.*

Locke's response was that common ownership of property does not necessarily give every co-owner a right to be consulted whenever it is used. Rather, all the co-owners have a right not to be harmed by its use. Locke believed that if someone's private use or consumption has not harmed strangers, the strangers' only interest in challenging it would come from motives not worth respecting, such as covetousness, envy, and laziness.

But if, by contrast, strangers are harmed by someone's taking a bite out of the common property for private property, then they have a legitimate right to complain. From this comes a fairly famous axiom of Locke's: The labourer owns whatever from the common he has intermixed with his labour, so long as 'enough, and as good', is left for everyone else. Locke reasoned that if enough and as good is left, then there is no ground for complaint.[44]

This seems reasonable. If many of us are on a desert trek and running out of water, and one happens upon a small pool of fresh water, we would think that person acts wrongfully if he tries to exclude all the rest of us, or if, after filling his own water bottle, he uses the pool as a latrine so it becomes unsuitable for drinking. But if all of us find springs or pools of fresh water sufficient for our needs, we would not think any of us wrongful if we kept our own spring to ourselves, and used it for any purpose we desired. That rightful exclusive use is the key to what we call 'property'.[45] Thus, the 'enough and as good' condition is crucial to Locke's justification of a natural right of property.

Imagine another example: An individual spends the day climbing trees in the forest to gather apples. By the end of the day she has a small heap of apples. Imagine further that upon completing her work, there are just as many good apples left on the trees for someone else to pick. Anyone who invests the same kind of labour can obtain just as many apples of equivalent quality – there is 'enough and as good' left. Then a stranger comes along and takes the heap of apples that the labourer has already picked.

Unless the stranger has some physical disability that prevents him from picking his own fruit, it is clear the stranger is acting that way solely to take advantage of

---

[44] See J. Locke, *Second Treatise*, chapter 5 at section 27. The proviso that 'enough, and as good' be left for others constitutes an additional 'do no harm' principle. See also L.C. Becker, *Property Rights: Philosophic Foundations*, Routledge & Kegan Paul (1977). Similarly, Locke's argument regarding waste suggests he saw nothing wrongful in taking property from someone to whom it had no value. J. Locke, *Second Treatise*, chapter 5 at section 37. If so, Locke would seem to view a non-harmful taking as non-wrongful, at least in the state of nature.

[45] Property includes more than a right of use. Typically it also includes, *inter alia*, a right to alienate and to bequeath. See Honore, 'Ownership', in L.C. Becker & K. Kipnis (eds.), *Property: Cases, Concepts, Critiques*, Prentice Hall (1984), 78, at 85. For discussion of property entitlements in the copyright context, see W.J. Gordon, *supra*, note 30, at 1343-1469. However, it is usually agreed that Locke's theory grounds a right of use and consumption much more securely than it does other property entitlements, such as a right to alienate. The entitlement probably most questionable in the Lockean scheme is the right to transmit by inheritance.

the labourer's pains. If using the other gatherer's labour did not motivate him, he would have picked his own apples, which would have been equally good. The stranger is acting wrongfully to so favour his own interest over another's. He is using the other's labour as a means toward his own ends, violating the very tenets of equality. He is harming the labourer by taking her labour, which is now inextricably tied to the apples that she gathered. Because he is acting wrongfully to take the labourer's pile, she has a right to exclude him from using the apples. She has a form of property in the apples.

Locke says the earth was given to us for the benefit of the industrious and rational, not for the benefit of those who are covetous.[46] What does it mean to covet in Lockean terms? I think it is something that we, in secular terms, can understand. It means to want what someone else has created; to choose one's self over the other who has invested his effort in it; to disregard that person's efforts and take the thing to one's self. If you want to use deontological language, it is a primary violation of the right of equal treatment.

The application of this theory to intellectual property is obvious. So obvious, in fact, that Locke has sometimes been misdescribed as if he himself created an explicit defence of intellectual property.[47] But, though that was not part of his project, applying Locke's property theory to the labour of the mind is intuitive and appealing: A creator takes something out of the common heritage – language, myth, artistic forms, and ideas. With this, she mixes something of her own: intellectual labour, artistry, taste, and judgment. The result is an intangible – a song, a story, a computer program – in which both common and individual elements are mixed. If, in taking from the common heritage, she left 'enough and as good' there for others to use, she would seem entitled to exclude strangers from what she has made. Similarly, she would seem entitled to demand compensation as a price for their using it. If so, she has a justifiable form of 'property'.

Thus, the theory suggests that, once the labourer has mixed her labour with the common, she has a right to call on either God, other people in the community, civil society, or the government to keep strangers from this new thing she has made. That is her right. But for every right that a property owner has, there is a corresponding duty on others. So what about the rest of us? Do we have nothing but duties once the labourer has acted? Let me just try to make clear what the rights and duties of the public are.

We have, under this view of Locke's, no right to another's pains, except if we are in great need. Aside from those extreme situations, strangers owe us no duties to

---

[46] 'He that had as good left for his improvement, as was already taken up, needed not complain, ought not to meddle with what was already improved by another's labour: if he did, it is plain he desired the benefit of another's pains, which he had no right to, and not the ground which God had given him in common', *Second Treatise of Government*, Chapter 5 at section 34.

[47] See E.W. Ploman & L.C. Hamilton, *Copyright – Intellectual Property in the Information Age*, Routledge & Kegan Paul (1980), at 13.

improve our lot. This is a norm quite unlike that of the pure economic or utilitarian perspective, which seems to say that all persons should be enlisted in creating the greatest net social product. The Lockean approach says 'no' to such instrumentalism. The consuming public does not have a right to the biggest and best. The public's right is preserved in its ability to make use of the common heritage. That entitlement is enshrined in the 'enough and as good' principle, which prevents new property from forming if the assertion of property rights would leave the public worse off in its use of that heritage. The public also has a right to act toward the created object in ways that do not take the creative person's labour.

I want to suggest that if you take the Lockean perspective seriously, you end up not with an unlimited right, but rather, with a very limited one. The example of American author Mark Twain will suggest that an unlimited right is an impossibility if we are going to have a culture at all. Twain is sometimes referred to as an advocate of extreme and perpetual copyright. But really, he could not have been. After all, in writing A Connecticut Yankee in King Arthur's Court, he borrowed from the many bards who had told King Arthur's tales in prior years. If Twain was going to be able to use images and stories that he learned through somebody else's efforts, and if he felt rightful in doing so, he must have had a conception of boundaries on those prior writers' initial rights. There are many such possible boundaries – perhaps ownership could subsist in expression and not ideas, or perhaps there could be some type of time limit on the ownership of expressions. But if there is to be more than one generation of author, some limitations on the claims of the initial generation are mandatory.

I suggest a conclusion that I defend at more length elsewhere: that our current copyright law gives authors more than they would get under Lockean natural rights. Sometimes the assertion of United States copyright law leaves the public worse off than it otherwise would have been in its ability to use the pre-existing heritage, and the law sometimes gives property rights far broader than are justified by the labourer's initial investment. Current copyright law gives more than a thoughtful authors' rights framework would justify.

It seems to me that there are at least three ways of handling that conclusion. First, if, in fact, current copyright law gives authors more than they would justifiably receive under natural rights, one response might be to amend the natural rights framework, or to junk it. A second response might be to amend copyright law, or junk that. A third response might be to investigate whether current copyright law gives back to the public – either in kind or in different form – benefits to compensate it for the losses it inflicts.

The latter is my favoured option. I argue that copyright law is justifiable under a natural rights framework if it takes from the public only fungible, commensurable losses for which the law fully compensates in other ways. And I think that US copyright law – at least until recently – did a fairly good job of providing such compensation, and should do so. In short, the authors' rights perspective ends up saying that the copyright statute must, to some extent, serve the public interest, which includes the interest of future creators, as well as the public.

This does not collapse the authors' rights and instrumentalist views together. For example, an author may deserve property rights, even if those rights do not lead to maximizing the sum of value in the world. All that is necessary under the Lockean approach is for the creative labourer to satisfy the 'enough and as good' proviso; if she does, then she has a legitimate property claim to exclude other people from taking the labour she has invested. Yet, the nature of the proviso and the limited nature of the claim do involve our law in some give-and-take. For purposes of practical administration and otherwise, we grant copyrights a scope far beyond these limits. Something must be paid for the erosion of the public's rights.

The easiest and least costly way to serve that goal – to leave the individual creator unharmed and give benefit to the public – is to cut off ownership at a limited term, particularly when the cut-off occurs after the author's death. Anything beyond the author's lifetime stretches the notion of protected the labouring author herself – and that protection is the Lockean focus. Although no particular specification is possible, I think this is a perspective that is more on the Eldred side in opposing the Bono extension than it is on Professor Miller's side in favouring it.

That, then, is the structure of my argument: Under an authors' rights view, the creative person's investment of labour should be protected, so long as she leaves 'enough and as good'. Our law gives creative persons – and their employers and assigns – much more than that. It protects more than the investment of labour, and gives rights even where 'enough and as good' may not be left. The public's rights are thus eroded. As a result, the law owes something to the public. One of the best ways to partly pay this debt is to limit the copyright term.

What remains to be specified are some of the ways in which our current law gives more scope to copyright than the Lockean view would justify. Let me then end by giving you three examples of things that we do protect by copyright, which I do not think a Lockean would protect.

The first such candidate is the extreme right over derivative works. Right now, a copyright owner can control any substantial use of his or her authorship, even if the second person is a creative individual who is doing something with the work that the original author never in a million years could have done themselves. In that case, a derivative work author causes the creator no harm at all, interferes in no way with the creator's initial plans, and may even give the creator new publicity and, therefore, new funds. There is no taking of the initial investment or interference with the creative person's foreseeable range of goals. Nevertheless, current copyright law imposes liability on this person who – unlike the stranger who stole the apples – is causing no harm. There may be practical reasons for such a choice, but it nevertheless goes much further than a Lockean analysis would justify.

Second, it is not clear that natural law would go any further than giving property during the life of the author itself. Even the right of transfer during life might be questioned.

For a third set of examples, I will refer back to my imagined piece of music that was created in 1931. Recall the new composer who wants to use it one hundred years later to comment on a period of economic tumult in her own life. She really has no substitute for the associations the music brings. She is not like the covetous stranger who uses the fruit of another's labour simply to save himself effort. She has a goal that can be defined independently from the saving of effort. If so, this user of the 1931 song is outside the class of persons whom Locke wished to restrain. In addition, her derivative work may be outside of the class of activities that would constitute an erosion of the original composer's investment.

The same may be true of a person who wants to collect twentieth-century songs for a history volume. Furthermore, enforcing copyright against this music historian might violate the proviso of leaving 'enough, and as good'. A historian in the state of nature had a freedom that copyright law will not allow to today's historian.

Describing our surroundings through art is one of the ways we navigate that described world. In virtually any view of human nature, making our own art or having access to others' art is essential for emotional and cognitive flourishing. So, when a historian uses others' images or sounds not simply to save himself labour, but because he and his audience need to understand the past to better navigate the present, he is not violating the tenets of equality. He is not like Locke's covetous stranger. If we borrow another's image, not to use it for its original purpose, but rather, because we need to describe our world accurately, the Lockean approach would not forbid us. Yet copyright today does so forbid us.

Moreover, in the state of nature, we could create art that described our surroundings. But when we need to describe the world around us today, we cannot be accurate if all we describe is natural woods and water. Rather, most of us seeking to represent our environment would describe created architecture, manmade sounds, and cultural symbols. If we are to have 'enough, and as good', we must continue to have the freedom to use our surroundings in our own art. Yet the copyright courts forbid such uses.

There are many plausible reasons why copyright law draws the lines here. Most notably, if the uses I describe were permitted, it could be administratively quite difficult to distinguish good-faith users from the commercially-motivated covetous strangers, who might disguise their pure parasitism under a cloak of independent artistic goals. Similarly, if unforeseen derivative uses were free of copyright restraint, determining foreseeability could embroil the courts in complex investigations into inherently uncertain counter-factuals. But though practical reasons may explain the grant of copyright in ways that erodes the public's entitlement, that erosion still requires compensation. A reasonably short copyright term is one way to make such repayment.

A short copyright term is also appropriate in Lockean terms. Labour is a purposive notion; random activity is not 'labour', for 'labour' is goal directed.[48] The core of the Lockean prohibition is the norm that the stranger should not harmfully interfere with goals the labourer's efforts seek to further.[49] It is hard to imagine that copying a work seventy years after death – a copy that may be made a century or more after the work was created – would interfere with the goals of the author seventy or more years before. In some real way, the use of the work in the far distant future is unforeseeable. We should follow the logic of the common law; as duties do not extend to the unforeseeable, neither should rights.

The tort analogy is instructive from the economic perspective as well. Both copyright law and personal injury law seek to affect behaviour by 'internalizing externalities'. That is, the legal doctrines seek to make decision-makers feel some of the effects to which their decisions and behaviours give rise. Copyright law allows people to capture benefits they generate. In copyright law, 'carrots' are given to plaintiffs to make them produce more creative works. In tort law, 'sticks' are imposed on defendants to make them engage less in destructive behaviour. In this way, torts and copyright mirror each other, operating in ways that are parallel but reversed.

There exists a constitutionally-mandated command that copyrights can only last for limited times. In two hundred years, all of today's copyrights will have expired. That is, an heir of a copyright owner who sues for non-consensual copying two hundred years from now will lose. Why? The logic is the same as in the tort case of no foreseeability. Imposing a duty on a copyist to pay royalties a hundred years after a book or movie is created will have no impact on an author's willingness to work hard today. Given discount rates and the difficulties of predicting that far in the future, the expectation of current benefit from such a far-distant right is minuscule, virtually unforeseeable. To impose liability would be to raise the price of books above the physical cost of manufacturing and distributing them for no incentive payoff. This not only wastes administrative costs (as imposing liability for unforeseeable harms also would do), but also imposes a deadweight loss on society. So plaintiff loses.

In the law of personal injury, a defendant need not pay for a harm unforeseeably (and thus not proximately) caused. This rule makes sense because, if this were not the rule, the court would be expending its resources to make the defendant pay when the obligation would have no incentive effect. In the law of copyright, copyright terms expire. If that were not the rule and copyrights were perpetual, copyright law would make defendants pay at times so far distant that the prospect of such payment would not add anything to the original author's

---

[48] Lawrence Becker argues that purpose is essential to the notion of 'labour' for one 'labours toward' a particular goal. See L. Becker, *Property Rights: Philosophic Foundations,* Routledge & Kegan Paul (1977), at 48-50; W.J. Gordon, 'Property Right in Self-Expression', in *Yale Law Journal* 102 (1993) at 1547-48.

[49] 'Not everything that we dislike or resent ... is harmful to us'. J. Feinberg, *Harm to Others: Moral Limits of the Criminal Law,* Oxford University Press (1984), at 45.

incentives to create new works, but would decrease the dissemination of information.

V.   Conclusion

Only copyright's limiting doctrines make copyright tolerable. This is equally true from the perspective of free speech, public welfare, or the autonomy and natural rights claims of downstream authors. Copyright's limits are the modes through which the conflicting demands of the various affected participants can be reconciled. Neither an authors' rights perspective nor an instrumentalist public-welfare perspective supports the long copyright term created by the CTEA.

Chapter 7

'Holding the Line' – the Relationship between the Public Interest and Remedies Granted or Refused, Be It for Breach of Confidence or Copyright

*Alison Firth**

I.   Introduction

Copyright and breach of confidence may both be used to regulate the flow of information. The extent to which this is possible, and the consequences of failure to control the flow, ultimately depend upon the availability of judicial remedies, in particular the injunction or restraining order. In breach of confidence and in copyright cases, common law courts have considered the notion of public interest when deciding how to address alleged breaches. The English Court of Appeal in *Ashdown v. Telegraph*[1] has somewhat revived the defence for copyright in England, after blows dealt by an earlier Court of Appeal decision in *Hyde Park v. Yelland*.[2] The tendency to refuse a remedy on the ground of a public interest in the disclosure of information has been joined by a small sister trend, recalling the discretionary nature of injunctions – consideration of the adequacy of damages when deciding whether to grant a permanent injunction. In the English case of *Ludlow Music Inc v. Robbie Williams*,[3] the court discussed the role of the permanent injunction and declined to award such an order on application in proceedings for summary judgment, although in subsequent proceedings an injunction was granted.[4]

---

[*]   Queen Mary, University of London.

[1]   *The Right Honourable Paddy Ashdown MP PC* v. *Telegraph Group Limited* [2002] Ch 149; [2002] RPC 5; [2002] ECDR 32; [2002] ECC 19; [2001] 3 W.L.R. 1368 ; [2001] 4 All E.R. 666; [2001] EMLR 44; [2001] HRLR 57. J. Griffiths, 'Copyright law after Ashdown – Time to deal fairly with the public', in *IPQ* 3 (*International Property Quarterly*) (2002) 240.

[2]   *Hyde Park Residence Ltd* v. *Yelland* [2001] Ch 143; [2000] 3 WLR 215; [2000] ECDR 275; [2000] E.M.L.R. 363; [2000] R.P.C. 604 (CA).

[3]   *Ludlow Music Inc.* v. *Robbie Williams* [2001] F.S.R. 19 (Nicholas Strauss Q.C. sitting as a Deputy High Court Judge).

[4]   *Ludlow Music Inc* v. *Williams (No.2)* [2002] E.M.L.R. 29; [2002] F.S.R. 57; [2002] E.C.D.R. CN6 (Pumfrey, J).

P.L.C. Torremans (ed.), Copyright and Human Rights, 131–155

The injunction's counterpart is damages in Equity.[5] On this point, Canadian jurisprudence in the shape of cases such as *Cadbury Schweppes* v. *FBI Foods*[6] is of particular interest to the intellectual property community. In *Cadbury*, the Supreme Court of Canada made much pertinent comment on damages in breach of confidence cases and held that a permanent injunction was inappropriate to restrain the defendant's use of 'not very special' commercial information.

II. Copyright, Breach of Confidence and Other Causes of Action

Although copyright protects expression whilst breach of confidence protects the underlying information,[7] in cases where the public has a serious interest in the disclosure of information, the form in which that information appears is often important. In *Fressoz and Roire* v. *France*,[8] a journalist received copy tax returns

---

5   'Common law' [initially discerned from general customary principles of law] and Equity [based upon conscience] developed in parallel in England and related jurisdictions. The two systems were merged by C19 Judicature Acts. 'Lord Cairns Act', the Chancery Amendment Act of 1858, by Section 2 (subsumed into Section 50, Supreme Court Act 1981) had made the common law remedy of damages available in lieu of an injunction, thus providing the courts with a mechanism for providing compensation for *future*, as well as past, breaches. Analogously, damages have been made available for past breaches of confidence: *AG* v. *Guardian Newspapers (No.2)* [1990] 1 A.C. 109, at 286 per Lord Goff: 'the remedy of damages, which in cases of breach of confidence is now available, despite the equitable nature of the wrong, through a beneficent interpretation of the Chancery Amendment Act 1858 (Lord Cairns Act)'. For a trenchant account of these matters and their relation to restitution, see D. Campbell, 'Hamlet without the Prince: How Leng and Leong use Restitution to extinguish Equity', in *Journal of Business Law* (2003) 131. The Canadian Supreme Court in *Cadbury Schweppes* v. *FBI Foods* [2000] FSR 491, rejected Lord Cairn's Act as a basis for damages in breach of confidence cases, holding the court's inherent Equitable jurisdiction to be the adequate and correct basis. In discussing relief to be granted in *Durand* v. *Molino* [2000] ECDR 320 (facts and decision as to liability), Pumfrey J held that equitable damages could be awarded in lieu of an order for delivery up: see G. Harbottle, 'Permanent injunctions in copyright cases: When will they be refused?', in *EIPR* (*European Intellectual Property Review*) (2001) 154, at note 8.
6   [2000] FSR 491.
7   In *Cadbury Schweppes* v. *FBI* [2000] FSR 491, at 504, the Supreme Court of Canada opined that 'whether a breach of confidence in a particular case has a contractual, tortious, proprietary or trust flavour goes to the *appropriateness* of a particular equitable remedy but does not limit the court's *jurisdiction* to grant it'. On the various bases for breach of confidence claims in England, see J. Hull, *Commercial Secrecy*, Sweet & Maxwell (2nd ed., 2003); J. Lang, 'The protection of commercial trade secrets', in *EIPR* (2003) 462.
8   Fressoz & Roire v. France (29183/95) [2001] 31 EHRR 28; comment at European Law Review, Supplement 25 (Human rights survey) (2000) 150; N. Bratza, 'The implications of the Human Rights Act 1998 for commercial practice', in *EHLRL* (*European Human Rights Law Review*) (2000) 1. J. Griffiths, 'Copyright law and the public's right to receive information: Recent developments in an isolated community', in E. Barendt and A. Firth (eds.), *Yearbook of copyright and media law* VI (2001-2), Oxford University Press (2002), at 29.

of the chairman of Peugeot, a large French car manufacturer. After checking against public domain material, the journalist wrote an exposé which was published with reproductions of the tax returns in the satirical magazine 'Le Canard Enchainé'. The journalist and a director of the publisher were convicted of handling stolen copies. In holding the convictions to be contrary to Article 10 of the European Convention on Human Rights (freedom of expression) the European Court distinguished between the underlying information (public domain) and the tax returns themselves, which might need to be reproduced to lend credence to the story. Likewise, it was argued in *Hyde Park* v. *Yelland* that, in order to refute public claims as to the length of time spent at a villa by the late Princess Diana and her companion Dodi Al-Fayed on the day before their death, it was necessary for a tabloid newspaper to publish security camera footage showing times. At first instance Jacob J held that Yelland had arguable defences and declined to grant summary judgment in favour of the claimant.[9] However, the Court of Appeal subsequently disagreed that printing the footage was legitimate[10] since the information could have been conveyed in a way that did not infringe copyright. The defence of public interest, to the extent that it exists in copyright, appears to be a residual defence, relied upon in these rare cases where the form in which information appears is highly significant. In these cases, copyright, privacy and commercial confidence are often intertwined. The public's right to be informed is also relevant to other torts, such as defamation.[11]

III. Guardians of the Public Interest

Solicitude for the public interest in the appropriate flow of information is not, of course, the courts' sole province. It can be found in international conventions,[12] national constitutions,[13] legislation, press or broadcasting codes, and in the notions of fair play, discretion and honourable conduct held by individual citizens. This paper examines the role of public interest considerations at the boundaries between full exclusivity of rights at one extreme, wholly uncontrolled use at the

---

[9] *Hyde Park Residence Ltd* v. *Yelland* [1999] E.M.L.R. 654; [1999] R.P.C. 655 (English High Court).

[10] *Hyde Park Residence Ltd* v. *Yelland* [2001] Ch 143; [2000] 3 WLR 215; [2000] ECDR 275; [2000] E.M.L.R. 363; [2000] R.P.C. 604 (Eng CA).

[11] E.g. *Dalban* v. *Romania* [2000] 8 BHRC 91 (ECHR), case comment 'Freedom of expression: conviction of journalist for criminal defamation', in *EHRLR* (2000) 84-85; *Thoma* v. *Luxembourg* (38432/97) noted at *EHRLR* (2001) 587.

[12] Ricketson, 'The boundaries of copyright: its proper limitations and exceptions: international conventions and treaties', in *IPQ* (1999) 56.

[13] For example, the constitutional provisions discussed by the Privy Council in *Observer Publications Limited* v. *Campbell 'Mickey' Matthew, The Commissioner of Police, The Attorney General* 2001 WL 395210 CA, a case on appeal from The Eastern Caribbean Court of Appeal of Antigua and Barbuda about the refusal of a broadcasting licence.

other extreme and several intermediate possibilities. Its focus is mainly on the role of the courts in common law and civil law jurisdictions, but we shall refer to analogous action by treaty makers and legislators.

IV. Ricketson's Spectrum

Professor Ricketson has suggested[14] a spectrum for copyright:

> **Ricketson**
> **Exclusive right > collective licensing > right to remuneration > free use**

A full[15] exclusive right does not necessarily empower an author to obtain fair return for use of a work; this will depend on the author's bargaining position, which may be bolstered by a collective agreement, restrictions on assignment or waiver of the right or other statutory backup.[16]

'Free use' can be further subdivided into:

a. the free use of otherwise protected material (termed 'free use' below); and
b. use which is free because the material in question enjoys no protection.

In the latter category belong the non-original work and its close relation, the insubstantial part of a copyright work. A similar spectrum may be drawn for confidential information. Since collective licensing is not usually employed for confidential information, that part of Ricketson's spectrum may be omitted.

> **'Modified Ricketson' spectrum for breach of confidence and copyright**
> **Exclusive right > right to remuneration > free use > beyond the bounds of protection**

This spectrum is *all* judicially conditioned, but in drawing and holding the lines between the different zones of the spectrum, availability of judicial remedies and the exercise of discretion by judges are of supreme importance. We shall use this

---

[14] 'International conventions and treaties', in *The boundaries of copyright*, ALAI study days, Cambridge 1998, published 1999, at p 5.

[15] For the distinction between full exclusive right and the possibility of prevention under the Rome Convention in the context of performers' rights, see J. Reinbothe and S. Von Lewinski, 'The WIPO Treaties 1996: ready to come into force', in *EIPR* (2002) 199, at 201.

[16] As with the new provisions of Section 32, German Copyright Act: K. Gutsche, 'New copyright legislation in Germany: Rules on equitable remuneration to provide 'just rewards' to authors and performers', in *EIPR* (2003) 366.

spectrum to explore the use of public interest considerations both for copyright and confidential information, in 'holding the line' between the categories.

The intermediate categories are not always in evidence. By way of example, one might consider the judicial 'experiments' in the US with tests for infringement of copyright in software: 'structure, sequence, organization', 'look and feel', 'abstraction-filtration'.[17] Adoption of the latter test moved much software copying from infringement of exclusive rights at the left of the spectrum to use of unprotected material at the right-hand end. It is submitted that the burgeoning of software patenting in the USA and the use of patents to protect online business methods owes much to the failure of copyright to protect software in the USA.[18] In the English High Court, Jacob J[19] in *Ibcos*[20] declined to apply the abstraction/filtration test to determine substantiality.

As regards the boundary between exclusive right of authors and collective licensing, collective licensing is sometimes said to be a response to market failure,[21] in that authors cannot hope to enforce their copyrights on an individual basis. Although the author trades her exclusivity for a right of remuneration by mandating a collecting society to licence works to third parties,[22] the collecting society in turn may benefit from the sanctions of exclusivity.[23] This will require appropriate standing, access to justice, and the possibility of injunctive relief.[24] A collecting society's standing to sue may be conferred by legislation or by transfer of exclusive rights from authors. Thus copyright collectively enforced may fall into the category of 'exclusive right' or 'right to remuneration', depending on the arrangements between the society and its members. Even those societies which take partial assignments or exclusive licences of their members' copyrights may

---

[17] For an overview of these concepts, see for example P. Samuelson, 'Economic and constitutional influences on copyright law in the United States', in *EIPR* (2001) 409; E. Derclaye, 'Software copyright protection: Can Europe learn from American case law? Part 2', in *EIPR* (2000) 56.

[18] For the death of 'strong copyright' in the USA, see Lea, 'Software: protection trends in the 1990s', in *Ent. LR* (*Entertainment Law Review*) (1995) 276.

[19] Now Jacob LJ, a judge of the Court of Appeal.

[20] [1994] FSR 275.

[21] S. Ricketson, 'The boundaries of copyright: its proper limitations and exceptions: international conventions and treaties', in *IPQ* (1999) 56; W.J. Gordon, 'Fair Use as market failure: A structural and economic analysis of the *Betamax* case and its predecessors', in *Columbia Law Review* 82 (1982) 1600, at 1620 to 1621. Of course, copyright itself may be regarded as an answer to market failure, e.g. P.B. Hugenholtz, 'Caching and copyright: the right of temporary copying', in *EIPR* (2000) 482; and Power, 'Digitization of serials and publications: the seminal objective of copyright law', in *EIPR* (1997) 444 and citations.

[22] A process characterized as voluntary compulsory licensing by C. Jehoram, 'The future of copyright collecting societies', in *EIPR* (2001) 134 at 135-6.

[23] E.g. *Phonographic Performance Ltd* v. *Maitra* [1998] 1 WLR 870; [1998] 2 All ER 638. Interim relief may be granted where the claimant is equitable rather than full legal owner, e.g. *Performing Right Society* v. *London Theatre of Varieties* [1924] A.C. 1, at 14.

[24] R. Fry, 'Copyright infringement and collective enforcement', in *EIPR* (2002) 516.

find themselves hampered by the limited nature of those rights. In an age of converging rights and for reasons of operational efficiency, collecting societies are merging[25] or engaging in joint enforcement ventures.

V. The Public Interest

The phrase 'public interest' eludes precise definition.[26] Considering the public interest in disclosure,[27] such an indefinite character is consistent with its role as a defence to otherwise legitimate restrictions upon freedoms. The public interest does *not* comprise all matters in which the public is *interested* as a matter of gossip or curiosity.[28] Rather, it covers matters of 'real' or 'legitimate' public concern, on such wide-ranging subjects as the propriety of seal hunting methods,[29] the conduct of security forces,[30] the identification of a self-publicizing extremist by non-domestic photographs,[31] the reliability of intoximeters,[32] the exposure of iniquity,[33] the correction of misleading information on a celebrity's habits,[34] the proper administration of justice,[35] the perils of Scientology[36] and possibly brief coverage of sporting fixtures[37] and other 'major events'.[38] The public interest in

---

[25] E.g., H.P. Knopf chronicles the merger of Canadian collecting societies in 'Copyright and the internet in Canada and beyond: convergence, vision and division', in *EIPR* (2000) 262.

[26] E.g. T. Dreier, 'Balancing proprietary and public domain interests: Inside or outside of proprietary rights?', in R. Dreyfuss, L. Zimmerman and H. First (eds.), *Expanding the boundaries of intellectual property. Innovation Policy for the Knowledge Society*, Oxford University Press (2001), at 297: 'while the term "public interest" is often cited, there is a certain vagueness inherent in it'.

[27] See, e.g. Bryan, 'The Law commission report on breach of confidence – not in the public interest?', in *Public Law* (1982) 188; Y. Cripps, *The legal implications of disclosure in the public interest*, Sweet & Maxwell (2nd ed., 1994).

[28] E.g. *British Steel Corporation* v. *Granada Television Ltd* [1981] AC 1069.

[29] *Bladet Tromso* v. *Norway* [2000] 29 EHRR 125.

[30] *Ogur* v. *Turkey*, noted at [1999] EHLR 531; *Surek* v. *Turkey* [1999] BHRC 339.

[31] *News Verlags GmbH & Co KG* v. *Austria* (31457/97) [2001] 31 EHRR 8; I. Simon, 'Picture Perfect', in *EIPR* (2002) 368. *Cf. Peck* v. *United Kingdom* [2003] 36 EHRR 41, where the aggrieved subject of published photos was held to have no cause of complaint.

[32] *Lion Laboratories* v. *Evans* [1984] 2 All ER 417.

[33] *Gartside* v. *Outram* [1856] 26 LJ Ch 113.

[34] *Campbell* v. *Mirror Group Newspapers Ltd* [2002] EMLR 30; [2003] HRLR 2.

[35] *Medcalf* v. *Mardell* [2003] 1 AC 120, a case on the wasted costs order.

[36] *Hubbard* v. *Vosper* [1972] 2 QB 84.

[37] G. Davies, *Copyright and the public interest*, Sweet & Maxwell (2nd ed., 2002), at p. 168-169 cites the French case of *FOCA* v. *FR3*.

[38] G. Davies, *Copyright and the public interest*, Sweet & Maxwell (2nd ed., 2002), at p. 168-169 cites French Law No 2000-719 of 1 August 2000 to permit broadcasting of such events on free television.

disclosure may of course be outweighed by a countervailing public interest[39] in respect for copyright[40] or the maintenance of confidentiality, for example the confidentiality of hospital records,[41] the ability of hospital staff to do their work without being harried by the press,[42] or more generally at the interim stage of litigation, pending trial of the merits.[43]

VI. Public Interest – the Exception or the Rule?

Although the public interest has been described above as a residual defence, is it really a starting point rather than a final consideration? The US Congressional power to enact copyright laws is premised upon society's interest in the progress of science and the useful arts.[44] In *Universities U.K. Ltd* v. *Copyright Licensing Agency Ltd*,[45] the UK Copyright Tribunal discussed the 'symbiotic relationship' between publishing and academia in serving the public interest in learning and scholarship. Austin puts it thus:

'In the Anglo-American tradition, the conceptual underpinnings of intellectual property rights have much to do with the public interest'.[46]

---

[39] The balancing act contemplated by Article 10(2) of the European Convention on Human Rights.

[40] *The Right Honourable Paddy Ashdown MP PC* v. *Telegraph Group Limited* [2002] Ch 149; [2002] RPC 5; [2002] ECDR 32; [2002] ECC 19; [2001] 3 W.L.R. 1368 ; [2001] 4 All E.R. 666; [2001] EMLR 44; [2001] HRLR 57.

[41] *X* v. *Y* [1988] 2 All E.R. 648; [1988] R.P.C. 379.

[42] *Nottinghamshire Healthcare National Health Service Trust* v. *News Group Newspapers Limited* [2002] E.M.L.R. 33; [2002] EWHC 409 (Ch D); [2002] R.P.C. 49 (Ch D).

[43] *Attorney General* v. *Punch Ltd* [2003] HRLR 14; [2003] EMLR 7; [2002] UKHL 50 (HL); confidentiality in the litigation process itself is discussed by R. Toulson and C. Phipps, *Confidentiality,* Sweet & Maxwell (1996). See, also, A.M. Joshua, 'Balancing the public interests: confidentiality, trade secret and disclosure of evidence in EC competition procedures', in *ECLR* (*European Competition Law Review*) (1994) 68.

[44] Article I, Section 8:
'The Congress shall have power ... to promote the Progress of Science and useful Arts, by securing for limited Times to Authors and Inventors the exclusive Right to their respective Writings and Discoveries.'
G. Davies, *Copyright and the public interest,* Sweet & Maxwell (2nd ed., 2002) discusses this 'underlying philosophy in the US law of copyright' at paragraphs 5-038 *et seq.*

[45] *Universities U.K. Ltd* v. *Copyright Licensing Agency Ltd, Design and Artists Copyright Society Ltd intervening* [2002] EMLR 35; [2002] RPC 36.

[46] G. Austin, *Private international law and intellectual property rights: a common law overview* (2001), WIPO/PIL/01/5, available at http://www.wipo.org/pil-forum/en/documents/.

Article 10 of the European Convention on Human Rights[47] puts freedom of expression first and exceptions second:

'1.   Everyone has the right to freedom of expression. This right shall include freedom to hold opinions and to receive and impart information and ideas without interference by public authority and regardless of frontiers. This article shall not prevent States from requiring the licensing of broadcasting, television or cinema enterprises.

2.   The exercise of these freedoms, since it carries with it duties and responsibilities, may be subject to such formalities, conditions, restrictions or penalties as are prescribed by law and are necessary in a democratic society in the interests of national security, territorial integrity or public safety, for the prevention of disorder or crime, for the protection of health or morals, for the protection of the reputation or rights of others, for preventing the disclosure of information received in confidence, or for maintaining the authority and impartiality of the judiciary'.[48]

The European Court of Human Rights has not ranked the various rights conferred by the Convention,[49] and allows a wide 'margin of appreciation' in Member States' implementation of the rights inter se. English[50] quotes the German Federal Constitutional Court as holding that neither privacy nor free speech 'can claim

---

[47]   T. Pinto, 'The influence of the European Convention on Human Rights on intellectual property rights', in *EIPR* (2002) 209.

[48]   Although there is debate as to whether Convention rights have 'horizontal effect' in creating rights between citizens: see, for example Morgan, 'Privacy, confidence and horizontal effect: "Hello" trouble', in *CLJ* (*Cambridge Law Journal*) (2003) 444, at 467-473. There seems little doubt, however, that Convention rights must be taken into account by the court when deciding whether or not to grant an injunction. Thus, in *The Right Honourable Paddy Ashdown MP PC v. Telegraph Group Limited* [2002] Ch 149; [2002] RPC 5; [2002] ECDR 32; [2002] ECC 19; [2001] 3 W.L.R. 1368 ; [2001] 4 All E.R. 666; [2001] EMLR 44; [2001] HRLR 57 one also finds the following statement:
> 'We would add that the implications of the Human Rights Act 1998 must always be considered where the discretionary relief of an injunction is sought, and this is true in the field of copyright quite apart from the ambit of the public interest defence under Section 171(3).'

[49]   J. Stratford, 'Striking the balance: Privacy v. freedom of expression under the European Convention on Human Rights', in M. Colvin (ed.), *Developing key privacy rights: The impact of the Human Rights Act of 1998*, Hart Publishing (2002), at p. 43 concludes that 'The Convention provides no obligatory point at which the balance must be struck between Articles 8 and 10'.

[50]   'Protection of privacy and freedom of speech in Germany', in M. Colvin (ed.), *Developing key privacy rights: The impact of the Human Rights Act of 1998*, Hart Publishing (2002), at p. 87, citing a 1973 case; the freedom of expression guaranteed by Article 10 of the European Convention on Human Rights appears in Article 5 of the German Constitution. For the right of privacy see A. Vahrenwald, 'Photographs And Privacy In Germany', in *Ent. LR* (1994) 205.

precedence over the other'. However, it appears that the courts of other states have historically used freedom of expression as the starting point. Freedom of expression has been characterized as the basic rule in France to which privacy is the exception.[51] Similar judicial comments may be found in UK case-law.[52] For example, in *Douglas, Zeta-Jones and Northern & Shell Plc.* v. *Hello! Ltd*:[53]

> 'English law, as is well known, has been historically based on freedoms, not rights. The difference between freedom-based law and rights-based law was memorably expressed by Lord Goff of Chieveley in the course of his speech in *Att.-Gen.* v. *Guardian Newspapers Ltd. (No. 2) [1990] 1 A.C. 109*, when he said he could see no inconsistency between English law on freedom of speech and Article 10 of the European Convention on Human Rights. He said at 283F:
>
> > "The only difference is that, whereas Article 10 of the Convention, in accordance with its avowed purpose, proceeds to state a fundamental right and then to qualify it, we in this country (where everybody is free to do anything, subject only to the provisions of the law) proceed rather upon an assumption of freedom of speech, and turn to our law to discover the established exceptions to it" '.

A less hierarchical approach was described in the breach of confidence case of *Imutran Limited* v. *Uncaged Campaigns Limited and Daniel Louis Lyons*:[54]

> 'In the case of subsection (4) it must be borne in mind that the courts emphasized the importance of freedom of expression or speech long before the enactment of Human Rights Act 1998. See Halsbury's Laws of England 4th ed. reprint Vol. 8(2) para. 107 and cases there cited. But neither those cases nor the provisions of s. 12(4) require the court to treat freedom of speech as paramount. There are many reported cases in which the court has had to balance freedom of expression or speech with other aspects of the public interest. See also Snell's Equity 30th ed. paras. 45-75.
>
> In those circumstances I do not consider that the subsection is intended to direct the court to lace even greater weight on the importance of freedom

---

[51] M. Colvin (ed.), *Developing key privacy rights: The impact of the Human Rights Act of 1998*, Hart Publishing (2002), at p. 11 and chapter 3 therein by C. Dupre, 'The protection of private life versus freedom of expression in French law', at p. 68-69.

[52] And in the legislation and case law of Commonwealth jurisdictions, such as New Zealand: Tobin, 'Freedom of expression and privacy in New Zealand', in M. Colvin (ed.), *Developing key privacy rights: The impact of the Human Rights Act of 1998*, Hart Publishing (2002), at p. 129-130.

[53] [2001] HRLR 26; [2001] QB 967; [2001] FSR 40; [2001] EMLR 9 (CA).

[54] [2001] ECDR 16; [2001] HRLR 31; [2001] EMLR. 21; [2002] FSR 2. *Wainwright and Another* v. *Home Office* [2003] UKHL 53, shows that Article 8 has not yet engendered a broad right of privacy in the UK.

of expression than it already does. As I said in para. 34 of my judgment in *Ashdown* v. *Telegraph Group Ltd* the requirement "to pay particular regard" contemplates specific and separate consideration being given to this factor.

I turn then to the claim for breach of confidence. I have been referred to the well known line of cases consisting of *Initial Services* v. *Putterill [1968] 1 Q.B. 396; Hubbard* v. *Vosper [1972] 2 Q.B. 84; Francome* v. *Mirror Group Newspapers Ltd [1984] 1 W.L.R. 892; Lion Laboratories Ltd* v. *Evans [1985] Q.B. 526; Re A Company's Application [1989] Ch. 477* and *A-G* v. *Observer Ltd [1990] 1 A.C. 109*. Each of them demonstrates that the public interest in disclosure may outweigh the right of the plaintiff to protect his confidences. They demonstrate that the court will also consider how much disclosure the public interest requires; the fact that some disclosure may be required does not mean that disclosure to the whole world should be permitted'.

This may be compared to the contextual approach of the Canadian courts to balancing the rights and freedoms conferred by the 1982 charter of rights.[55] On the balance between freedom of speech and privacy, Australian law has been described as establishing '*ad hoc* balances between the public interest in freedom of expression and the protection of privacy', resolving conflicts through 'pragmatic compromise'.[56]

Many of the cases[57] and much literature[58] on freedom of expression concern what may loosely be called political speech. However, public interest cases appear to defy meaningful categorization.[59] This may be evidence of the 'pragmatic genius of the common law'[60] but may also be a sign that the public interest is a more general and fundamental consideration. It is submitted that the public interest in

---

[55] Russell, 'The impact of the charter of Rights on privacy and freedom of expression in Canada', M. Colvin (ed.), *Developing key privacy rights: The impact of the Human Rights Act of 1998*, (2002), at p. 119-121 cites *Big M Drug Mart* [1985] 1 SCR 295; *Dagenais* v. *CBC* [1994] 3 SCR 835; *R* v. *Mills* [1999] 3 SCR 668.

[56] Lindsay, 'Freedom of expression, privacy and the media in Australia', in Colvin (ed) *Developing key privacy rights: The impact of the Human Rights Act of 1998*, Hart Publishing (2002) at pages 195 and 160.

[57] E.g. *R (on the application of Pro-Life Alliance)* v. *BBC* [2003] 2 All ER 977; [2003] 2 WLR 1403; [2003] ACD 65; [2003] EMLR 23; E. Barendt, 'Free Speech and Abortion', in *Public Law* (2003) 580.

[58] With honourable exceptions, e.g. C.R. Munro, 'The value of commercial speech', in *CLJ* (2003) 134 and citations. I. Hare, '*Is the privileged position of political expression justified?*', in J. Beatson and Y. Cripps (eds.), *Essays in honour of Sir David Williams QC,* Clarendon Press (2000).

[59] *Hyde Park Residence Ltd* v. *Yelland*, [2000] 3 WLR 215 (Eng CA), per Mance LJ, dissenting.

[60] C. Forsyth, 'The protection of political discourse: pragmatism or incoherence', in J. Beatson and Y. Cripps (eds.), *Essays in honour of Sir David Williams QC,* Clarendon Press (2000).

fact operates at four stages in the determination of rights. First, the public interest may be served by establishment or recognition of a private right – to confidence, private life, or author's right.[61] Secondly it is the basis for 'everyday' exceptions to private rights, such as the exceptions and limitations to copyright.[62] Thirdly it may provide a defence to a claim, which is likely to be exceptional and residual where legislation provides a system of specific defences. Fourthly, it may enter into the exercise of judicial discretion how precisely to enforce a right.

This means that, far from being an impermissible extension of freedom of speech or of the exceptions and limitations to copyright, the public interest may be taken into account at each stage to ensure that a system of rights is working reasonably fairly.[63] The analysis is supported in the EU and elsewhere by acceptance that intellectual property may be overridden by competition law,[64] constitutional law,[65] media, contract and consumer laws.[66] Furthermore, proper consideration of a public interest or a competition argument in a copyright case

---

[61] Recital 9 of Directive 2001/29/EC asserts that copyright and related rights should be harmonized at a high level to encourage creativity in the interests of 'authors, performers, producers, consumers, culture, industry and the public at large'.

[62] Now somewhat harmonized within the EU by Articles 5 and 6 of Directive 2001/29/EC on the harmonization of copyright and related rights in the Information Society.

[63] See also the preamble to the Draft Protocol to the WIPO Performances and Phonograms Treaty concerning Audiovisual Performances: 'Recognizing the need to maintain a balance between the rights of performers in their audiovisual performances and the larger public interest, particularly education, research and access to information'. S. Von Lewinski, 'The WIPO diplomatic conference on audiovisual performances: A first resume', in *EIPR* (2001) 333.

[64] For the EC, see O. Vrins, 'Intellectual property licensing and competition law: some news from the front – the role of market power and double jeopardy in the EC Commission's new deal', in *EIPR* (2001) 576; see also, G.V.S. McCurdy, 'Intellectual property and competition: Does the essential facilities doctrine shed any new light?', in *EIPR* (2003) 472. For the US, Antitrust Guidelines for the Licensing and Acquisition of Intellectual Property, 59 Fed. Reg. 41, 339 (1994). For recognition of antitrust competence in the context of the Berne Convention, see S. Ricketson, 'The boundaries of copyright: its proper limitations and exceptions: international conventions and treaties', in *IPQ* (1999) 56. 'Although Article 17 has been interpreted as being restricted to matters of censorship, it has also been acknowledged by successive Revision Conferences that Member States still retain certain rights to regulate the rights of copyright owners where this is necessary for the control of monopolistic and other anti-competitive practices.'

[65] Clashes between US trade secret law and the Constitutional first amendment (free speech) are said to be rare – e.g. R. Milgrim, *Milgrim On Trade Secrets*, LexisNexis (1967), at 12.06 (as updated at 2002), but P. Samuelson has predicted that first amendment defences will increase: 'Resolving Conflicts Between Trade Secrets and the First Amendment', (Draft as of March 20, 2003) posted at http://www.sims.berkeley.edu/~pam/papers/TS%201st%20A%203d%20dr.pdf.

[66] T. Dreier, 'Balancing proprietary and public domain interests: Inside or outside of proprietary rights?', in R. Dreyfuss, L. Zimmerman and H. First (eds.), *Expanding the boundaries of intellectual property. Innovation Policy for the Knowledge Society*, Oxford University Press (2001), at 309-312.

will necessarily satisfy the 'three-step test' required by Article 13 TRIPS. This argument will be elaborated next.

VII. Copyright, Competition Law and the Three-Step Test[67]

It would be a serious error to see intellectual property rights and competition law as irreconcilable opponents that fight for supremacy. Instead one should start by looking at the way in which intellectual property rights fit into our modern society and how their existence can be justified.[68] Why are these intangible property rights created? Economists argue that if everyone would be allowed to use the results of innovative and creative activity freely, the problem of 'free riders'[69] would arise.[70] No one would invest in innovation or creation, except in a couple of cases where no other solution would be available,[71] as it would give them a competitive disadvantage.[72] All competitors would just wait until someone else made the investment, as they would be able to use the results as well without investing money in innovation and creation and without taking the risks that the investment would not result in the innovative or creative breakthrough it aimed at.[73] The cost of the distribution of the knowledge is, on top of that, insignificant.[74] As a result

---

[67] I am grateful to Prof. Paul Torremans for his assistance in drafting this section of the essay.

[68] See in general P.L.C. Torremans, *Holyoak and Torremans Intellectual Property Law*, Butterworths (3rd ed., 2001), pp. 12-25.

[69] See R.P. Benko, *Protecting Intellectual Property Rights: Issues and Controversies*, American Enterprise Institute for Public Policy Research (AEI Studies 453) (1987), at 17.

[70] Inappropriability, the lack of the opportunity to become the proprietor of the results of innovative and creative activity, causes an under-allocation of resources to research activity, innovation and creation: see K. Arrow, 'Economic Welfare and the Allocation of Resources for Invention', in National Bureau for Economic Research, *The Rate and Direction of Inventive Activity: Economic and Social Factors*, Princeton University Press (1962), at 609–625. The role of licensing income in support of the 'never-ending task' of mapping the United Kingdom was referred to in *Her Majesty's Stationery Office and Another* v. *The Automobile Association Limited and Another* [2001] E.C.C. 34; allegations of abuse of dominance, contrary to Article 82 EC Treaty, were struck out.

[71] E.g. a case where the existing technology is completely incapable of providing any form of solution to a new technical problem that has arisen.

[72] See R. Ullrich, 'The Importance of Industrial Property Law and Other Legal Measures in the Promotion of Technological Innovation', in *Industrial Property* (1989) 102, at 103.

[73] One could advance the counter-argument that inventions and creations will give the innovator an amount of lead time and that the fact that it will take imitators some time to catch up would allow the innovator to recuperate his investment during the interim period. In many cases this amount of lead time will, however, only be a short period, too short to recuperate the investment and make a profit. See also E. Mansfield, M. Schwartz and S. Wagner, 'Imitation Costs and Patents: An Empirical Study', in *Economic Journal* (1981) 907 at, 915 *et seq.*

[74] See R.P. Benko, *Protecting Intellectual Property Rights: Issues and Controversies*, American Enterprise Institute for Public Policy Research (AEI Studies 453) (1987), at 17.

the economy would not function adequately because we see innovation and creation as an essential element in a competitive free market economy. In this line of argument innovation and creation are required for economic growth and prosperity.[75] In this starting point one recognizes very clearly elements of public interest, i.e. as the needs of society. Property rights should be created if goods and services are to be produced and used as efficiently as possible in such an economy. The perspective that they will be able to have a property right in the results of their investment will stimulate individuals and enterprises to invest in research and development.[76] These property rights should be granted to someone who will economically maximize profits.[77] It is assumed that the creator or inventor will have been motivated by the desire to maximize profits, either by exploiting the invention or creation himself or by having it exploited by a third party, so the rights are granted to them.[78]

But how does such a legally created monopolistic exclusive property right fit in with the free market ideal of perfect competition? At first sight every form of a monopoly might seem incompatible with free competition, but we have already demonstrated that some form of property right is required to enhance economic development as competition can only play its role as market regulator if the products of human labour are protected by property rights.[79] In this respect the exclusive monopolistic character of the property rights is coupled with the fact that these rights are transferable. These rights are marketable; they can, for example, be sold as an individual item. It is also necessary to distinguish between various levels of economic activity as far as economic development and competition are concerned. The market mechanism is more sophisticated than the competition/ monopoly dichotomy. Competitive restrictions at one level may be necessary to promote competition at another level. Three levels can be distinguished: production, consumption and innovation. Property rights in goods enhance competition on the production level, but this form of ownership restricts competition on the consumption level. One has to acquire the ownership of the

---

[75] See R.P. Benko, *Protecting Intellectual Property Rights: Issues and Controversies,* American Enterprise Institute for Public Policy Research (AEI Studies 453) (1987), Chapter 4 at 15, and US Council for International Business, *A New MTN: Priorities for Intellectual Property,* (1985), at 3.

[76] J. Lunn, 'The Roles of Property Rights and Market Power in Appropriating Innovative Output', in *Journal of Legal Studies* (1985), 423, at 425.

[77] M. Lehmann, 'Property and Intellectual Property – Property Rights as Restrictions on Competition in Furtherance of Competition', in *IIC* 20 (*International Review of Industrial Property and Copyright Law*) (1989), at 11.

[78] For an economic-philosophical approach see also Mackaay, 'Economic and Philosophical Aspects of Intellectual Property Rights', in M. Van Hoecke (ed.), *The Socio-Economic Role of Intellectual Property*, Rights Story-Scientia (1991), pp 1-30.

[79] M. Lehmann, 'Property and Intellectual Property – Property Rights as Restrictions on Competition in Furtherance of Competition', in *IIC* 20 (1989), 1, at 12.

goods before one is allowed to consume them and goods owned by other economic players are not directly available for one's consumption. In turn, intellectual property imposes competitive restrictions on the production level. Only the owner of the patent in an invention may use the invention and only the owner of the copyright in a literary work may produce additional copies of that work. These restrictions benefit competition on the innovative level. The availability of property rights on each level guarantees the development of competition on the next level. Property rights are a prerequisite for the normal functioning of the market mechanism.[80] Or, to take the example of patents: 'patents explicitly prevent the diffusion of new technology to guarantee the existence of technology to diffuse in the future'.[81] Copyright and the restrictions on copying and communication to the public which it imposes are needed to enhance further creation of copyright work, which is clearly what is required and desirable from a public interest point of view. This is the only way in which copyright can in the words of the American Constitution play its public interest role 'to promote science and the useful arts'.[82]

Not only does this go a long way in demonstrating that the copyright system right from its inception is influenced heavily by public interest imperatives and that the balance which it tries to achieve between the interest of the rightholders and of the users-public is based on public interest considerations. Competition law is also used as a tool to regulate the use that is made of copyright in a later stage. Excesses that can not be reconciled with the justification for the existence of copyright, i.e. that do not serve to achieve the public interest aims of copyright, will come to be seen as breaches of competition law. Yet again the public interest is involved, this time in regulating the use of the exclusivity granted by copyright.[83] The *Magill*[84] and *IMS*[85] cases are good examples in this area.

Magill was concerned with the copyright in TV listings.[86] The broadcasters who

---

[80] M. Lehmann, 'The Theory of Property Rights and the Protection of Intellectual and Industrial Property', in *IIC* 16 (1985), 525, at 539.

[81] R. Benko, *Protecting Intellectual Property Rights: Issues and Controversies*, American Enterprise Institute for Public Policy Research (AEI Studies 453) (1987), Chapter 4 at 19.

[82] US Constitution, Article 1, Section 8, clause 8.

[83] See P.L.C. Torremans, *Holyoak and Torremans Intellectual Property Law*, Butterworths (3rd ed., 2001), pp. 302-309.

[84] Joined cases C-241/91 P and C-242/91 P *Radio Telefis Eireann and Independent Television Publications Ltd* v. *EC Commission* [1995] ECR I-743, [1995] All ER (EC) 4161.

[85] Case C-481/01 *IMS Health* v. *NDC Health*, pending, the Advocate General delivered his opinion on 2 October 2003, available at http://curia.eu.int/; Order of the President of the Court of Justice of 11 April 2002 in case C-481/01 P(R); Order of the President of the Court of First Instance of 10 August 2001 in case T-184/01 R and Order of the President of the Court of First Instance of 26 October 2001 in case T-184/01 R both available at http://curia.eu.int/.

[86] The English cases of *ITP/BBC* v. *Time Out* [1984] FSR 64 had established the subsistence of copyright in such listings.

owned the copyright refused to grant a licence to Magill, to produce a comprehensive weekly TV listings magazine for the Irish market. The case shows clearly that there is nothing wrong with the copyright as such. The problem is clearly situated at the level of the use that is made of the copyright. Here again the starting point is that it is up to the rightholder to decide which use to make of the right and that as such a refusal to licence does not amount to a breach of competition law. But the Court of Justice argued that a refusal might in exceptional circumstances constitute an abuse.[87] These exceptional circumstances involved the following in this case. The broadcaster's main activity is broad-casting; the TV guides market is only a secondary market for them. By refusing to provide the basic programme listing information, of which they were the only source, the broadcasters prevented the appearance of new products which they did not offer and for which there was a consumer demand. The refusal could not be justified by virtue of their normal activities. And, by denying access to the basic information which was required to make the new product, the broadcasters were effectively reserving the secondary market for weekly TV guides to themselves.

In essence, the use of copyright to block the appearance of a new product for which the copyright information is essential and to reserve a secondary market to oneself is an abuse and cannot be said to be necessary to fulfil the essential function (reward and encouragement of the author) of copyright. Here again one clearly sees the public interest input. Competition law is used to make sure that copyright is used according to its proper intention, i.e. in the public interest. Any abuse of the right against the public interest will constitute a breach of competition law.[88]

IMS Health[89] is the current complex follow up case. IMS Health had developed a brick structure to facilitate the collection of marketing data on the German pharmaceutical market. It owned the copyright in that brick structure and refused to grant a licence to its potential competitors. In comparison with *Magill* a number of complicating factors arise. First of all it is not entirely clear whether there is a secondary market involved at all, as IMS Health and its competitors both whished to operate on the primary market for the collection of pharmaceutical data in Germany and secondly it is also not clear whether in the circumstances the emergence of a new product would be blocked, as the competitors were only interested in copying IMS's block structure without necessarily providing the user with a different product as a

---

[87] Joined cases C-241/91 P and C-242/91 P *Radio Telefis Eireann and Independent Television Publications Ltd* v. *EC Commission* [1995] ECR I-743, [1995] All ER (EC) 4161, at paragraphs 54 and 57.

[88] P.L.C. Torremans, *Holyoak and Torremans Intellectual Property Law*, Butterworths (3rd ed., 2001), pp. 302-309.

[89] Case C-481/01 *IMS Health* v. *NDC Health*, pending, the Advocate General delivered his opinion on 2 October 2003, available at http://curia.eu.int/; Order of the President of the Court of Justice of 11 April 2002 in case C-481/01 P(R); Order of the President of the Court of First Instance of 10 August 2001 in case T-184/01 R and Order of the President of the Court of First Instance of 26 October 2001 in case T-184/01 R both available at http://curia.eu.int/.

result of such use. The main point in IMS Health is however not as much the question whether the requirements of reserving a secondary market to oneself and of blocking the emergence of a new product can be defined in a more flexible way, but rather the question whether these two requirements need to be met cumulatively or whether meeting one of them is sufficient to trigger the operation of competition law. The definitional problems really come down to defining the boundaries of the public interest on this point and the question whether the requirement apply in a cumulative manner defines when the threshold for an intervention by competition law in defence of public interest concerns is met.

It is therefore also obvious that proper consideration of a public interest argument in a copyright case will necessarily satisfy the three step test.[90] We are here by definition not concerned with the first part of the argument developed above, i.e. the public interest input in designing the rules of copyright themselves as a bundle of rights that are awarded in the public interest. We are rather concerned with the stage at which the exercise of these rights is interfered with for public interest reasons. First of all, such an interference will only occur in special cases, i.e. when public interest concerns are raised by a certain use of copyright. Secondly, the interference will not conflict with the normal exploitation of the copyright work, as it will only occur when copyright is used for purposes for which it was not intended and which cannot be justified under the economic justification for the existence of copyright. In such circumstance the use that is affected is clearly not normal use. And thirdly, there cannot be an unreasonable prejudice to the legitimate interests of the copyright owner. Any legitimate interest concerns the correct, i.e. justifiable, use of copyright by the rightholder. Such use is not affected in the first place. This explains why all three stages of the test are satisfied.

We shall now consider how other aspects of the public interest govern the setting and enforcement of boundaries on the 'modified Ricketson' spectrum.

VIII. Exclusivity Versus Right to Remuneration

As mentioned earlier, authors may voluntarily convert their exclusivity into a right to remuneration by mandating a collecting society to administer the right. In the case of reprographic copying, German and other countries' laws permit private copying of works, subject to the payment and distribution of levies on machines such as photocopiers, fax machines, scanners and CD writers.[91] This system may

---

[90] Article 13 TRIPS Agreement 1994.

[91] Schaal, 'The copyright exceptions of Article 5(2)(a) and (b) of the EU Directive 2001/29', in *Ent. LR* (2003) 117, sets forth the relevant provisions of the German Urheberrechtsgesetz or Copyright Act of 1965 and case law on its application to newer copying technologies. Recital 37 of Directive 2001/29/EC merely asserts that national reprographic schemes do not create barriers to the internal market, although Recital 38 makes distinction between analogue and digital private copying.

be regarded as an involuntary conversion of exclusive rights into a mere right to remuneration. In this case, the collecting societies do not take over any rights of exclusion against users. The system is permitted by Article 5(2)(a) of Directive 2001/29 on copyright in the information society and is being retained[92] and extended to a wider range of works, subject to the ability of authors to use technical copy-protection measures.[93] Distribution of reprographic levies must inevitably be an inexact science. Rosenblatt[94] refers to claims by users that even collecting societies' standard tariffs are not in the public interest but they provide at least some correlation between use, payment and reward to creators.

The 'rental and lending' Directive 92/100/EEC harmonized the laws of EC Member States with regard to the rights of authors and performers over commercial rental and public lending. Article 2(5) contains a mandatory provision that, by entering into a film production agreement, a performer is presumed to have transferred his or her rental right to the producer. The performer may contract to the contrary and in any event has an unwaivable right to equitable remuneration for rental. A preamble to the Directive makes clear that such remuneration may comprise a single contract payment.

Where exclusive rights are conferred and retained, judges might be expected to uphold them by granting injunctions to restrain unauthorized use. In *Shelfer* v. *City of London Electric Lighting Company*,[95] the English Court of Appeal held that only in exceptional cases should the court refuse injunctions to prevent continuing damage to property. An attack on this principle was launched in *Phonographic Performance Ltd* v. *Maitra*,[96] where it was argued that the grant of an unlimited injunction to restrain future infringement amounted to an abuse of process. The argument was rejected, even although such an injunction might also operate as a lever to obtain payment for past infringement. The court affirmed that the owner of exclusive rights was, in general, entitled to prevent unlicensed use and to grant licences on such terms as they thought fit.

However, the remedy of a final injunction may sometimes be refused, even though infringement of rights has been established. In *Ludlow Music Inc* v.

---

[92] Schwarz, 'Germany: Copyright – Legislation', in *Ent. LR* (2002) N74; see also J. Liholm, 'GEMA and IFPI', in *EIPR* (2002) 112 for information on collecting societies.

[93] Section 95(a); Recital 39 of Directive 2001/29/EC states that an exception for private copying should not inhibit the use of technological protection measures or their enforcement but Article 6(4) obliges rightsholders or Member States to enable a user with legal access to benefit from the exception – principles difficult to reconcile.

[94] H. Rosenblatt, 'Copyright assignments: rights and wrongs – the collecting societies' perspective', in *IPQ* (2000) 187: 'Some users express concern that set tariffs are not in the public interest and argue on this basis for non-exclusivity. However, the amount of remuneration set by a collecting society may be subject to public supervision such as a reference to the Copyright Tribunal.'

[95] [1895] 1 Ch 287.

[96] [1998] 1 WLR 870, [1998] 2 All ER 638.

Williams (No.1)[97] the claimant sought summary judgment for infringement of copyright. Despite giving judgment in the claimant's favour on infringement, Nicholas Strauss, QC, sitting as a deputy high court judge, refused to grant an injunction. He reiterated the general principle that, in the absence of special circumstances, property rights would be enforced by injunction, so that a defendant could not buy the ability to infringe rights by payment of damages. Noting the original reason for this general rule – the inadequacy of damages as a remedy in respect of future acts – the judge held it arguable that there had been acquiescence by the claimant, whose original complaint mentioned only financial compensation, thus suggesting that the claimant was interested only in money. There was a further hearing[98] by Pumfrey J of the claims to relief, at which the defendant argued that damages in lieu of an injunction could and should be awarded under Section 50 of the Supreme Court Act 1981[99]. In the outcome, an injunction was awarded to prevent future pressings of the disputed record track, but the defendant was not restrained in relation to existing pressings. 'Exceptional' circumstances were held to be present in *Banks* v. *EMI Songs Ltd (formerly CBS Songs Ltd) (No.2)*.[100] The defendant had received assurance from a friend that he, not the claimant, was the author of a disputed song. By the time of the hearing as to remedies, the claimants' song had been used for eleven years and had enjoyed its commercial success in their hands.

Although the decision in *Ludlow Music* has been criticized by Phillips and others,[101] it is submitted that the existence of a discretion to grant or refuse an injunction is an important power and safeguard of the public interest. There is implicit support for this in the case of *Biogen* v. *Medeva*,[102] where the defendant had pleaded that an injunction restraining the manufacture or sale of its hepatitis B vaccine[103] would lead to loss of human life and/or avoidable damage to human health. The claimant asked the court to strike out this part of the defence, but the court declined to do so.

The Supreme Court of Canada considered the propriety of granting a final injunction for breach of confidence in *Cadbury Schweppes* v. *FBI Foods*.[104] In that

---

[97] 'The risk that rewards: copyright infringement today', in *Ent. LR* (2001) 103. See also, G. Harbottle, 'Permanent injunctions in copyright cases: When will they be refused?', in *EIPR* (2001) 154.
[98] [2002] FSR 57; [2002] ECDR CN6; Robinson, 'Copyright – lyrics – remedies', in *Ent. LR* (2003) N-38.
[99] The statutory successor to Lord Cairns' Act.
[100] [1996] EMLR 452.
[101] By Phillips, 'The risk that rewards: copyright infringement today', in *Ent. LR* (2001) 103. See also, G. Harbottle, 'Permanent injunctions in copyright cases: When will they be refused?', in *EIPR* (2001) 154.
[102] [1993] RPC 475.
[103] Allegedly superior to the claimant's vaccine.
[104] [2000] FSR 491.

case the defendant had for nearly six years been marketing a product originally developed using information confidential to the plaintiff's predecessor in title. The product could have been developed without breach of confidence, leading the court to conclude that the information was not very special. In the circumstances the court took the view that a money remedy was adequate, limited to a twelve month period within which an alternative product could have been developed. In the circumstances the court of first instance had been justified in refusing an injunction.

In *Ashdown* v. *Telegraph*,[105] the English Court of Appeal recognized that the public interest might militate against the grant of an injunction, but leave a claimant free to seek remuneration or damages for use of material protected by copyright as well as confidentiality:

> 'For these reasons, we have reached the conclusion that rare circumstances can arise where the right of freedom of expression will come into conflict with the protection afforded by the 1988 Act, notwithstanding the express exceptions to be found in the Act. In these circumstances, we consider that the court is bound, in so far as it is able, to apply the Act in a manner that accommodates the right of freedom of expression. This will make it necessary for the court to look closely at the facts of individual cases (as indeed it must whenever a "fair dealing" defence is raised). We do not foresee this leading to a flood of litigation.
>
> The first way in which it may be possible to do this is by declining the discretionary relief of an injunction. Usually, so it seems to us, such a step will be likely to be sufficient. If a newspaper considers it necessary to copy the exact words created by another, we can see no reason in principle why the newspaper should not indemnify the author for any loss caused to him, or alternatively account to him for any profit made as a result of copying his work. Freedom of expression should not normally carry with it the right to make free use of another's work'.

A defence of public interest may therefore prevent a claimant for exercising full exclusive rights, but does not necessarily deny a claim to remuneration.

IX. Exclusive Right or Right to Remuneration Versus Free Use

In the case of texts and speeches of public importance, the Berne Convention provides that signatory states may refrain from conferring protection, or may permit certain uses. For example, Article 2(4) provides that for official texts of a

---

[105] *The Right Honourable Paddy Ashdown MP PC* v. *Telegraph Group Limited* [2002] Ch 149; [2002] RPC 5; [2002] ECDR 32; [2002] ECC 19; [2001] 3 W.L.R. 1368 ; [2001] 4 All E.R. 666; [2001] EMLR 44; [2001] HRLR 57.

legislative, administrative or legal nature, protection is a matter for the state concerned, rather than a specific obligation (Stockholm revision onwards). Ricketson[106] refers to the public policy reasons for making these texts available to all and asserts that they should not be subject at all to private proprietary restrictions. He notes that most national laws, including those of Germany, Italy, Japan and Mexico, excluded protection for official texts, although in the UK they are copyright but subject to 'permitted acts', so may be used freely in appropriate circumstances. The public interest argument here seems to be that copyright ensures investment in their publication and distribution, especially where a publisher 'adds value'. Lambert suggests that the US case of *Veeck* v. *Southern Building Code Congress International Inc*[107] demonstrates the desirability of the UK's combination of copyright & permitted acts.[108] Berne Article 2*bis* (1) allows countries of the Berne Union to exclude political speeches and speeches delivered in the course of legal proceedings from copyright protection, wholly or in part whilst Article 2*bis* (2). Again, Ricketson[109] points to recognition of public interest arguments for keeping such speeches out of copyright. Considerable latitude is given by Article 2*bis* (2) as regards the protection of lectures and other addresses, subject to permitted uses justified by informatory purpose. However, collections of these works by their authors must be accorded full exclusive rights: Article 2*bis* (3).

Articles 10(1) and (3) of Berne provides for mandatory free use of acknowledged quotations from published works, provided that the use is compatible with fair practice and justified in degree. Article 10(2) is permissive as to fair use for illustration in publications, teaching, broadcasts and recordings. 10*bis* permits Berne Union countries to make exceptions to copyright for the reporting of current events. Such exceptions seem to work well in national laws although *Hyde Park Residence Ltd* v. *Yelland*[110] demonstrates that a public interest defence may be desirable in relation to an *unpublished* work. It is submitted that the Court of Appeal's holding that Mr Yelland's newspaper did not need to use actual CCTV footage to refute an exaggerated claim by Mr Al Fayed is unconvincing.

From time to time defendants attempt a quotation defence in relation to whole works. An interesting example of this occurred in *Queneau* v. *Christian Leroy*[111] where the defendant had digitized an entire collection of poems, although each visitor to his web site could display only one poem at a time. Not surprisingly, the

---

[106] S. Ricketson, *The Berne convention: 1886-1986*, Kluwer (1987), at paragraph 6.67.

[107] Court of Appeals for the Fifth Circuit: Circuit Wiener and Stewart JJ. and District Judge Little, 2 February 2001, http://www.ca5.uscourts.gov/opinions/pub/99/99-40632- cv0.htm.

[108] Lambert, 'Access to legislation on the internet: An English lawyer's reflections on *Veeck* v. *Southern Building Code Congress*', in *Ent. LR* (2001) 145. P. Leith, 'Owning legal information', in *EIPR* (2000), 359, discusses legal publishing in the UK.

[109] S. Ricketson, *The Berne convention: 1886-1986*, Kluwer (1987), at paragraph 6.16.

[110] [2001] Ch 143; [2000] 3 WLR 215; [2000] ECDR 275; [2000] EMLR363; [2000] RPC 604 (CA).

[111] [1998] E.C.C. 47 (Trib Gde Inst Paris).

tribunal held that the defendant's activity did not fall within the 'brief quotation' defence of Section L.122-5-3 of the French Intellectual Property Code. The court observed that poems viewed by visitors to the web site were not intended to be incorporated in another work to which it contributed a 'pedagogical, scientific or informative element'. Furthermore, it was possible in principle to reconstitute the entire work by juxtaposing successive 'quotations'.

In another French case, *Fabris* v. *Société Nationale de Television France 2*,[112] the claimant was holder of moral rights and co-owner of economic rights in the works of the deceased artist Utrillo. The defendant televised a one-off news report of an exhibition of Utrillo's works. The 128-second news broadcast showed twelve of Utrillo's paintings without permission. In proceedings for infringement of copyright, the court of first instance dismissed the claim, holding that the use of the entire work did not fall within the short quotation exception of Article L.122-5. However, the court accepted the argument that the report was justified by the television viewers' right to receive up-to-date information of a cultural event in a current news item about the work or its author. It was relevant that the report was not in competition with usual forms of exploitation of the work.[113] The claimant appealed. The Court of Appeal confirmed that the short quotation exception did not apply to the showing of the whole works. It went on to reject as 'baseless' the defendant's reliance upon a right of communication under the European Convention on Human Rights, since showing the paintings was clearly not essential. However, the Court of Appeal did at least entertain the argument and further referred to Article 1 of the first additional Protocol to the Convention, 'every natural or legal person is entitled to peaceful enjoyment of his possessions', which the court viewed as substantially guaranteeing the right to property, tangible or intangible. Thus the *Cour d'Appel* can be seen engaging in the exercise of balancing of public interests.

In Austria the quotation defence under the Copyright Act applied to words but not to pictures. In *R.* v. *Re Quotation of News Pictures*[114] the public interest was held to justify applying the quotation defence by analogy to pictures, the court recognizing that these days, pictures are of more and more importance in the news media.

The phrase 'justified by informatory purpose' in Berne Article 2*bis* (2) suggests public interest may demand more lenient criteria for copying works of fact, the line between restricted and free use being drawn to favour the user. In *Ravenscroft* v.

---

[112] [2003] E.C.D.R. 13 (C d'A Paris).

[113] The editors of *Copinger & Skone James on Copyright* suggest that this factor would be of little weight today in respect of substantial copying under UK copyright: paragraphs 8-37, n. 33. It would of course be germane to alleged fair dealing: e.g. *Sillitoe* v. *McGraw-Hill* [1983] FSR 545. J. Griffiths, 'Copyright law after Ashdown – time to deal fairly with the public', in *IPQ* (2002) 240.

[114] [2002] E.C.C. 20 (OGH Austria).

Herbert,[115] a comment to this effect was based upon the author's presumed intention to add to society's corpus of useable knowledge:

'The author of a historical work must, I think, have attributed to him an intention that the information thereby imparted may be used by the reader, because knowledge would become sterile if it could not be applied. Therefore, it seems to me reasonable to suppose that the law of copyright will allow a wider use to be made of a historical work than of a novel so that knowledge can be built upon knowledge.'

A similar approach may be discerned in map cases. In the early English case of *Sayre* v. *Moore*[116] the court held that there would be infringement only if a derivative map was a 'servile imitation' (it wasn't). In *Geographia* v. *Penguin*,[117] Whitford J observed:

'In a map case, even if, on a close examination, there be some apparent similarity in the finer features the question is always going to remain as to whether having regard to the quantity and quality of the information taken there has been any real prejudice to the interests of the copyright owner'.

However, the public interest in access to copyright works is generally served by exceptions and limitations. Where exceptions are clear and reasonably up-to-date, courts will refrain from elaborating them with public interest arguments. For example, in *Phonographic Performance Ltd* v. *South Tyneside Metropolitan Borough Council*[118] the court rejected the defendant's argument that since as a local authority it performed social welfare functions, it could rely on Section 67, which permitted charitable organizations to play copyright works.

A public interest in laughter is served by the defence of parody, in some jurisdictions a specific defence,[119] in others an aspect of fair dealing or fair use.[120] Courts in most jurisdictions would agree with the analysis of the Dutch court in *Rowling* v. *Byblos*, that:

'The aim of making a parody of another's work is to create humour, not competition'.

---

[115] [1980] RPC 193 at 206. In this case the defendants' taking was held sufficient to infringe.

[116] (1785) 102 ER 139.

[117] [1985] FSR 208.

[118] [2001] RPC 29.

[119] See e.g. Gimeno, 'Parody of songs: a Spanish case and an international perspective', in *Ent. LR* (1997) 18.

[120] E. Gredley and S. Maniatis, 'Parody: A fatal attraction? Part 1: The nature of parody and its treatment in copyright', in *EIPR* (1997) 339; Hayhurst, 'Canada: Copyright – copyright in fictional characters – parody as fair dealing for the purpose of criticism', in *EIPR* (2000) No. 55 (*Productions Avanti Cine-Video Inc* v. *Favreau*); F. Macmillan, 'The cruel C: Copyright and film', in *EIPR* (2002) 483.

If these conditions are satisfied, free use may be allowed, but the courts are quick to detect a competitive motive. Because parody relies upon the public's familiarity with the material used, it does not tend to arise in breach of confidence cases.

X. Free Use Versus No Protection

Arguments that protection should be denied outright may be based upon the notion that the material should be positioned in the public domain, free for use by all, or upon the contrasting principle that iniquitous material should be used by none, and should certainly not lead to benefit or recovery by a claimant. The case of a non-original work falls into the first category, as does the idea that non-substantial taking should be permitted.

The exceptions for short quotations or fair dealing deal with the situation where the quantity of the work used would normally require authorization, but (to use the words of the 'three-step test') but the use is for 'certain special cases which do not conflict with a normal exploitation of the work and do not unreasonably prejudice the legitimate interests of the right holder'.[121] If a sufficiently short or non-original portion of a work is used, no infringement is committed. A short cut may be to consider whether the portion would attract copyright, although the UK courts have been prepared to contemplate the notion that a substantial taking of a copyright work may occur even where the taking would not independently attract copyright. This is in contrast to the position in the US and other jurisdictions.[122] Altered, as opposed to partial, copying[123] often gives rise to problems of substantiality in copyright – has the expression been taken or the idea, the form or the content?[124] Even in the UK, where the idea/expression or content/form dichotomy has received less judicial attention than elsewhere, the extreme case of *Bowater Windows Ltd* v. *Aspen Windows Ltd*[125] shows that where only common-place ideas are taken, there will be no infringement.

The equivalent in breach of confidence cases involves information which lacks the necessary quality of confidence because it is trivial[126] or commonplace, such as

---

[121] Berne Article 9(2); TRIPS Article 13; Directive 2001/29/EC Article 5(5).

[122] See the comparisons in *IBCOS Computers Ltd* v. *Barclays Mercantile Highland Finance Ltd* [1994] FSR 275; *cf. John Richardson Computers Ltd* v. *Flanders (No.2)* [1993] FSR 497.

[123] H. Laddie, P. Prescott and M. Vitoria, *The modern law of copyright*, Butterworths (3rd ed., 2000), paragraph 3.130.

[124] T. Dreier, 'Balancing proprietary and public domain interests: Inside or outside of proprietary rights?', in R. Dreyfuss, L. Zimmerman and H. First (eds.), *Expanding the boundaries of intellectual property. Innovation Policy for the Knowledge Society*, Oxford University Press (2001), at p. 304 and citations.

[125] [1999] FSR 759.

[126] *Coco* v. *AN Clark (Engineers) Ltd* [1969] RPC 41 at 48; *AG* v. *Guardian Newspapers Ltd* [1988] 3 All ER 545, per Lord Goff.

workplace procedures concerned with personal health and cleanliness and janitorial cleaning in *Ocular Sciences* v. *Aspect Vision Care*.[127]

A public interest could be claimed in the protection of morals, the prevention of crime, the exposure of iniquity and the principle that turpitude should not be rewarded. In both breach of confidence and copyright cases, courts have denied protection or remedies because of the unacceptable nature of the information or work. A classic statement was made in *Gartside* v. *Outram*,[128] that 'there is no confidence as to the disclosure of iniquity'. Not every human weakness amounts to 'iniquity' and the courts are slow to characterize personal behaviour as such.[129] In the case of hypocrisy of public figures, however, public interest favours the correction of false impressions.[130]

Given that iniquity will not be protected by confidence, is copyright recognized in iniquitous works? There is venerable English case law to this effect. It was suggested in *Glyn* v. *Western Feature Film Co*,[131] that an immoral work should be denied copyright. The House of Lords were divided on this issue in *Spycatcher*,[132] but it is submitted that the better view is that the courts will decline to enforce copyright where restricted acts such as publication and sale would operate against the law or the public interest.[133] This approach is consistent with the early case of *Lawrence* v. *Smith*,[134] where the court declined to continue an *ex parte* injunction in relation to medical lectures which were said to be 'hostile to natural and revealed religion and denied the immortality of the soul'. The turpitude of a work should therefore be relevant to remedies rather than the subsistence of rights. A similar approach has been adopted in Switzerland in *Re Copyright In Maps and Plans*.[135] The case concerned a 'Map for Men', whose purpose was summed up in the caption 'What's where, streetwalkers, bars where prostitutes gather, brothels, strip shows, drag, gay clubs, bars for connoisseurs, dancing dives and many others'. The court reasoned that although the work constituted a guide to 'opportunities for the conclusion of contracts which private law classifies as immoral, the explanatory notes attached to it are nevertheless statistically unique

---

[127] [1997] RPC 289.

[128] [1856] 26 LJ Ch 113, characterized by Bingham LJ as public interest in *AG* v. *Guardian* [1988] 3 All ER 545.

[129] *Stephens* v. *Avery* [1988] Ch. 449; A v. B [2000] E.M.L.R. 1007.

[130] *Woodward* v. *Hutchins* [1977] 1 WLR 760; 2 All ER 751; *Campbell* v. *MGN Ltd* [2002] EMLR 30, [2003] HRLR 2; *Campbell* v. *Frisbee* [2002] WL 32273641.

[131] [1916] 1Ch 261

[132] *AG* v. *Guardian Newspapers (No 2)* [1988] 3 All ER 545.

[133] In *Hyde Park Residence Ltd* v. *Yelland* [2000] 3 W.L.R. 215, Aldous LJ listed situations where the court might refuse to enforce copyright – where a work was immoral, scandalous or contrary to family life, or was injurious or incited or encouraged others to act in a way which was injurious to public life, public health and safety or the administration of justice.

[134] Jac. 471, cited in *Bowman* v. *Secular Society* [1917] A.C. 406.

[135] [1985] E.C.C. 549 (ObG Zurich).

and thus entitled to copyright protection'. However, although copyright subsisted, the offending of morals could be an obstacle to publication. In the circumstances the claimant could not claim loss-of-profit damages for another's publication. Any copyright protection should be limited to an injunction to prevent copying and publication.

XI. Conclusion

At the boundaries between each of the categories in the 'modified Ricketson' scheme, courts everywhere use their powers to grant remedies consistent with the competing public interests in disclosure and confidentiality, freedom of expression and the protection of intellectual property.

Chapter 8

Rights of Privacy, Confidentiality, and Publicity, and Related Rights

*Peter Jaffey**

I.   Introduction

This paper compares claims in the areas of privacy, confidentiality, 'rights of publicity' and merchandizing rights and related and overlapping areas including defamation and intellectual property. The objective is to highlight the confusion and incoherence that is liable to result from a failure to separate distinct categories based on different principles. Although the principal concern is with English law, the arguments are of more general relevance. Two important themes are the different ways in which legal regimes can regulate the disclosure and transmission of information, and the importance of the distinction between rights of ownership and rights against harm, in relation to information and other intangibles.

II.   Privacy and Confidentiality

Until recently it was said straightforwardly that there was no right of privacy in English law, and there were cases that gave striking support to this proposition. In the notorious *Kaye* v. *Roberston*,[1] newspaper journalists entered the hospital room of the claimant where he was bedridden and recovering from a serious accident, and took a photograph which was published without the claimant's consent. The court described this as a 'monstrous invasion of privacy',[2] but denied that there was any right of privacy in English law.[3] In the light of this case and others, the

---

*   Professor of Law, Brunel University. I am grateful to Ken Oliphant for his comments on a draft of this essay.
[1]   [1991] FSR 62.
[2]   *Ibid.* at 70, per Bingham LJ, using Griffiths J's expression in *Bernstein* v. *Skyviews* [1978] QB 479, 489.
[3]   The court contrived to give some protection on the unsatisfactory basis of injurious or malicious falsehood. This applied only because the court found (1) a false implication that the photograph was consented to by the claimant and (2) a pecuniary loss in the form of the loss of the commercial value of the story. Such a false implication is not a necessary characteristic of a breach of privacy, and the loss identified is based on the value of the claimant's story for commercial exploitation, not the value of his privacy, and the implication is that if the claimant would not have been willing to sell his story he should have no claim.

P.L.C. Torremans (ed.), *Copyright and Human Rights*, 157–181
© *2004 Kluwer Law International. Printed in the Netherlands.*

absence of a right of privacy has long been controversial. The enactment of the Human Rights Act 1998, giving effect to the European Convention on Human Rights, has revived the issue, in the light of Article 8 of the Convention, which provides in paragraph (1):[4] 'Everyone has the right to respect for his private and family life, his home and his correspondence'. In recent cases the courts have taken the position that, although there is still no action for breach of privacy as such, the right of privacy under Article 8 does now receive satisfactory protection, principally through the ancient action for breach of confidence, as it has been developed by the courts.

II.1. THE LAW OF CONFIDENTIALITY

The basis of the law of confidentiality is a matter of controversy. In the simplest case, C confides in D, who has agreed to keep the information confidential, and the law prohibits D from divulging the secret. More commonly, although D has not made an explicit undertaking of confidentiality, it is clear that there is an agreement to keep the information confidential, but one that is unspoken and indeed need not be expressed because of the nature of the relationship and the circumstances: there is, in other words, a confidential relationship, carrying with it an implied undertaking of confidentiality. In such cases, the law can in principle be explained in terms of agreement or contract, broadly understood.[5]

Say C confides in D1 and D1 conveys the information to D2. It is established that D2 can also incur a duty not to publish the information.[6] It is sometimes argued that D2's duty is a duty not to interfere with the performance by D1 of his duty of confidentiality, or not to induce D1 to breach it.[7] But this explanation is plausible only where D2's disclosure makes him complicit in a wrong by D1, as for example where D1 relayed the information to D2 with a view to D2's disclosing it. If D1 intended D2 to keep the confidence, D2's breach cannot plausibly be understood as wrongful on the ground that it procured or assisted in a breach by D1.[8] The point is even clearer where D2 eavesdrops on C confiding in D1. It may

---

[4] Subject to the proviso in paragraph (2).

[5] As noted in W.R. Cornish & D. Llewelyn, *Intellectual Property*, Sweet & Maxwell (5th ed., 2003), 8-06. Historically the claim was governed by equity rather than common law and so would never have been regarded as a matter of contract. The difficulty at common law would have been the inadequacy of the common law remedy of pecuniary damages compared to the equitable remedy of injunction.

[6] See e.g. *Attorney-General* v. *Guardian Newspapers (Spycatcher)* [1990] AC 109.

[7] See e.g. *Campbell* v. *Mirror Group Newspapers* [2003] QB 633, paragraph 66; W.R. Cornish & D. Llewelyn, *op. cit.* in footnote 5, 8-06.

[8] The fact that by making the disclosure D2 destroys the value of D1's undertaking to C does not mean that D2 has induced a breach or unlawfully interfered with its performance: see *RCA* v. *Pollard* [1983] 1 Ch 135; *Douglas & Zeta-Jones* v. *Hello!* [2003] EWHC 786 at paragraph 243, per Lindsay J.

have been thought at one time that in such a case D2 incurs no duty to keep the information confidential because D2 is clearly not an accessory to a breach by D1,[9] but it now seems clear that D2 can be bound by a duty of confidentiality in such a case,[10] and this surely cannot be understood as incidental to or dependent on the undertaking of confidentiality by D1.[11] On what basis, then, is D2 bound by a duty of confidentiality?[12]

Where C has given personal information to D1 in confidence,[13] disclosing the information is liable to cause harm to C: it is liable to cause him embarrassment or humiliation or to demean him in the eyes of some people – this is why C wanted the information kept confidential.[14] The duty of D2 not to disclose the information must be based, not on D1's undertaking to maintain its confidentiality, but on a duty arising under the general law not to cause C harm of this sort by revealing the information. Thus the basis of the claim must surely be, not that the information was divulged to D1 in confidence, but that the information was private. The fact that the information was divulged in confidence merely demonstrates its private nature and the fact that its disclosure is liable to cause harm to C. This seems to be the only plausible basis for the duty binding third parties.

The principal condition for a duty of confidentiality to arise is said to be that the information 'must have been imparted in circumstances importing an obligation of confidence'.[15] On its most natural interpretation, this means that the information must originally have been communicated or acquired in a confidential relationship in the sense explained above, i.e. subject to an actual express or implied agreement to respect confidentiality. In some cases, it seems that the absence of a genuine confidential relationship in this sense was enough to preclude any legal duty of confidentiality.[16] But it now seems clear that there is no

---

[9]   This may have been the position of Megarry VC in *Malone* v. *Metropolitan Police Commissioner* [1979] Ch 344, 375-7.

[10] *Francome* v. *Mirror Group Newspapers* [1984] 1 WLR 892, *Attorney-General* v. *Guardian Newspapers (Spycatcher)* [1990] AC 109.

[11] Lord Goff in *Attorney-General* v. *Guardian Newspapers (Spycatcher)* [1990] AC 109, 281 referred to the 'public interest in the maintenance of confidences', but if this does not refer to enforcing undertakings of confidence or preventing interference by third parties in the performance of such undertakings, then it is not clear what it can really mean other than, as argued below, the protection of privacy.

[12] It is sometimes said that D2 is bound by a duty of good faith or a duty not to act unconscionably, but without elaboration these expressions fail to disclose any meaningful basis for a claim.

[13] As to information that is not personal, see the section below concerning trade secrets.

[14] See, *infra*, text at footnote 55. Where the confidential information concerns a third party, it is the third party's privacy that is in issue.

[15] *Coco* v. *Clark* [1969] RPC 41, 47, per Megarry VC.

[16] See e.g *Malone* v. *Metropolitan Police Commissioner* [1979] Ch 344.

requirement of a genuine confidential relationship in this sense. Thus in *Attorney-General* v. *Guardian Newspapers (No 2) (Spycatcher)*,[17] Lord Goff said:

> '[I]n the vast majority of cases ... the duty of confidence will arise from a transaction or relationship between the parties ... But it is well settled that a duty of confidence may arise in equity independently of such cases ...' He also said that a duty of confidence could arise when 'an obviously confidential document, such as a private diary, is dropped in a public place, and is then picked up by a passer-by'.[18]

A personal diary is not a communication made subject to a confidential relationship, but it is clearly private.

A good example of this point is provided by *Hellewell* v. *Chief Constable of Derbyshire*.[19] Here Laws J took the view that when the police take photographs of suspects who are subsequently convicted, although the police are free to distribute the photographs for the purpose of promoting law and order, their freedom to do so is subject to constraints to protect the suspect's privacy. It is clear here that the protection is not based on any undertaking of confidentiality given by the police, or on any confidential relationship in the sense above. The police are empowered to take the photographs without giving any such undertaking. As the judge said, the duty of confidentiality protects the claimant's right of privacy. Laws J also said:[20]

> 'If someone with a telephoto lens were to take from a distance and with no authority a picture of another engaged in some private act, his subsequent disclosure of the photograph would ... as surely amount to a breach of confidence as if he had found or stolen a letter or diary in which the act was recounted and proceeded to publish it'.

Clearly there is no confidential relationship between the photographer and the subject; indeed, the same is true of the diary.[21]

These cases begin to reveal the transition in the law of confidentiality from the idea of an undertaking of confidentiality, arising from a confidential relationship, as the *justification* for a duty of confidentiality or non-disclosure, to the idea of a duty of confidentiality or non-disclosure as the *remedy* to protect a right of privacy. The transition is disguised by the ambiguity in the expression 'circumstances importing an obligation of confidence'. This seems originally to have been intended to refer to a genuine confidential relationship in which there was an actual, though tacit, confidentiality agreement, but was subsequently

---

[17] [1990] 1 AC 109, 281.
[18] *Ibid.*
[19] [1995] 1 WLR 804.
[20] *Ibid.* at 807.
[21] Although maybe not of correspondence.

understood to mean circumstances in which it is justified to impose a duty of confidentiality, viz., where disclosure would infringe a right of privacy. The same ambiguity can be found in the expression 'confidential relationship', since one might take it to refer to a situation where, by virtue of the claimant's interest in his privacy, the defendant incurs a duty of confidentiality. Where a confidential relationship (and not privacy) is said to be the basis of the law in such circumstances, a fiction is at work in disguising the true basis of the law.

Thus even before the need arose to take account of Article 8, in relation to private matter the law of confidentiality could only be understood on the basis that its function was to protect privacy. More recently, in response to Article 8 the courts have made this more explicit. This is well illustrated by the recent case of *X & Y* v. *News Group Newspapers*,[22] where an injunction was issued prohibiting the media from revealing the new name of the applicant who had been notorious under her original name as a convicted murderer.[23] In *Douglas & Zeta-Jones* v. *Hello!*,[24] Sedley LJ, taking account of Article 8 and the state of the common law, said:[25] 'The law no longer needs to construct an artificial relationship of confidentiality … it can recognize privacy itself as a legal principle …' And most recently and explicitly in *A* v. *B*, Lord Woolf CJ said:[26] 'A duty of confidence will arise whenever the party subject to the duty is in a situation where he either knows or ought to know that the other person can reasonably expect his privacy to be protected'. He added:[27] 'The bugging of someone's home or the use of other surveillance techniques are obvious examples of such an intrusion'. On the basis that a field of law should be defined by reference to the rationale for the claim, the law of confidentiality should now really be described as the law of informational privacy, i.e. the law restricting disclosure of information on the ground that it is private. The defendant incurs a duty of confidentiality not because of a confidential relationship in a natural sense, but in order to protect privacy.[28] For reasons discussed below, however, the courts have been at pains to insist that there is no tort of breach of privacy, only a tort of breach of confidence that protects privacy.

II.2. THE LIMITS OF INFORMATIONAL PRIVACY

There are two main problems that arise concerning the right to informational privacy. The first is the scope of the right: when is there a reasonable expectation

---

[22] [2003] EWHC 1101.

[23] *Cf. Venables* v. *News Group Newspapers* [2001] Fam 430.

[24] [2001] QB 967.

[25] *Ibid.* at paragraph 126.

[26] [2003] QB 195, 207.

[27] *Ibid.* See also *WB* v. *Bauer Publishing* [2002] EMLR.

[28] The Data Protection Act 1998 also confers a right of privacy in some circumstances: see *Campbell* v. *Mirror Group Newspapers* [2003] QB 633.

of privacy, such as to generate the right of confidentiality? In *A* v. *B*, Lord Woolf said that 'usually the answer to the question whether there exists a private interest worthy of protection will be obvious'.[29] He also quoted from the judgement of Gleeson LJ in *Australian Broadcasting Corpn* v. *Lenah Game Meats*:[30] 'The requirement that disclosure or observation of information or conduct would be highly offensive to a reasonable person or ordinary sensibilities is in many circumstances a useful practical test of what is private'. One suspects that Lord Woolf may have been too sanguine in thinking that particular cases will not raise difficulty on this point. But at least it seems clear that the claimant in *Kaye* v. *Robertson* would have been protected. Similarly it is surely clear that someone who is surreptitiously photographed in private using a long lens camera is covered, certainly if he appears or acts in a way that he would not in public.[31]

Lord Woolf also quoted from the judgment of Gleeson LJ to the effect that there is no hard and fast line between what is public and what is private.[32] An activity may not be private even though it occurs on private property and is not open to the public. On the other hand, there can presumably be an expectation of privacy sufficient to justify a right of confidentiality in respect of what is said or done in a public place or is open to the gaze of strangers who happen to be in the vicinity: for example where someone is lying injured in the road after an accident. The latter point is illustrated by the case of *Peck*, a case from the UK in the European Court of Human Rights.[33] In *Peck*, the applicant had been filmed on a closed circuit television (CCTV) used for security purposes by the local authority. The applicant was seen with a knife which he subsequently used to attempt suicide, although the suicide attempt was not caught on film. The film was subsequently shown on television in a programme about CCTV. The court held that the English law of confidentiality was inadequate to protect the applicant because it did not apply where the claimant was in a public street. This would have been indisputable as a statement of English law at one time, but following the recent cases it must be open to question.

An interesting case on this point is *Douglas & Zeta-Jones* v. *Hello!*.[34] Here the

---

[29] [2003] QB 195, 206.
[30] [2001] 185 ALR 1, 13.
[31] This is the position under the Press Complaints Commission Code of Practice, referred to by Woolf CJ in *A* v. *B*, at 209, which the Human Rights Act 1998 by Section 12 requires the courts to take account of. In *Spencer* v. *United Kingdom* (1998) 25 EHRR CD 105 before the European Commission of Human Rights, one alleged invasion of privacy was the taking of a telephoto picture of the claimant in a private garden of a hospital. It was held that the applicant had not established that there was no claim in English law, although one can have some sympathy with the applicants' view that at the time the authorities did not support such a claim.
[32] [2001] 185 ALR 1, 13.
[33] *Peck* v. *United Kingdom* [2003] EMLR 15.
[34] Interim proceedings [2001] QB 967; final proceedings [2003] EWHC 786.

claimants held a large wedding with several hundred guests and imposed a condition on everyone attending that no-one other than the claimants' authorized photographers was permitted to take photographs. The restriction was enforced by tight security. This was in accordance with an arrangement with OK! Magazine, and the intention was that the claimants would be able to select photographs that showed them at their best, to be published exclusively by OK! An unauthorized photographer entered and took clandestine photographs which he sold to a rival magazine, the defendant Hello! The claimants asserted a right to stop the publication by the defendant. One can ask first what the position would have been if no confidentiality or security arrangements had been put in place. Would the nature of the occasion in itself have given the claimants a right of privacy? It would not seem apt to say, applying Gleeson LJ's formula, that it would be 'highly offensive' to publish photographs of such an occasion.[35] But it is not clear that there is no reasonable expectation of privacy. One can at least say that the point is not obvious.[36]

What then is the effect of the arrangements to secure confidentiality? Leaving aside the question of the duty imposed on people who attended by the conditions of entry, and the liability of third parties as accessories in a breach of this duty, can one infer from the fact that the claimants made these arrangements that they regarded the occasion as a private one, and is this sufficient to establish that they did indeed have a reasonable expectation of privacy even if they otherwise would not have done? There seems to be no reason why this should not be the case. If the claimants wanted to have an occasion where they could be confident that no photographs would be published, so that they could feel free to look and behave as they might at home, say, why should they not be able to do this?[37] The fact that the claimants also intended to release specially selected photographs to preserve and enhance their public image does not seem to undermine this right. But it is worth observing that this does not imply that because celebrities have a particular commercial interest in their public image they consequently have a right to control or monitor the publication of photographs of themselves in general, or that they have an expectation of privacy in circumstances in which others would not.

The second main problem is in what circumstances the right of privacy is overridden by a countervailing interest in disclosure. Some judges have suggested that this would be an insuperable problem, or at least one that requires a legislative solution.[38] No doubt difficult questions can arise, but it is an issue that

---

[35] As noted by Lindsay J, at paragraph 192.

[36] The issue is really a matter of convention, in the sense that there is no ground for complaint if the claimant ought to have appreciated that there was no reasonable expectation of privacy in the circumstances and taken care to act accordingly.

[37] Subject to any public interest justification for disclosure in respect of particular events.

[38] See e.g. *Malone* v. *Metropolitan Police Commissioner* [1979] Ch 344, 373, per Megarry VC; *Wainwright* v. *Home Office* [2002] QB 1334, paragraph 60, per Mummery LJ.

already has to be addressed in connection with the public interest defence in confidentiality and copyright. The recent privacy case of *Campbell* v. *Mirror Group Newspapers*[39] showed that in addition to the established right to disclose wrongdoing the public interest justifies overriding the right of privacy in order to correct a false reputation cultivated and exploited by a celebrity.[40]

II.3. INFORMATIONAL PRIVACY AND THE 'BLOCKBUSTER TORT' OBJECTION

As noted above, there is now in reality a right of privacy in English law, and the English courts consider that the law now provides protection in accordance with Article 8. But most judges still insist that there is no 'freestanding' tort of privacy in English law,[41] merely a tort of breach of confidence, which protects privacy.

The discussion above has concerned informational privacy, the protection of private information against disclosure. This is of course why the appropriate remedy is an order against disclosure or publication, just as for the original case of confidentiality where the private information was initially divulged in a confidential relationship. Privacy is often taken to be a broader concept than informational privacy.[42] In the United States, the right of privacy is famously said to be 'a right to be left alone',[43] and the Restatement of Torts, adopting the famous analysis by Prosser,[44] reflects the idea that the right to be left alone is a fundamental right that supports a number of more specific rights, of which a right against the disclosure of private information is only one.[45] Another specific right said to be an aspect of the general right of privacy is a right of seclusion or right against intrusion. This would appear to include rights against physical intrusion into the home and against intrusive noise or smells. On this understanding, the right of privacy appears to underlie at least part of the law of trespass, assault, and

---

[39] [2003] QB 633, paragraph 43. See also the earlier case of *Woodward* v. *Hutchins* [1977] 1 WLR 760.

[40] The clash between privacy and freedom of expression is now addressed through the balancing of Articles 8 and 10 of the European Convention on Human Rights: see *A* v. *B* [2003] QB 195, paragraph 4; *Douglas & Zeta-Jones* v. *Hello!* [2001] QB 967, paragraph 136.

[41] E.g. *Khorasandjian* v. *Bush* [1993] 727, 744; *Wainwright* v. *Home Office* [2002] QB 1334 paragraph 57, paragraph 96ff; [2003] UKHL 53 (HL), paragraphs 16-19 and 29-35; see also *X & Y* v. *News Group Newspapers* [2003] EWHC 1101, paragraph 14; *A* v. *B* [2003] QB 195, 206; *cf. Campbell* v. *Mirror Group Newspapers* [2003] QB 633, paragraph 70.

[42] See e.g. S. Deakin, A. Johnston & B. Markesinis, *Tort Law*, Oxford University Press (5th ed., 2003), 701-3.

[43] The formulation is apparently attributable to T. Cooley, *Cooley on Torts* (2nd ed., 1888), 29, although it is generally associated with the famous article by S.D. Warren & L.D. Brandeis in *Harvard Law Review* 4 (1890) 193.

[44] Restatement (Second) of Torts (1977); W. Prosser, 'Privacy', in *California Law Review* 48 (1960) 383.

[45] For a brief survey, see D.A. Anderson, 'An American Perspective', in S. Deakin, A. Johnston & B. Markesinis, *op. cit.* in footnote 42, 735-739.

nuisance.[46] Indeed 'a right to be left alone' might seem broad enough to cover any form of harm to or constraint of the individual and so to underlie much of the law of tort. As considered further below, the right against 'false light portrayal' and the right against 'appropriation of personality' are also identified as elements of the general right to be left alone in the Restatement and are recognized in some jurisdictions in the US. Furthermore, in the US the right of privacy has notoriously been invoked as the basis for the protection of certain liberties, for example to use contraception, have an abortion, or engage in homosexual relations.[47] In this context, privacy seems to refer to what in other contexts is described as autonomy, and is concerned with a right to be free to take certain decisions bearing on the conduct of one's life free of state interference. This is again very broad – it amounts to a general criterion for limiting the scope of civil and criminal law.

Thus there is an important issue whether a right of informational privacy is an element of a broader and more fundamental right of privacy, which would mean that the recognition of a right of informational privacy entails as a matter of principle the recognition of such a broader right. Indeed the controversy over the recognition of a right of privacy in English law has involved discussion of harassment in particular as well as informational privacy. In the recent case law some judges have been particularly insistent that no right of privacy has been or should be recognized in English law, unless introduced through legislation in Parliament, apparently mainly because they have assumed that this would have broad implications beyond informational privacy. For example, in *Malone* v. *Commissioner of the Metropolitan Police*,[48] where the judge said that a right of privacy could be introduced only by Parliament and not by the courts because of its very broad and indefinite character, he clearly understood the right of privacy to include a right against physical intrusion as well as a right to informational privacy. In *Kaye* v. *Robertson*, as mentioned above the court again insisted that the courts were unable to remedy the absence of a right of privacy, and Leggatt LJ referred to the 'right to be left alone' in US law and the four heads of privacy that have sprung from it.[49] In *Khorasandjian* v. *Bush*,[50] Peter Gibson J said simply that the argument for a right of privacy 'was not open to him in the light of the decision of this court in *Kaye* v. *Roberston*, confirming that English law has recognized no such right'. But this was not a case of informational privacy; it was a case where

---

[46] See e.g. S. Deakin, A. Johnston & B. Markesinis, *op. cit.* in footnote 42, 701. In the US, it appears that many such cases actually concern intrusive means of acquiring and revealing information, and so are really a matter of informational privacy: see D.A. Anderson, *op. cit.* in footnote 45, 737-8.

[47] E.g. *Griswold* v. *Connecticut* 381 US 479 [1965]; *Roe* v. *Wade* 410 US 113 [1973]; see e.g. J. Rubenfeld, 'The Right of Privacy', in *Harvard law Review* 102 (1989) 737.

[48] [1979] Ch 344, 372-3, Megarry VC.

[49] [1991] FSR 62, 70-71, per Bingham and Leggatt LJJ.

[50] [1993] QB 727, 744.

the defendant had harassed and pestered the claimant, in particular by making unwanted telephone calls.

More recently in *Wainwright* v. *Home Office*,[51] where the claimants had been subjected to a strip search on a prison visit, in the Court of Appeal Mummery LJ said:

> '[T]here is no tort of invasion of privacy. Instead there are torts protecting a person's interests in the privacy of his body, his home and his personal property. There is also available the equitable doctrine of breach of confidence for the protection of personal information, private communications and correspondence'.

He continued:[52] 'I foresee serious definitional difficulties and conceptual problems in the judicial development of a 'blockbuster' tort vaguely embracing such a potentially wide range of situations'. Similarly Buxton LJ insisted that all the cases where privacy had actually been protected were actions to prevent disclosure of information, and he inferred that they could all be explained in terms of breach of confidence without any need for a tort of breach of privacy:[53] 'These cases therefore do nothing to assist the crucial move now urged, that the courts in giving relief should step outside the limits of confidence, artificial or otherwise'. Buxton LJ was right to reject the 'crucial move' but he was wrong to say that this is a move from confidentiality to privacy. It is a move beyond informational privacy to some other supposed notion of privacy. Buxton LJ's approach is misleading as an analysis of the case law, since it suggests that confidentiality supplies a basis for the claims distinct from privacy, which as discussed above is not the case. It suggests that he was deceived by the fiction referred to above. This point causes some inconsistency, or at least the appearance of inconsistency, in Lord Hoffmann's recently released judgment in *Wainwright* in the House of Lords. Lord Hoffmann also rejected the possibility of a tort of invasion of privacy, because he denied that the law recognized or ought to recognize a 'high-level principle of invasion of privacy', but he did accept that the action for breach of confidence 'might as well be renamed invasion of privacy'.[54]

In a case where there is no genuine confidential relationship, there is a fiction involved in saying that the basis of the law is a deemed confidential relationship, and the fiction simply obscures the true basis, which is the right of informational privacy. The fiction disguises the fact that the justification for the claim is now not the maintenance of the claimant's confidences but his interest in informational

---

[51] [2002] QB 1334, paragraph 57 per Mummery LJ.
[52] *Ibid.* at paragraph 60.
[53] *Ibid.* at paragraph 99. The passage continues: 'This court was called on to consider making that move in *Kaye* v. *Roberston*. It declined to do so'. But *Kaye* v. *Roberston* was about informational privacy and so in that case the court was not asked to make the move.
[54] [2003] UKHL 53, paragraphs 29-30.

privacy. It would be better to accept that the action for breach of confidence (in relation to private information) is really an action for breach of privacy, but that privacy, properly understood, is informational privacy.

There is a clear rationale for protecting informational privacy.[55] Most people are concerned about what other people think about them, about their reputation in the broadest sense. This is based on general self-consciousness, on a disquiet at being evaluated on the basis of limited information by strangers, and on a fear of prejudice. Consequently most people behave differently in different contexts, showing more restraint in public and revealing weaknesses, sensitivities and abnormalities only in private. By enabling people to prevent the dissemination of private information, the right of privacy protects their reasonable expectations concerning the nature of their audience. The case where there is an express undertaking of confidentiality or a confidential relationship is covered by this principle, but the principle is broad enough to justify protection whenever it was reasonable to assume in the circumstances that information divulged or information about behaviour would not be publicised. This is the reasonable expectation of privacy that now underlies the law of confidentiality. This rationale is distinct and limited to informational privacy. It is not derived from a broader principle or value that requires the recognition of a broader right of privacy of which informational privacy is merely an element. Thus it is misconceived to assume that in recognizing that English law has a right of informational privacy – which is now simply an accurate statement of the law – the courts have also implicitly recognized or are bound to recognize a 'right to be left alone' or some form of right of autonomy as a concrete legal right, or more particularly a right against intrusion or harassment. Furthermore, as considered further below, a right of informational privacy does not entail a right against 'false light portrayal' or a right against 'appropriation of personality'. This is consistent with the position (if not the terminology) in *Wainwright* in the House of Lords, where, as noted above, Lord Hoffmann accepted that the action for breach of confidence could reasonably be renamed 'invasion of privacy', but denied that there was a general tort of invasion of privacy based on a 'high-level principle of invasion of privacy'.[56]

---

[55] There is a large literature on the nature and rationale of privacy, e.g. R. Gavison, 'Privacy and the Limits of the Law', in *Yale Law Journal 89* (1980) 421; J. Rubenfeld, *op. cit.* in footnote 47; R.C. Post, 'Three Concepts of Privacy', in *Georgia Law Review* 89 (2001) 2087, discussing J. Rosen, *The Unwanted Gaze: The Destruction of Privacy in America*, Random House (2000); D. J. Solove, 'Conceptualising Privacy', in *California Law Review* 90 (2002) 1087.

[56] [2003] UKHL 53, paragraphs 29-30. The difficulty with the judgment is that it appears to accept that informational privacy is an instance of the broader concept of privacy which prompts the question why ii is treated differently. *Cf.* S. Deakin, A. Johnston & B. Markesinis, *op. cit.* in footnote 42, 712-3, arguing for a general right of privacy encompassing physical intrusion and 'appropriation of personality' as well as disclosure of private information, but without offering a general concept of privacy to explain this. I have not considered the scope of the jurisprudence of the European Court of Human Rights on the scope of the right of privacy under Article 8, or the question of its 'horizontal effect' in private law.

III. Confidentiality as the Ownership of Trade Secrets

There is a further objection to the argument above that the law of confidentiality protects privacy. This is that in many cases where confidential information is protected, the information is not private at all, but commercial, i.e. a trade secret, or know-how concerning industrial or commercial activities.[57] Protection for trade secrets cannot be explained in terms of a right of privacy, and so, one might object, the law of confidentiality cannot be regarded as based on privacy. But the point here is that there is a fundamental divide in the law of confidentiality that has not been formally recognized in English law. Only part of what is described as the law of confidentiality is based on a right to informational privacy. What then is the basis of the law of trade secrets? Again, it cannot be the principle referred to above that someone who has undertaken to keep a confidence should be bound by his undertaking, since again trade secrets can be protected from disclosure by third parties who gave no such undertaking and whose disclosure cannot be understood as making them complicit in the breach of such an undertaking by someone else.

The justification for protecting a trade secret is that it is the property of the claimant. This explains why a third party is bound by a duty of confidentiality even though he did not give an undertaking of confidentiality and is not complicit in a breach of such an undertaking by anybody else. But of course this explanation is incomplete. Why should the claimant have ownership of the confidential information? The only plausible answer is that ownership of a trade secret is justified as a means of providing an incentive or reward for the creation of value. A right of ownership achieves this by securing to the owner the power to exploit the property by exclusive use, licensing or sale. On this understanding the right to a trade secret is a form of intellectual property, in terms of both its proprietary nature and its rationale, and of course the law of trade secrets or know-how is commonly associated with patent law and treated in this way.

The two different rationales for protecting confidential information – privacy and property[58] – characteristically raise different types of issue. The justification for the first category is simply to protect against a certain type of harm, and the existence of a claim depends on whether the claimant has a legitimate interest in privacy and whether there is countervailing interest in the disclosure of the information. For the second category, the fundamental issue of principle is whether it is justified to give the right-holder the right to all the value to be made from exploiting the information. The two different rationales support different types of legal regime. First, if the claimant has a right of ownership of information, designed to secure to him the commercial value of the information, he should be

---

[57] A well-known example is *Seager* v. *Copydex* [1967] 2 All ER 415.
[58] There has been some discussion in the literature of whether the right to confidential information can or should be understood as a property right: see e.g. W.R. Cornish & D. Llewelyn, *op. cit.* footnote 5, 8-50.

able to license the use of the confidential information or sell it by transferring his right of ownership. By contrast, in the case of a right of privacy, designed to protect the claimant from personal harm caused by the disclosure of private information, the purpose of the law is not to secure to the claimant the commercial value of the information, or in other words to empower him to sell the information or licence its use, although there is no reason why he should not be free to waive his right of privacy. For example, a newspaper that paid for a waiver of privacy in order to be free to publish private information would not thereby acquire the right to prevent third parties from publishing the information, as would the purchaser of a trade secret. Secondly, in the case where the claimant has a right of ownership, he should be entitled to what might be called a 'use claim', that is to say, a claim for payment of a reasonable licence fee as a remedy for unauthorized use of the confidential information, as an alternative to a claim for compensation for loss caused by the disclosure of the confidential information.[59] This is justified on the basis of the claimant's right to the 'use-value' of the information, as an element of his ownership of it. But in the case of the right of privacy, there is no basis for such a claim, and the normal remedy will be compensation for the harm caused by the disclosure.[60]

The essential difference between the two categories is not the type of information or the context, but the nature of the right and its relation to the information in question, i.e. whether it is a right of ownership of confidential information as property, or whether it is a right against a certain type of harm. One would expect that the right of ownership would subsist in respect of industrial or technical or business information or 'know-how', but in principle there can be ownership of personal information. For example, in *Douglas & Zeta-Jones* v. *Hello!* one issue considered by Lindsay J was whether unauthorized wedding photographs constituted a trade secret, and whether their publication could be prevented on this basis.[61] This point is considered further in the last section below.

---

[59] I.e. where the information is still confidential and there has been no loss to the claimant through the defendant's use. As to the use claim in general, see P. Jaffey, *The Nature and Scope of Restitution*, Hart (2000), Chapter 4. In the ownership case, the claimant can of course and normally will make a claim for compensation for loss, but this is damage to the property, which is the right to the exclusive value of the information.

[60] Leaving aside the question of 'disgorgement' to remove the profits of wrongdoing, or exemplary or punitive damages or 'disgorgement' to remove the profits of wrongdoing: see P. Jaffey, *op. cit.*, Chapter 11.

[61] [2003] EWHC 786, paragraph 195.

IV. Privacy, Defamation, and 'False Light' Portrayal

IV.1. PRIVACY AND DEFAMATION

The interest in privacy – i.e. informational privacy – arises from people's sensitivity to other people's opinions and judgments about them. It is concerned, in a broad sense, with reputation, although there is no requirement for the claimant actually to show that his reputation has been adversely affected in anyone's eyes: it is better to say that the right of privacy is based on a legitimate concern about reputation.[62] There is an obvious question of the relationship of privacy to defamation. Consider the famous case of *Youssoupoff* v. *MGM*.[63] The claimant succeeded in a claim for defamation in respect of a false statement by the defendant that she had been the victim of a rape. It has been argued that such a case involves artificially stretching the law of defamation, because the reputation of the claimant is not lowered in the eyes of 'right-thinking people' as the conventional test for defamation requires, and that it might be better regarded as a case of invasion of privacy.[64] Indeed, it has been argued that this reveals the basic distinction between defamation and privacy, namely that the former is concerned with reputation in the eyes of right-thinking people and the latter with reputation in the eyes of what might be called 'wrong-thinking people', which would include people who are liable to be prejudiced against someone who has been raped.[65] The implication is that defamation and privacy could operate in tandem to deal with protection of reputation, the distinction between the two turning on whether reputation in the eyes of 'right-thinking' or 'wrong-thinking' people is in issue, and this would avoid the need to stretch the law of defamation in this artificial way.

It is no doubt fair to say that the right of privacy is often concerned with protecting against the prejudice of 'wrong-thinking' people. Private matters are particularly prone to be the subject of prejudice.[66] But this is surely not the basis for the distinction between defamation and privacy. First, the problem of damage to reputation amongst 'wrong-thinking people' can also arise in respect of matters that are not private at all – an example might be the statement that the claimant at one time had an official position in a certain political party. The development of the law of privacy will leave unresolved the question of the proper scope of this aspect of the law of defamation. In any case, on one view the 'right-thinking people' test is not an accurate statement of the current law of defamation, and a

---

[62] *Cf. supra*, text at footnote 55.

[63] (1934) 50 TLR 581.

[64] This argument is advanced by M. Tugendhat, 'Privacy & Celebrity', in E. Barendt, A. Firth *et al.* (eds.), *The Yearbook of Copyright & Media Law 2001/2*, Oxford University Press (2002), 13.

[65] *Ibid.*

[66] E.g. matters of sexuality or medical conditions, where people are prone to be prejudiced and to take account of irrelevant matters: see M. Tugendhat, *op. cit.*

statement can indeed be defamatory if it is liable to harm the claimant's reputation in any significant section of the community.[67]

Furthermore, the idea that privacy is about reputation in the eyes of wrong-thinking people and defamation about reputation in the eyes of right-thinking people implies that if the law of defamation is understood to have this broader scope, it could subsume the law of privacy.[68] But this ignores a basic feature of privacy. By contrast with defamation, privacy is not concerned with the falsity of statements. It is concerned with protecting against loss of reputation (in a broad sense) resulting from the disclosure of *true* private information, for example the true information that the claimant has been raped, or rather statements about private matters *irrespective of their truth or falsity*. (It cannot be relevant whether the information is true or false, because otherwise the claimant would have to show the truth of the statement, or the defendant would escape liability by showing its falsity, and yet the claimant's right of privacy should empower him to suppress the information without having to bring its truth into consideration at all.) Thus the point in *Youssouf* is not that the claimant had a grievance that was strictly a matter of privacy rather than defamation; it was that the claimant had two distinct grievances, one the publication of a falsehood, and the other an invasion of privacy, namely the statement about private matters, whether true or false. Although it might seem that subsuming privacy under an expanded notion of defamation might seem a compact way to bring together two forms of protection for reputation, broadly understood,[69] to the contrary it is surely preferable for the two categories to be kept distinct, even if both are relevant in some circumstances, because they have distinct rationales and raise distinct issues. The essence of the law of defamation is to protect reputation against inaccuracy, whereas the essence of the law of privacy is to protect reputation from being influenced by private information whose disclosure might be unfairly prejudicial, even if true.[70]

IV.2. 'False Light' Portrayal

In the United States, many jurisdictions recognize a tort of 'false light' portrayal. As mentioned above, the tort is recognized in the Restatement of Torts and was

---

[67] J.G. Fleming, *The Law of Torts*, LBC (9th ed., 1998), 583.

[68] There have at various times been proposals for legislation to modify the law of defamation to protect privacy by withholding the defence of justification if the statement relates to a private matter – the claimant would sue for defamation and if the matter is private then the defendant would be liable irrespective of truth or falsity: see J.G. Fleming, *op. cit.*, 613. This would no doubt have served a useful purpose in providing some protection for privacy in the absence of an explicitly recognized right of privacy.

[69] The range of statements that would count as defamatory would have to be wide enough to encompass all types of private information.

[70] And so even though it would enhance the accuracy of reputation amongst entirely dispassionate and objective parties.

identified by Prosser as one of the four privacy torts derived from the 'right to be left alone'.[71] It appears that the tort is committed where the defendant depicts the claimant in a false light and the depiction would be highly offensive to a reasonable person.[72] The claim clearly has an affinity with defamation. Often it operates in tandem with defamation, and some US jurisdictions have denied the existence of the tort on the ground that it subverts the law of defamation.[73] The development of the tort in the US raises the question whether it is a necessary aspect of a right of privacy and so should be recognized in English law by virtue of the development of a fully-fledged right of privacy in accordance with Article 8.

Some commentators in the US regard false light portrayal as an aspect of informational privacy, on the basis that informational privacy is concerned with a right to control information about oneself and that this extends to suppressing false information in some circumstances.[74] Some false light cases do indeed appear to concern the exposure of private information.[75] In such cases, the portrayal is presumably 'highly offensive' because of its private nature. The question then is why there is no ordinary claim for informational privacy to suppress the information irrespective of its truth or falsity. The answer may be that the defendant is entitled to publish the information, despite its private nature, because of the legitimate public interest in the events in question, but that this defence is available only if the account is true, or at least if the defendant has not been reckless as to its truth. On this basis, the claim can be explained entirely in terms of the ordinary claim for informational privacy.

In other cases of false light portrayal it appears that the information is not private and the claim cannot be understood in terms of informational privacy. For example, the case might concern aspects of the professional life of the claimant that are entirely in the public domain, and not in any sense private.[76] But there is no reason to think that such a claim is based on some broader right of privacy of which informational privacy is also an aspect. The issue here is simply whether the claimant's reputation has been damaged by a false account of his life. It is in principle a matter for the law of defamation, and if the law of defamation is inadequate the reason may be the difficulty considered above, that the false

---

[71] *Supra*, text at footnote 43.

[72] With knowledge or recklessness as to falsity.

[73] See e.g. D. Zimmerman, 'False Light Invasion of Privacy: The Light that Failed', in *New York University Law Review* 64 (1989) 364; B.R. Lasswell, 'In Defence of False Light: Why False Light Must Remain a Viable Cause of Action', in *South Texas Law Review* 34 (1993).

[74] See the discussion in D.J. Solove, *op. cit.* in footnote 55, 1109-1115.

[75] E.g. *Time Inc* v. *Hill* 385 US 374 [1967], concerning the claimants' experiences whilst they were being held hostage; *Wood* v. *Hustler Magazine* 736 F.2d 1084 [1984], concerning the publication of a nude photograph of the claimant in circumstances arguably implying that the publication was with consent.

[76] See the case discussed in M. Stohl, 'False Light Invasion of Privacy in Docudramas: The Oxymoron which Must Be Solved', in *Akron Law Review* 35 (2002) 251.

account is not liable to lower his reputation amongst 'right-thinking people'.[77] It is surely not helpful to address this issue by way of the development of a different tort that circumvents this possible limitation in the law of defamation without directly considering whether it is justified.[78]

V. Publicity and Merchandizing

V.1. Privacy as the Ownership of Image: the Right of Publicity

In the United States, the general right of privacy has also been understood to give rise to a tort of 'appropriation of personality', which is committed by a defendant who without permission uses the name or image of the claimant (generally a celebrity) for commercial purposes, typically to promote the sale of a product by exploiting the claimant's appeal to consumers.[79] This is said to be based on a 'right of publicity'.[80] The idea of the right of informational privacy as a right to control personal information might lead to the misconception that this tort is an aspect of informational privacy as described above. But again this is not the case. The right to prevent the commercial use of one's public image does not relate to private information; indeed the commercial use of a public image does not involve the transmission of information at all (unless it is understood as an endorsement).[81] That is not to say that such a right is not justified. But it has to be justified on different grounds from a right against invasion of informational privacy.

Furthermore, there is an important distinction that is often disregarded in connection with the concept of appropriation of personality. This is the formal distinction made above in connection with informational privacy and trade secrets, between a right against harm to the claimant, and a right of ownership.[82] The point is that it is one thing to recognize that a celebrity has a right against the use of his image for commercial purposes on the ground that the association with a commercial product or activity causes harm to an interest of his that should be protected, possibly an interest in reputation or dignity or autonomy; and it is quite another to say that a celebrity *owns* his image, and so is entitled to its commercial

---

[77] See M. Stohl, *op. cit.* There are procedural differences between the torts that do not provide a principled basis for recognising two different torts.

[78] B.R. Lasswell, *op. cit.* in footnote 73, 170, suggests that false light privacy protects against emotional disturbance whereas defamation protects reputation, but protection for reputation is surely designed to protect against emotional disturbance caused by damage to reputation (as surely is false light privacy). See also D. Zimmerman, *op. cit.*, n 431ff.

[79] This is the fourth category of privacy identified by Prosser and incorporated in the Restatement of Torts. A standard example is *Carson* v. *Here's Johnny Portable Toilets* [1983] 698 F 2d 831.

[80] The term comes from *Haelen Laboratories* v. *Topps Chewing Gum* 202 F.2d 866 [1953].

[81] It is does not convey information about the product, or about the celebrity. An endorsement does convey information: viz., that the product meets the standards of the celebrity.

[82] *Supra*, text following footnote 58.

value. The latter right would be designed to enable the celebrity to license his image and realize its commercial value, whereas the former would be designed to save him from a certain type of harm. In the United States, it appears that the law has moved from the former to the latter without appreciation of the distinction: thus it is said that this form of privacy claim 'often seems to have more to do with commerce than with personal privacy'.[83] This point will be returned to below, after a brief discussion of the law of trade marks, which, as will be seen, impinges on the same issue from a different direction.

V.2. TRADE MARKS: THE INFORMATION FUNCTION

The principal function of a trade mark has always been said to be the 'origin function'. This should be understood in the following sense.[84] A trade mark tells a consumer that the quality and attributes of the product bearing the mark are under the control of some person (whoever it may be) who uses or authorizes the use of the mark to signify this fact. For this reason the consumer can infer that a product bearing a certain trade mark will have the quality and attributes that he has come to associate with products that he has previously encountered bearing the trade mark. Thus the trade mark is a simple and powerful tool for communicating information,[85] albeit information that is vague and impressionistic and not entirely reliable. The use of a trade mark to communicate information allows a producer to build up and exploit a reputation in his products, viz., goodwill. This goodwill is valuable to the trader because it attracts custom. It represents the fruits of his efforts in providing products that have the quality and attributes that satisfy customers.

The law of trade mark infringement prohibits the deceptive use of the claimant's trade mark.[86] It is only because the trade mark conveys information that its unauthorized use can be deceptive. The law of trade mark infringement thus reflects the information-related function of trade marks. It might seem that

---

[83] D.A. Anderson, *op. cit.* in footnote 45, 738. Anderson also notes that this right is assignable and inheritable as property unlike other privacy rights.

[84] As defined in the text, the origin function is not the function of revealing the identity of the manufacturer or distributor of the product, which is how it is sometimes understood. The function of a trade mark is not a question of law: identifying the function is a matter of explaining social and economic practices.

[85] This understanding is associated with the economic analysis of trade marks; see e.g. W.M. Landes and R.A. Posner, 'The Economics of Trademark Law', in *Trademark Report* 78 (1988) 267.

[86] The law of trade marks encompasses the common law of passing off and the statutory law of registered trade marks. By preventing deception in this way, the law remedies the particular harm suffered by the trade mark owner as a result of the deception, and also sustains the trade mark system in general against the degradation in its efficacy as a means of communication that would result from deceptive use. See footnote 92 below.

the law of trade marks is the counterpart of the law of defamation, protecting commercial reputation or goodwill as opposed to personal reputation. In fact a closer commercial equivalent to defamation is injurious or malicious falsehood,[87] which concerns false statements that damage the claimant's business and products, including his goodwill. The law of trade mark infringement has a different function: it is characteristically concerned not with causing damage to the claimant's goodwill, but with deceptive use of the claimant's trade mark by which the defendant exploits the claimant's goodwill for his own benefit, typically by diverting custom to himself. There is no equivalent in defamation. This is an example of what was referred to above as a 'use claim',[88] and it reflects the fact that the law of trade marks protects goodwill as a form of property belonging to the claimant, whereas personal reputation is not property in this sense under the law of defamation.[89]

V.3. The Non-information-related 'Image' Function of a Trade Mark

Trade marks can also have an important effect that is not concerned with communicating information to consumers.[90] A trade mark can acquire an 'image' through advertising. The image embodies attitudes or feelings or 'values' that the producer through advertising has managed to associate with the trade mark. If a trade mark has such an image, consumers may be influenced to purchase the product by their attraction to the image or their desire to associate themselves with it. Insofar as a trade mark operates through its image, it does not communicate information to consumers about the product. This non-information-related, image-based function can be described as the advertising or merchandizing function.

Trade mark owners see their trade marks as embodying and protecting a mixture of goodwill and image, and therefore serving both information-related and non-information-related functions. The concept of 'brand', although originally understood to mean a trade mark having the traditional information-related function, is now generally used more broadly to refer to a trade mark as the repository of the advertising image of the product as well as its reputation in the quality and attributes of the product.

In principle, the justifications for supporting the two functions are quite different. Protecting the pure trade mark or origin function and the ownership of goodwill is easily justified because it merely prohibits the provision of false

---

[87] Injurious or malicious falsehood extends to damage to reputation but is not confined to it.

[88] See, *supra*, footnote 59 and text.

[89] Similarly, goodwill is transferable but personal reputation is not.

[90] The aesthetic appearance of a trade mark may in itself induce some consumers to buy the product, but a stronger effect of the aesthetic appeal would be to enhance the efficacy of the trade mark as a sign communicating information about the product.

information and thereby sustains the ability of producers to convey information to consumers and to profit from the reputation in their products that they have established amongst consumers. But protection for the merchandizing function cannot be justified in this way. It is not concerned with prohibiting deceptive statements in order to promote the supply of true information. The unauthorized use of an image cannot in itself be deceptive because its purpose is not to convey information, or at least not information about the product. With respect to the merchandizing function, the question is whether it is right to recognize ownership of an image cultivated through advertising and exercising an emotional appeal to consumers. Can it, for example, be justified as a way of rewarding and encouraging the investment of the trader in the development of the image? Are such images valuable things that traders ought to be rewarded for developing?[91] Nevertheless the protection provided by the law of trade marks, even if intended to protect the pure trade mark or origin function, in practice inevitably also provides protection for the merchandizing function, i.e. it supports trade mark owners in developing and exploiting the image of their trade marks.[92]

V.4. Protecting Images for Merchandizing Through the Law of Trade Marks

A trade mark's image can receive protection through the law of trade marks as discussed above. A different issue is whether the law recognizes a merchandizing right – i.e., an exclusive right to use or license an image for commercial purposes – in respect of the images of celebrities, cartoon characters, or other things or events that may be appealing to consumers. In the absence of explicit merchandizing rights in English law, claimants have sometimes sought to secure the exclusive right to such images through the law of trade marks, by an action in passing off or by seeking to register the image as a trade mark. However, as discussed above, an image designed for merchandizing is distinct in function from a trade mark, or at least a trade mark in its pure trade mark or origin function; by contrast with a trade mark, such an image does not purport to convey information, and so its use (whether authorized or not) cannot be deceptive. Since, as explained above, deceptiveness is the essence of trade mark infringement, English law has in general denied any protection of an image for merchandizing through this avenue.[93]

---

[91] See e.g. M. Madow, 'Private Ownership of Public Image: Popular Culture and Publicity Rights', in *California Law Review* 81 (1993).

[92] In modern times, trade mark regimes have increasingly recognized that non-deceptive 'dilution' can constitute dilution, e.g. tarnishing of the trade mark or blurring of its distinct. This is readily understood to be intended to protect the image of a trade mark and so to support the advertising or merchandizing function of a trade mark, but it is also explicable in terms of the origin function, i.e. in terms of its effect in hindering communication with consumers.

[93] The leading cases are *Lyngstrad* v. *Anabas Products* [1977] FSR 62; *Wombles* v. *Wombles Skips* [1977] RPC 99; *Tavener Rutledge* v. *Trexapalm* [1975] FSR 179; and more recently *BBC*

The attempt to found merchandizing rights on trade mark law has found more success in other jurisdictions. But this has depended on establishing deceptiveness in some artificial way;[94] in reality, deceptiveness is not really in issue at all. One might argue that this is a reasonable fiction by which to make a natural extension to the law in order to generate merchandizing rights in law. But the move away from deceptiveness and the promotion of supply of information means that a different justification of the claim is required and this issue is obscured by the fiction.

The right of publicity discussed earlier is a merchandizing right in their image for celebrities. It was suggested that the argument for a right of publicity based on the general right of privacy was unconvincing. The argument for a merchandizing right arising from the law of trade marks and goodwill is an attempt to establish the same right (although not confined to celebrities) from a different direction, and the discussion above shows that it is also unconvincing.

VI. Intellectual Property and Ownership of Intangibles

The law of intellectual property is concerned with the ownership of ideas or information or certain other types of valuable intangible.[95] An intellectual property right is a right of ownership in the sense discussed above.[96] It is designed to secure to the owner the commercial value of the intangible created, as a reward for the work and effort involved in creating it and the contribution it makes to the society, rather than to provide protection from harm or to compensate for harm.[97] Thus an intellectual property right-holder can make a use claim as explained above as well as a simple claim for compensation for harm; and he can license and sell his right.

---

cont.

   Worldwide v. *Pally Screen Printing* [1998] FSR 665. For the same reason, registration of a merchandizing mark has been denied on the ground that the mark is not capable of acting as a trade mark because it will not be so understood by consumers: *Elvis Presley Trade Marks* [1999] RPC 567.

[94] E.g. it might be argued that the consumer is deceived because he mistakenly thinks that the use of the merchandizing mark was authorized, i.e., a misrepresentation 'as to licensing': see e.g. *Dallas Cowboys Cheerleaders* v. *Pussycat Cinema* 604 F.2d 200 [1979] and *Boston Athletic Association* v. *Sullivan* 9 USPQ 2d 1960 [1989] in the United States; *Pacific Dunlop* v. *Hogan* [1989] 87 ALR 14 in Australia; and in the English courts *Mirage Studios* v. *Counter-Feat Clothing* [1991] FSR 145; see further P. Jaffey, 'Merchandising and the Law of Trade Marks', in *IPQ* (1998) 240.

[95] This refers to 'non-exclusive' intangibles, which can be used by different people at once, not intangible transferable wealth or money.

[96] Text following footnotes 58 and 82.

[97] But some aspects of intellectual property law are concerned with protecting against harm e.g. moral rights in copyright, or copyright where it protects privacy in unpublished works, rather than with securing the value of the intangible to the right-holder.

In English law, it seems that generally intellectual property rights have not been recognized by the common law, only through a statutory regime:[98]

'[C]ourts of equity have not in British jurisdictions thrown the protection of an injunction around all the intangible elements of value, that is, value in exchange, which may flow from the exercise by an individual of his powers or resources whether in the organization of a business or undertaking or the use of ingenuity, knowledge, skill or labour'.

There appear to be certain exceptions to this, however. First, in the law of confidentiality, although the right of privacy is a right against harm, not a right of ownership of private information, as suggested above the right to a trade secret does appear to be a right of ownership, and it is recognized at common law. It is not obvious that this is justified, although it is easy to see how it has happened. Employers can clearly impose binding obligations of confidentiality on their workers, but why should this necessarily lead to a right of ownership of the information? If the trade secret concerns an invention, should it not be required to be patented and regulated by the statutory patent regime, which is designed to secure an appropriate return to the inventor, and accordingly limits the term of protection?

Secondly, in the law of trade marks, goodwill is a form of intangible property (by contrast with personal reputation, which as discussed above is not recognized as a form of property in the sense above), and it is protected at common law through the law of passing off. This is justifiable, it seems, because goodwill is distinct from other forms of intellectual property in an important respect alluded to above. Normally recognizing an intellectual property right has the drawback of imposing a significant cost on consumers. For example, a patent or copyright allows the right-holder to exclude competitors from selling a product incorporating the protected matter and the effect is to raise prices to the consumer in order to confer a return to the right-holder in excess of what he would otherwise get through the market. It is a complex question involving empirical issues to determine what sort of regime is justified, arguably a question that the courts are not qualified to answer and this may be why it is appropriate for the recognition of intellectual property rights to be left to the legislature. But the protection of goodwill does not impose any such cost on consumers; to the contrary, the protection of goodwill also benefits consumers by facilitating the supply of information to them.

Thirdly, in recent years there has been a tendency towards recognizing merchandizing rights – rights of ownership of images whose appeal to consumers can promote the sale of products. As discussed above, one argument for this in connection with celebrities is the argument for the right of publicity recognized in

---

[98] *Victoria Park Racing* v. *Taylor* [1937] 58 CLR 479, per Dixon J at 509.

US law as an aspect of the law of privacy. As pointed out above, the distinction has often been missed here between a right against harm to an interest of the celebrity caused by the commercial use of his image and the celebrity's right of ownership of his image. In fact neither is plausibly based on a right of informational privacy, and this is particularly clear in the case of the latter. As mentioned above, another argument for merchandizing rights has come from the law of trade marks, through the attempt to characterize an image as a trade mark. This is also misconceived, because an image does not communicate information about the product, and so its use is not deceptive and does not fall within the scope of trade mark infringement, at least as it is conventionally understood. Although image and goodwill are often confused, they are not the same in principle and ownership of image cannot be justified in the same way as ownership of goodwill. The effect of these two lines of argument, if they were to succeed in establishing a merchandizing right or a right of publicity, would be to circumvent the traditional aversion to the judicial recognition of intellectual property rights in the common law, without addressing or overcoming the objection mentioned above.

Douglas & Zeta-Jones v. *Hello!* provides an interesting set of facts to illustrate some of these issues.[99] As discussed above, the issue in that case was on what basis, if any, the claimants could prevent the publication of photographs of their wedding, taken by an unauthorized photographer despite arrangements to secure confidentiality. There are a number of possible types of claim. There is the possibility, certainly in the case of an authorized photographer or invited guest, of a right based on contract and interference with contract. Also there is the possibility of a right of informational privacy.[100] Then there is the possibility of an argument for a right of ownership of image, i.e. a right of publicity or merchandizing right, which is not dependent on confidentiality or the privacy of the occasion.[101] It was argued above that there is no basis for developing such a right out of the right of informational privacy, or out of the law of trade marks.

There is also the possibility of a right to the photographs as a trade secret. Lindsay J in the final proceedings concluded that there was indeed such a right,[102] although he did not make the distinction suggested above between ownership of confidential information and a right of privacy. The implication of the judge's discussion of the point appears to be that, if information is valuable, and reasonably effective measures can be taken to keep it secret, then there is a right of

---

[99] See also P. Jaffey, 'Privacy, Publicity Rights, and Merchandising', in E. Barendt, A. Firth *et al.*, *op. cit.* in footnote 64.

[100] *Supra*, text following footnote 34. Also there is the possibility of passing off if an endorsement can be found.

[101] There may be some suggestion of such a right in the judgment of Sedley LJ in the interim proceedings, who described the claimants' right to privacy as a 'commodity' that had been 'traded'. [2001] QB 967, 1007. This is why the court considered that damages were an adequate remedy, which was crucial in the interim proceedings.

[102] [2003] EWHC 786, paragraph 195ff.

ownership of it. The fact that it is practicable to keep information confidential by subjecting people to conditions of confidentiality certainly means that it is in practice possible to secure the full market value of the information. But why should this justify a right of ownership? Compare the case where the claimant organized an event that generates valuable information, but it is not practicable for the claimant to keep it secret and so control its release and realize its commercial value for himself. In *Victoria Park Racing* v. *Taylor*, the claimant organized a sporting event, and the defendant commentated on it from a vantage point outside the stadium. As the quotation above shows,[103] the fact that the claimant had generated the value exploited by the defendant did not mean that he was entitled to prevent the defendant commentating on it or to exact a licence fee from him.

Consider also the case of *Sports & General Press Agency* v. *'Our Dogs' Publishing Co.*[104] Here the claimant sought to prevent the defendant from publishing photographs of a sporting event put on by the claimant, who controlled entry but had not imposed any condition of confidentiality or restriction on taking photographs. It was held that he had no right to prevent the publication of photographs or demand payment. But if the claimant does not have the exclusive right to publish photographs of the event just by virtue of being the person who organized and managed it, why should he acquire this right – a right against the whole world – through the imposition of confidentiality conditions on particular people who attend the event, as Lindsay J implied in *Douglas & Zeta-Jones* v. *Hello!*?

VII. Conclusion

The action for breach of confidence in English law has evolved from protecting confidentiality to protecting privacy. But privacy must be understood to mean informational privacy: the right of privacy is a right against the disclosure of private information, and the interest it protects is, broadly speaking, the interest in being free from public scrutiny in circumstances when it is reasonable to act on this assumption. The English courts insist that there is no tort of privacy. This is because of an assumption that the recognition of such a tort would mean recognizing a more general, fundamental right of privacy going beyond the right to informational privacy and supporting the recognition of other specific new rights, for example rights against physical intrusion, harassment, 'false light' invasion of privacy, or the 'appropriation of personality'. But these are either reducible to a right of informational privacy or are quite distinct claims that have different rationales and are based on different interests.

---

[103] *Supra*, footnote 98. See also K. Gray, 'Property in Thin Air', in *Cambridge Law Journal* (1991) 252.

[104] [1917] KB 125, which was mentioned by Lindsay J, paragraph 222.

In addition to enforcing express or implicit undertakings of confidentiality against the parties who accepted them and third party accessories, the law of confidentiality in English law includes a law of informational privacy and a law of trade secrets or know-how. Whereas the right of informational privacy is a right against a certain type of personal harm caused by the disclosure of information, the right to a trade secret or 'know-how' is a right of ownership of confidential information.

The right of informational privacy is concerned with reputation, inasmuch as it responds to a general concern with the way in which private information will affect other people's opinions. In some circumstances, a defamation claim can arise from the same events as a claim for breach of privacy. The two are distinct because defamation is concerned with false statements that damage reputation, whereas privacy is concerned with the disclosure of private information irrespective of its truth or falsity, and without any requirement to show that reputation has actually been adversely affected. 'False light' privacy is reducible in principle to either informational privacy or defamation.

The 'right of publicity' amounts to a right of ownership of image for celebrities. It is said to be a type of privacy right, but it is not based on the same principle as informational privacy and the recognition of a right of informational privacy provides no support for the recognition of a right of publicity. The right of publicity is a type of merchandizing right, and it is sometimes argued that merchandizing rights can be established through a natural development of the law of trade marks. This is also unconvincing, because trade marks are in principle concerned with communicating information to consumers, whereas merchandizing images do not communicate information but operate purely through their inherent appeal to consumers.

For good reason, the common law has generally avoided recognizing intellectual property rights of ownership in the intangible products of labour, leaving it to the legislature to enact an appropriate regime. The recognition of the ownership of confidential information is an exception and so would be the recognition of a merchandizing right or right of publicity.

INFORMATION LAW SERIES

GENERAL EDITOR

Prof. P. Bernt Hugenholtz
Institute for Information Law
University of Amsterdam
The Netherlands

TITLES IN THE SERIES

1. Egbert J. Dommering & P. Bernt Hugenholtz (eds.), *Protecting Works of Fact: Copyright Freedom of Expression and Information Law* (1991), ISBN 90-6544-567-6.
2. Willem F. Korthals Altes, Egbert J. Dommering, P. P. Bernt Hugenholtz & Jan J.C. Kabel (eds.), *Information Law Towards the 21st Century* (1992), ISBN 90-6544-6273.
3. Jacqueline Seignette, *Challenges to the Creator Doctrine: Authorship, Copyright, Ownership and the Exploration of Creative Works in the Netherlands, Germany and the United States* (1994), ISBN 90-6544-876-4.
4. P. Bernt Hugenholtz (ed.), *The Future of Copyright in a Digital Environment* (1996), ISBN 90-411-0267-1.
5. Julius C.S. Pinckaers, *From Privacy Toward a New Intellectual Property Right in Persona* (1996), ISBN 90-411-0355-4.
6. Jan J.C. Kabel & Gerard J.H.M. Mom (eds.), *Intellectual Property and Information Law: Essays in Honour of Herman Cohen Jehoram* (1998), ISBN 90-411-9702-8.
7. Ysolde Gendreau, Axel Nordemann & Rainer Oesch (eds.), *Copyright and Photographs: An International Survey* (1999), ISBN 90-411-9722-2.
8. P. Bernt Hugenholtz (ed.), *Copyright and Electronic Commerce: Legal Aspects of Electronic Copyright Management* (2000), ISBN 90-411-9785-0.
9. Lucie M.C.R. Guibault, *Copyright Limitations and Contracts: An Analysis of Contractual Overridability of Limitations on Copyright* (2002), ISBN 90-411-9867-9.
10. Lee A. Bygrave (ed.), *Data Protection Law: Approaching its Rationale, Logic and Limits* (2002), ISBN 90-411-9870-9.
11. Niva Elkin-Koren & Neil Weinstock Netanel (eds.), *The Commodification of Information* (2002), ISBN 90-411-9876-8.

12. Mireille van Eechoud, *Choice of Law in Copyright and Related Rights. Alternatives to the Lex Protectionis* (2003),
ISBN 90-411-2071-8.
13. Martin Senftleben, *Copyright, Limitations and the Three-Step Test. An Analysis of the Three-Step Test in International and EC Copyright Law* (2004),
ISBN 90-411-2267-2.
14. Paul L.C. Torremans (ed.), *Copyright and Human Rights. Freedom of Expression – Intellectual Property – Privacy* (2004),
ISBN 90-411-2278-8.